All That We Are

RAJESH PARMAR

First published 2019 in the United Kingdom by Rajesh Parmar
allthatweare@mailfence.com

ISBN 978-1-5272-4059-9 (print)
ISBN 978-1-5272-4066-7 (ebook)

Printed in the United Kingdom by KDP

Cover artwork courtesy of Kay Jacobs, USA
www.kayellyn.com

All images sourced and licensed from https://www.shutterstock.com

Contents

Figures

Thank You

I send my sincere gratitude and appreciation to the many inspirational people I have met along the way.

Tracy Baker, UK
www.psychictracy.co.uk

Jerry Humphreys, UK
www.senseofknowing.co.uk

Billie LeuFung, Norway
www.BillieLueFung.com
http://divinemindintelligence.com/

Ara Parisien, Victoria, BC
https://araparisien.com/

Rosa Oh, Healer
rosaoh214@yahoo.com

Carol Clarke, UK
welshseer15@aol.co.uk
welshseer@hotmail.co.uk

Introduction

In moments of stillness we may pause and ask age old questions. What is the purpose of all this? Why am I not happy despite having all this abundance? Why am I here? Where do I go from here? What is Karma? What is Incarnation? These questions lead to a pursuit toward the meaning of reality and life. What is presented herein are points for reflection and not statements of fact or absolute truth. The perspectives are intended to stimulate thought in an eclectic and unfiltered manner. The statement and concepts may provide an answer to questions we silently seek to understand humanity, society and reality. General Quantum physics, esoteric and metaphysical concepts are used to stimulate reflection and encourage movement toward the inner spirit.

The text will find its way to those who are in resonance with it. The perspectives are for those who question their place in the world, seek to create a fuller human experience and expand personal awareness. The reader is taken on an exploration into our physical reality, to derive purpose to their chosen life, understand what transcends and what is temporary. The content should be discerned to determine what resonates and settles within. It is prudent to allow the spirit, heart and mind to process what is read. A plethora of theosophy, esoteric and metaphysical material is available for study from noted philosophers, sages, yogis, gurus, researchers and scholars. This text is offered from a personal understanding of *All That Is* from experiences, interactions and expressions.

The term God will not be used and is replaced by *Source* to refer to the infinite, unknowable and *All That Is*. Humanity has degraded the meaning of the term God. The term God is used by religion in all of its forms to separate groups and nations, create prejudice, pervade dogma, lead the uninitiated into war, manipulate, control and mask our injustices. The term infinite spirit will be used to describe the soul. The journey to expanded perception and awareness is endless as the unknowable is infinite. To move perception beyond the physical into the interdimensional is to embark upon an endless journey of self-rediscovery and the frequency of *Source*.

The Life Divine is a body of work that encompasses the teachings of Sri Aurobindo. This book was pivotal to understanding my own inner thoughts and feelings which at the time I was unable to order. The reader is advised to consider all perspectives and information on the path to self-awareness and understanding of divine law. This book does not look to debate nor convince. Each and every incarnation will come to an end regardless of what established belief or doctrine is followed. The ultimate truth will be revealed in the end. There is one true beginning, middle and end. The atheist and nihilist embrace the notion their spirit and body will simply disappear as they believe it never existed. They do not accept the infinite spirit uses the body to support its life experience. Upon end the infinite spirit departs and merges back into its core of stateless energy. Human ignorance, egoistic intellectualism has dissolved truth, reality of *All That Is* and the frequency of love.

The origin to expansion is to accept the infinite spirit inhabits a physical body to experience life. The physical body is a vessel and will cease to live when the spirit decides the experience has served its purpose. The fractal of our eternal spirit will depart and re-emerge in the spiritual realm or home. The spirit or the 'I' is a divine fractal of *Source* and is always connected to its frequency. The infinite spirit never leaves home. A fractal of the 'I' animates the body and is always connected to its core in the spirit realm. The infinite spirit exists in a complete state of awareness. It is everywhere and in everything. From this state sojourns into physical life are designed and the adventure begins. A common misconception is that life is imposed upon the infinite spirit. This is untrue. Free will exists in infinite state as it does in physical form. What is read should be felt. Follow what resonates and detach from the egocentric intellectualism clouding the heart.

The novelist and Nobel Laureate William Faulkner was once asked. "'Mr. Faulkner, some of your readers claim they still cannot understand your work after reading it two or three times. What approach would you advise them to adopt?' Faulkner replied, 'Read it a fourth time.'"

Discernment is important when considering subjects outside the spectrum of the mind. This and other books provide concepts for consideration and are not the answer. It is only the ego that purports what is stated is the truth. Any assertion that a doctrine, book or perception can truly understand infinite *Source* consciousness, the absolute unknowable and indescribable is mere fantasy. To perceive beyond the mind is to open the heart to emotion and feeling. It is not to republish aged theosophy or propagate established spiritual, esoteric or new age doctrines and practices. Be open to experiment with what is presented. Travel the fantastic path inward, open the self to knowledge, feeling, awareness and changes to perception. Allow personal beliefs or established doctrines to be questioned and the ego to fall away.

Flow through the content in its entirety as questions that arise may be answered in later chapters. Humanity exists in bubbles of varying forms and importance. Humanity long ceased venturing into the infinite spirit. Instead we focus on processing life through the mind. Include into study new practices such as meditation, gratitude and prayer. From this state discern what is received. Discernment is from within and not seated in the mind. Feel what is read through the heart, be still and if it resonates reflect upon it. It will either resonate true or not.

There is no person or persons, book or books that define the ultimate reality. A person cannot fully comprehend the true aspect of home or *Source* itself whilst in the crudeness of the body. It is unfathomable until the fractal of our core returns and becomes unburdened by the humanness of being human. Whatever notion is held of home is personal and will evolve if the consciousness remains open and independent of religious or philosophical doctrines. If an established doctrine or belief brings love and comfort hold it but not so tightly that it restricts. There is no right or wrong path back to *Source*, God or whatever other name we wish to assign to our spiritual origin. The importance is that we embark upon the journey to return to it. Make the journey what you wish it to be. All spokes lead to the center.

Perspectives change as expansion continues. Discern and render the information internally and develop continually. Avoid regarding any person or book as the *Source* of truth. This does not and will not exist. We have access internally to the *Source* of truth and information. We need only ask. The external experience is the catalyst to seeking information and understanding. The internal is the engine through which true discovery is achieved. Seek to challenge and stimulate study and the internal adventure. The key message is there is a single absolute truth. We will all experience it in the end after the veil is lifted. All that has been, is and can ever be emanates from this absolute unity of consciousness and presence. You are a fractal of the One or *Source*. The universal theatre is a canvas of limitless beauty and all possibility in which we expand through every emotion.

Imagine

The human experience is a duality in its most brutal form. Why is it this way? Is it supposed to be like this or can it be changed? Some esoteric practitioners suggest some are here to observe, others are here to feed the duality forcing us to expand and the rest are here for expansion and adventure. The reality is all of these are possible. We incarnate with the intention of expansion and a physical adventure. We design life experiences with the highest intention yet many repeat old paradigms and tendencies. These repeating patterns encourage further sojourns into the human theatre. We have the free will choice to create through positive intent or direct our actions, words, thoughts and intent toward strengthening the duality.

We own the responsibility to change what has been allowed to establish itself. There are those who look outward for a saviour or a being to change what we collectively experience rather than take ownership of the duality. The wait for a second coming or a saviour is a futile one and will lead to disappointment. The doctrine of a saviour is part of the illusion of the human theatre and is not of *Source*. We incarnate many times into multiple avatars and worlds. New age suggests two types of tendency. There are earthbound spirits who repeatedly incarnate into the human theatre. There are star people or spirits who incarnate into many worlds and in an array of avatars across the cosmos. The reality of these categories is not important. What is fundamental is that we incarnate many times until we come to a point in expansion where we see no purpose to further physical life experience. This fundamental truth should be a consideration as we traverse the life experience in the present. We should be mindful of what we allow in the life we experience in the now as we may choose to incarnate into what we leave behind. Reincarnation exists and there is no forced life of suffering as a punishment for past deeds. We design and choose every incarnational experience. The law of life is ownership and responsibility. We as infinite spirits own every action, word, thought and intent. We own our choice to incarnate. We own the outcome of every sojourn. We own our expansion and reconnection with *Source* or the lack thereof. We are the owners of our eternal destiny and trajectory. This is an absolute.

That which emanates from *Source* is based upon unlimited and infinite free will. The law of free will exists in the universal theatre as it does when we are in pure spirit. Each sojourn into life is designed in alignment with the intended expansion of the true self. The choice to incarnate as a human or any other lifeform in the cosmos is taken from a state of grace and infinite awareness. We design our template for the next incarnation when in a state of being everywhere and in everything. We are pure energy in a state of infinite grace and peace. We are not burdened by the physical impositions of being in an avatar, the mind and the body. We design predetermined experiences, interactions and major decision markers. These are specific to the intended purpose of the incarnation. Free will determines if we follow our intended path or redirect our lives down different paths. The choices we make at these junctures when presented with the signs, synchronicities, numbers, symbols, events, people and places determine our individual timeline. There is no separation. A ripple in our individual timeline affects the human collective and universal canvas.

All that exists has a purpose. There is nothing in the seen and unseen that exists by chance. Everything has intention and a reason for being. We privately seek purpose to life yet look outward to others, the mind and science to provide the answers. The only way to understand purpose is through the inner journey, the infinite spirit and thus *Source*. Free will allows negative and positive action. We contribute to the human collective through an elevated heart centred frequency or disconnection leading toward harm or disturbance to others. Free will governs choice. The free will of another can in horrific ways affect or end a life through the imposition of unplanned and uninvited action. Free will is a universal law and all pervasive. We are here to fulfil our incarnational intent. We knowingly enter the human duality with the awareness we will be subject to our own and others free will. Free will is unavoidable.

The Buddhist definition of nirvana is of transcendence. It is a state where inequality, suffering, desire and low vibrational tendency no longer have influence or power. It is balanced Karma. Imagine a human experience where the majority have expanded to an elevated frequency. There has been a shift inward toward the self, a connectedness to true reality and one another. We have transformed the human experience into an overwhelming vibration of love, joy, service to others, inner knowing and connectedness. We see life as an incarnation and temporary sojourn from home. The influence of duality is lessened and we are sovereign of government, control systems, myopic social movements and self-professed diviners of *Source*. The yin and yang aspects of matter are tilted toward higher frequency. True liberty and freedom of thought is regained. We act with others in mind replacing the agenda prospering the few.

We seek to be of service and are in harmony to form our own unique experience. We have evolved beyond overriding selfishness and egoistic intellectualism. Political, social and cultural ideologies are muted and intention guided through expanded perception. We become detached from lower vibrational tendencies of war and greed. We understand our place in the Universe and that we share expansion with innumerable lifeforms. We are one. We no longer perceive humanity as the pinnacle of intelligent life.

Poverty is replaced with the sharing of the abundant resources and technological innovation. Education is based on truth, true reality and unbounded possibility open to the spirit. Systems supporting opportunity are not dependent on another being poor for the profit of the few. Innovation is shared and collaborated openly across nations supporting food production and renewable resources. The digital era is steered toward the service to humanity and not used to enforce a greater myopia of perception. We recognise the divine right to clean unadulterated air, water and food. Cash crops driving deforestation are relegated to the recesses of the mind. We have grown to consume only what we need creating a balanced emotional, physical and spiritual wellbeing.

Means of exchange are equitable and not controlled, allowing all nations to work as one yet free to follow independent paths. The indelible rights of each person are implicit. Opportunity, education and care available to all and not rationed dependent on status, corporate control or wealth. The development of consciousness is nurtured creating a stage where each person is supported as they create their unique life experience. The majority see each other as one, supporting growth and limiting judgement. The universal theatre is seen as a fantastic tapestry of adventure, freedom and expansion. Each incarnation revealing its challenges and joys with the spirit working toward high frequency expansion.

Imagine a limited government to manage services and one that truly serves the people, is accountable and transparent. Imagine no government at all. We do not incarnate to become a single homogenous nondescript tracked, microchipped, digitally distracted herded species. We do not incarnate to be governed by a one world government dictate or religion telling us what to believe, hate and love. We incarnate to experience difference and diversity. We incarnate to interact with cultures, nations, languages, environments, perspectives, thoughts and ideals. That is the purpose of the human experiment. This is the reason it exists. We must cease removing the intent for the human experience. We incarnate to bring unity and collaboration through difference.

The human experience is intended to be of freedom, sovereignty and cultural variety. Incarnational life is intended to be a series of fantastic experiences and inward movement toward the spirit. It is a free will opportunity to follow our intended path or stray into other corridors of experience. Take a moment to close the eyes, free the mind and allow sight from within. It is a timeline that can be brought into manifestation through individual and collective free will. Incarnation is a choice. For the majority this will be repeated sojourns into the human theatre. What do you wish to return to? Humanity has yet to realise what is commonly referred to as the golden age where humanity was in harmony with *Source* and its inner spirit.

The opportunity for a different reality is not a dream or the foundation of a socialist or communist ideology. It is what we are here to recreate. It will be the derivative of expansion and spiritual involution. We are offered every second, minute and hour of every day the opportunity to recreate the golden age. Ideologies are human creations. We can either work in harmony and progress or perpetuate the ongoing brutal duality. It is a choice. Be prepared to own that choice and relive it over multiple incarnations. That is the reality.

> "The Universe breathes, inhaling and exhaling as man breathes; and every light unit, atom and molecule breathes; and as everything in the firmament above and the waters below breathes."
>
> Walter Russell.

The Distraction

We incarnate into life knowing the paradigm into which the adventure will playout. Our infinite spirit embarks upon life from a state of grace and knowing. We design our incarnations into the physical experience when out of the body. Physical life is embarked upon with absolute intent and an awareness challenges will be presented during our sojourn into the human experience. Our infinite spirit is aware of the many distractions and manipulations of the human theatre including the limitations of the five senses. We incarnate for the purpose of expansion. Expansion is achieved through the inward adventure toward true sovereign free will, love, liberty and freedom. These are not solely physical attributes but expressions of the true spirit.

Our infinite spirit seeks to fulfil the intention of life through expansion. We expand toward the silent unseen spirit by opening the mind, the ego and the heart. We begin to observe the theatre and overcome the challenges, manipulations and duality of the human playground. The spirit seeks to emerge into the surface self to guide the creation of our wonderful physical experience. We enter a dichotomy of an infinite presence shifting into an experience where limitation and detachment from *Source* is imposed. The challenge before us is to rediscover the true nature of the self and the fulfilment of our life intent or purpose. The alternative is to lose sovereignty over the self, allow the manipulation of the mind and separation from the spirit. Free will determines the outcome. There are numerous blogs, online channels and researchers discussing the hidden control systems and matrix of the human experience. They discuss in-depth the mechanisms of perception management and the herding of the un-awakened masses. It is not critical to study the theatre of illusion as it will be implicitly presented by the inward journey. If the inward journey is embarked upon, true sight becomes open through expanded intuition. It is unavoidable to see the theatre in which we live. It is not implicit that inward expansion is an outcome of research into the human theatre and its manipulations. The awakening movement is necessary but directed by the mind. The following is a reminder of those distractions.

An Uncomfortable Truth

We are infinite spirit. We are having a human experience. Humanity is a species amongst innumerable lifeforms in the Universe. As infinite spirits having a human experience we possess unlimited potential and access to all possibility. We seem to allow the few to create the global trajectory of the human experience. We are at a stage in human development where we should alter our perceptions and advance beyond the physical illusion, division and war into universal unity with one another and harmony. We are, to date, collectively far from this state. We are openly creating a prison for our perceptions and are vulnerable to rooting ourselves in the manipulated experience. The prison is not physical but energetic. We have become detached from our inner spirit and have through egoistic intellectualism dismissed *Source*. Through the process we have forgotten what we are and no longer see each other as one. We have become distracted by identity politics, status and materialism. We have confused opinion over truth. We direct energy into myopic transient movements rather than nurturing transcendental expansion. The prison bars are the distractions and manipulations of the human theatre which are highly successful in their outcome. The evidence is in the experience. We measure connectedness with degrees of separation, six, four or two. The reality from a universal perspective is that there is no separation as all is one.

It is an uncomfortable reality that despite our capacities confusion has been replaced clarity, connection reduced to division and charity given with judgement. Oneness is confounded with prejudice, freedom is diminished by control and inner perception is replaced by programmed thought and myopia. We are mired by hypocrisy and contradiction. We live in a world abundant with life and resources yet there is starvation and poverty. Charity is accompanied with judgement of the receiver as being worthless or lazy. It is not for us to judge another for their choices or state we find them. We should give openly through the heart. It is equally the free will of the receiver to use what they are offered in any way they wish, if it brings them joy or a respite from their circumstances. Through free will life can take a negative turn at any crossroad placing a person in a position to ask for help from a stranger.

We have collectively allowed the implicit human right to be cared for when ill and basic support services to be destroyed and linked to political and material ideologies. We desire unity, togetherness and understanding yet some silently hold prejudice, racism and separation. Identity and gender politics are used as a commodity in the unceasing agenda driven human theatre. Sovereign freedom of thought and critique are controlled through social credit, de-platforming, self-censorship and excessive correctness. These all form a barrier toward our inalienable divine gift of liberty, freedom, sovereignty and infiniteness.

The inward journey will open the mind, the ego and the heart toward our true inner self. To expand is to express infiniteness in life. Infiniteness in life is to be free of artificial systems of perception. The human theatre will be what it is collectively directed to become. The individual contribution to collective transformation occurs when our actions, words and thoughts are directed by our divine sovereignty over the paradigms of the external theatre. We can expand and project an elevated frequency of thought and action in a manipulated theatre and not be of it.

Everything we have ever been, are and will be is recorded in the Quantum or Akashic field. We create many possible timelines in our individual and collective lives. We have many incarnations on Earth and other planets. We are not human. We are an infinite spirit having a human experience. We enter human life to feel and experience every emotion whether positive or negative. The force of energy directed into a thought, an idea, a word or an action will create one or more outcomes. All possibility are outcomes or experiences. These form timelines. The timeline we experience will depend on which we individually direct our focus. Collective timelines also exist and follow the same universal principle. Our current timeline seems unchanging and one of constant fear, division and agenda driven politics gestating inner and collective disharmony.

The Theatre
The Universe is the theatre and the Earth the stage for our human experience. We are the actors. Life is governed by

universal cause and effect or karma. Natural law is our inner conscience, moral and ethical vibration. Universal law cannot be circumvented. Natural law is subject to free will. We have free will to ignore our inner consciousness and innate moral and ethical vibration. We can ignore our intuition and inner elevated frequency and immerse into the material world. Human law is an artificial creation supporting norms and values in society. Human law is a derivative of natural law. Human law is a reminder of our innate vibration of unity, moral and ethical behaviour. We seem as a species to need to be reminded of our innate nature. Human law is broken every minute throughout the world. We can use the tree as a metaphor to describe the fall toward the physical. It is equally valid if we wish to understand the barriers to return from physical attachment toward *All That Is* or *Source*. We enter incarnation from all possibility into the physical body. We experience the physical illusion which becomes more powerful as it imposes forgetting upon our open senses upon birth. We slowly become attached to the material and perceptions are distracted by the distractions of the human theatre. The detachment to the inner being is solidified through the mind and ultimately egoistic intellectualism. We become blind to true reality through intellect and perceived exceptionalism. We truly become attached to the physical and identify with our body, gender, culture, colour, and identity group. Through these mechanism we divide, justify war and create socio and economic inequality. The inward journey toward *All That Is*, is a difficult path. It will force us to confront our egoistic self and self-awarded intellectualism. To return to the self is to traverse through the layers of ego, mind and illusion to which we have become attached.

All That Is

Illusion
Attachment
Distraction
Mind
Ego

Physical

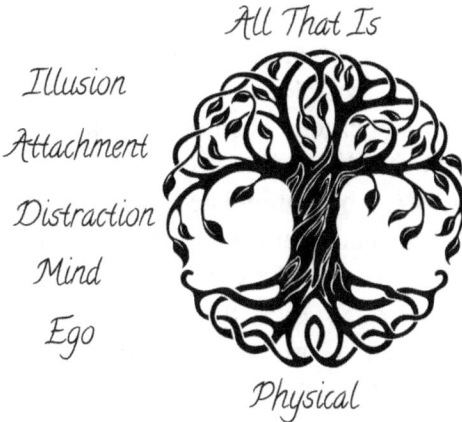

Figure 1: The Theatre

We interact with the human theatre through the physical body and its five senses of touch, taste, smell, sight and sound. The body is the conduit or vessel through which the spirit engages the physical world and creates the experience. We form our perceptions through the senses. Energy is the basis of everything that exist in the Universe. The infinite spirit is all possibility and an expression of the manifested and un-manifested *Source* consciousness. *Source* created the Universe through thought and intention. The Universe from inception become a canvas of experience transformed through cause and effect. The Universe is in perpetual motion of destruction, transformation and creation. It follows universal law. The Universe is expanding not through an omnipotent influence but through the cause and effect of forces in constant motion. The constituents of the Universe create anew and transform the old. Quantum physics uncovers ever more wonders of the infinite cosmos and its eternal expansion. The Universe contains dark matter or un-manifest creational energy. Matter is energy measured as waves and vibrational frequency.

In metaphysical science the unseen is dark matter, energetic waves of invisible forces. The Universe is regarded as an observable energetic cosmos of forming matter and un-manifest possibility. Metaphysical philosophy states universal energy can be manipulated for positive or negative intent. It is thought and intent that transmutes infinite energy into form. *Source* is thought, consciousness and presence. *Source* is not matter. *Source* is the origin and sum of all that exists. The Universe is an energetic expression of *Source* created for the sole intention to allow life to take form and create experiences and outcomes. There may be multiple universes within the sum of *All That Is*. *Source* is limitless possibility and everything is within the One. Humanity is an expression of *Source*. The Earth is the home of our experience. Everything that exists absorbs into *Source*, as it is within it. *Source* does not manipulate the Universe. The Universe just is. We just are. The future of the Universe and everything that exists within it is absolute free will and governed by universal law.

Source has no limitation. Limitation is a physical expression and state the mind imposes upon our external self. Spiritual and intuitive limitation is nurtured by the manipulations and distractions. To interact with the human experience we must perceive it to be real. We touch solid objects, feel the heat of the Sun and the cold of the snow. We experience what it is to be human and physical. There are some among us who have retained opened sensory perceptions and observe wider wavelengths of reality. Others through meditation and other practices have developed their inner sight into spectrums beyond the limited five senses.

There are many charlatans in the esoteric and spiritual practices. The legitimate intuitive possesses clairvoyance, clairaudience and clairsentience. This elevated cognition is sight beyond sight. They are the true mystics and psychics. Evidence of wider realms of perception can be observed in daily in life. We often will see a newborn baby or child staring or conversing with something unseen. An animal will focus on a presence invisible to the human senses. We should not dismiss what we are unable to observe or measure. Our five senses operate in a limited spectrum of light. We are unable to observe all that exists outside our limited spectrum of perception. We are not born without inner sight. As the human experience closes down our inner sight the veil between the illusion and home becomes thickened. We have allowed the distractions to take root. We have built a wall of the mind, the ego and identification with the body. The ultimate outcome is the total detachment from *Source*, the 'I' and loss of purpose.

The Body

We are an infinite spirit having a human experience and not are not physical beings with a spirit. We designed the fundamental aspects of our incarnational experience. We own the experience including the body used to live it. Absolute identification with the body is the first distraction. Identification with our avatar is used to divide humanity at a base physical level. We create prejudices through appearance, size and shape. Being attracted to another by their physical appearance is a natural state. It is the focus on the physical which distracts from sufficient investigation into what resides beyond. The impressionable compare themselves with others creating a sense of inferiority and develop emotional issues. The focus on the physical is further reinforced through archaic cultural dogma, advertising, society and social media. The outcome is distraction and blindness to the presence of our inner spirit pressing against our external being waiting for an embrace. We have become through complete identification with the body completely human in unshakable fashion. We are not human or the body. These are avatars or vessels used to experience the universal theatre. The infinite spirit animates the body. Without the infinite spirit the body dies and has no life. The heart and other organs are the engine and the mind its processor. Esoteric, metaphysical and mystical philosophy have stated this truth for thousands of years. These truths have been lost.

The human experience is real as we perceive it. We are physical in the sense of being in a body in an observable plane of experience. We interact with the physical. We are born biologically one of two genders. We can logically associate with our body and external self with a name and professional title. The challenge arises when we solely identify with these labels and delete any awareness beyond them. The infinite spirit incarnates into realms of experience. The infinite spirit is interacting with the experience and all the personas it offers.

The Ego
It is not negative to have an ego. A balanced ego is required to sustain self-confidence and assertiveness. With a balanced ego the imposition of external distractions is limited and inner awakening has an opening. We all have periods along our physical sojourn where we suffer from an inflated ego and arrogance. It is a natural course of the experience. The goal is to recognise the role of the ego in limiting expansion. An imbalanced ego develops narcissism and

self-importance. Excessive ego prevents expansion of perception, awareness and inner knowing. Ego promotes self-awarded intellectualism and exceptionalism. It feeds status, identification with material possessions, racism and prejudice. It demands respect and recognition.

Pride and vanity are expressions of ego. Healthy pride is a balanced view of achievement. Excessive pride leads to the devaluing of others and arrogance. Excessive ego, pride and arrogance create blindness to others, self-importance and selfishness. Ego will prevent reflection of established notions of truth and it will develop a demonisation and suppression of others. Ego suppresses the courage to assess and bring to the surface internal baggage for healing. Ego reinforces the sense of personal perfection, vanity and narcissism leading toward further immersing into the mind and the physical. Ego does not question itself and accepts no other reality or truth. Narcissism is a common expression of the ego. Narcissism instils a sense of righteousness and imposes unachievable standards upon others. Online communities attack each other because they perceive themselves as right and everyone else as wrong. An egoistic personality is unable to accept that it can be manipulated and assumes everyone else is misled.

The Mind

Over millennia the mind has been the frontline to control perception of the masses. The great unwashed are controlled through fear, feeding the ego and creating division physically, emotionally, mentally, spiritually and energetically. To control billions there must exist distractions to divert attention from liberation through the rediscovery of the inner self and the sovereignty of free will. We are aware before entering life that the human experience will drive perception toward the mind and that it will be subject to manipulation. The manipulations are highly effective control mechanisms and the persistence of ignorance. We should reflect holistically at the universal theatre and consider if what we experience is mere coincidence or are interconnected and intentional movements. Fear, vulnerability and powerlessness are fertile soil for the manipulation of perception. There are no coincidences or chance experiences. The Universe is interconnected and the law of connectedness pervades everything. Nothing happens without the free will of the individual or the collective.

Mind and imbalanced ego are mutually inclusive. Mind is the foundation to the loss of true perception and awareness. We are upon birth bombarded by established concepts of reality, truth and dogma. Our minds are enforced as the only processor of reality, perception and awareness. Many still assert that the mind creates consciousness or is its foundation. Our consciousness is silently steered to control what we interpret through the mind and accept as programmed beliefs. We have become intellectually egoistic in our measurement of self and others. This condition promotes a self-awarded intelligence supplemented by the methodical dumbing down of critical thinking and intellect. The culminating effect is a mass herded society.

The human mind is a powerful organ able to propel humanity forward in innovation, technology, sciences, investigation and analysis into the wider nature of existence. To achieve our potential we must cease being the creators of blindness to the realities of existence. The mind focuses on measurement and analysis and is distracted from the connection to universal intelligence accessed through the infinite spirit. Our fixation with the all-powerful mind supports the effectiveness of the layered manipulations. The mind rejects concepts that are beyond the programming of the normal and focuses on the political, societal and divisive camps of belief. We think constantly but not in concert with the heart or the inner spirit. We should step away from the distractions and the creeping technocratic virtual world. We should open our minds, remove established doctrines, religious dogma and political, societal and cultural influences.

The egoistic mind and the materialist self seeks to achieve what is desirable or of value. Buddhist call this attachment or a hungry ghost driven by insatiable desires. These insatiable desires draw us toward physical planes of existence and influence a return for another sojourn. Attachment to the physical sustains in some a feeling that something is missing and deepens a sense of unease. This is not to say that the materialist life experience is negative but should be balanced through the heart and spirit. Every incarnation is a divine experience. The path is a choice to seeking fulfilment only in the material or to allow the spirit to rise and create through the heart with mind the subordinate.

We find ourselves filling every minute with activity fulfilling cultural expectations, societal judgements, chasing the perfect life, juggling multiple jobs to feed a family, single parenting, pursuing material objects of success and countless other pressures. This paradigm is a manifestation of the human experience and is not created by *Source*. Through these realities, our minds are tunnelled into the myopia of the individual, family, community or national bubble. The mind is seldom able to spend time simply being present. The mind convinces us that if we are not engaged in activity we are unproductive, lazy, and not progressing in the daily material race. The mind replaces the inner journey with looking to others, science and social media to provide an understanding of life, humanity and the Universe. Take a moment to reflect. Are our personal perceptions, decisions and awareness truly guided by the inner spirit or are they silently formed by the distractions and manipulations of the material world? The simple practice of stillness or mindfulness and being present in the moment will start the process toward greater truth and provide the answer.

The Distractions

The material world presents us with the *carrot on the stick*. It states we must be in relentlessly achieving to accumulate material objects and wealth as these are measures of success and are fulfilling pursuits. Desire is a powerful emotion and is fed by the media and focusing the mind on attainment. From the moment that we feel desire the environment feeds that emotion and continues nurturing it throughout life. We have been conditioned to measure our successes against the material objects we accumulate and to value power, control and status. This paradigm is akin to the snake eating its own tail and is never satisfied. Healthy desire can be defined as ambition, goals and objectives balanced and pursued with conscience, integrity, sincerity, justice and consideration of others. Our system is designed to move perception and awareness into the myopia of day-to-day physical life. We operate through the mind and are governed by the ego. Modern life barely finds minutes in the day for reflection, which propagates this self-destructive cycle.

We live in a world seemingly led by psychopathic and sociopathic tendency and leaders. The majority of world leaders are detached from society and pursue agendas not congruent with the lives of those who cyclically elect them to govern their everyday lives. It would seem chaos and control are the fertiliser for ongoing war and destruction. We could argue that perpetual chaos and war is used indirectly or directly to maintain the status quo. A fine line exists between manipulation and the emergence of our true nature. If the journey is embarked upon with persistence and faith it is impossible for external distractions and manipulations to block expansion. We develop inner sight and expose the reality of the human experience. Any hidden agendas are revealed. Logic states that if we are reconnected with the inner spirit the physical illusion would no longer hold dominance. The show would become as clear as if it were on a movie screen. The universal theatre is a movie with humanity one of many actors.

Sovereignty is lost through the act of free will. Humanity gives power to others to dominate and control leading to abuse, ego and corruption. The human experience is not yet at a frequency where this paradigm can be avoided. However, all possibility and potential exist. Consider a scenario where the majority grow to use their true inner being, unity, sovereignty and free will to governing actions, words, thoughts and intent. Would it need leaders, politicians, systems, controls, governments, military and religion? Would hate, separation, fear and war exist? They would not as the vibration to support them would be diminished. Without an energetic vibration and frequency to support an action it cannot manifest itself. Society functions in harmony when directed through the inner spirit led by free will, self-determination and inner knowing.

The Illusion

The illusion is the Universe and our experience within it. It is an illusion as it is not true home. We do not originate from it nor are of it. We are infinite spirits having a human experience. We incarnate into the universal theatre to experience life and expand. There are multiple illusions. There is the illusion the Universe is our origin and we are simply creations of it. The second illusion is the human theatre with which we interact. We observe it as a series of unconnected attributes or events. We observe it as random and coincidental. The reality is quite the opposite. The third illusion is the virtual world that is steadily becoming reality. We may introduce an additional layer of illusion with artificial intelligent beings replacing human interactions. These are experiences absorbed into the One. The line we should not cross is becoming technology through implants, microchipping and the deluded illusion of becoming superhuman.

The physical body is a transient form, an avatar which does not exist beyond the material. The body is simply a vessel to experience being human. We use it and leave it when the experience is over. Awareness of *Source* or true self is not attained through the body or the mind. We expand through feeling, intuition, inner knowing and free will. In the end even the egoistic intellectual will have the true reality unveiled. If we truly wish to remove attachment from the illusion we should open the mind to all possibility, study and investigate new paradigms and concepts. Our true origin is *Source*. We are expression of the One. Everything has an infinite spirit and is aware. We are energy with consciousness. We exist so that *Source* can feel all possibility within the Universe. We along with every possible form of life in the cosmos are conduits to all possibility. As we create and experience we absorb into the One. We are all within the One. The illusion is the world. The illusion is that we are human.

We incarnate into an avatar. The film Avatar depicted the process through which we experience different worlds and lifeforms. Our spirit enters an avatar and animates it. Through the body we experience life, create experiences and expand our inner being. We all exit life. We do so when the experience has served its purpose, through unintended harm or other reasons. Life will end. Our spirit will exit the body and return to our true home. The body will expire and return as energy to the expanding cosmos. This is the illusion. We have forgotten the illusion exists and have become detached far from our true reality.

Gurus and mystics attempt to teach us the reality to existence. To remove perception away from the illusion and create balance we should question everything and accept nothing through the ego and the mind. The mind and the ego will fix perception and awareness. The transformation is from within. We should not dismiss the reality of incarnational life. It is real as we experience it. We incarnate with intention. We should embrace incarnational life and seek to derive from it what we intended and create a wonderful physical adventure along the way. We should develop so that our inner self becomes the origin of our actions, words, thoughts and intents.

The illusion consists of dimensions. Dimensions are states of energetic frequency and perception. They are not physical places. As we expand inner sight we are able to perceive and interact with wider spectrums or dimensions. It is said humanity operates in the third dimension. The third dimension is said to be associated with fear, chaos, anger, hatred as well as belonging, love and kindness. It is a powerful base Chakra frequency. The highest of frequency is that of *Source* and love. Humanity demonstrates love in numerous ways and has the potential to experience a universally aligned existence. Having potential does not imply expansion. Once we realise the illusion, embrace it, experience it, derive growth and adventure from it we will also elevate the dimensional frequency through which we nurture it.

The Awakening

Humanity is entering an era where the hidden is becoming visible and awareness of the human experience is rising. It is called the awakening. The collective experience has an opportunity to move into a higher vibrational dimensional state if it chooses. The vibration is always within the self and not external. We have expanded exponentially technologically. Technology is a duality and can aid or hinder human expansion. Technology can by stealth blight sovereign thinking. Through the absorption into the online virtual Universe which together with identity politics and divisive agendas directs humanity into further separation. The opportunity to transform is always present should we wish to allow our consciousness to step out of the march of masses.

The awakening has a tendency to remain in the mind. The awakening is underpinned by religious, ideological and political camps of belief. The outcome is a fixation on conspiratorial exposure and not a reconnection to the inner spirit. Those who have awakened concentrate solely on exposure as the driver to the changes they seek. The alternative or new media seek to shine light upon that which was hidden and at times align with their own ideology. The paradox is that one matrix is replaced by another, thus avoiding inner expansion. Traversing the inner journey will implicitly bring awareness of the universal theatre through inner sight. The absurdity of the human theatre becomes less important. As an outcome of expansion we cease to participate in and give power to the human theatre. We replace it instead with sovereign thinking, free will and self-determination to guide our actions, words, thoughts and intent. The inner journey has no religious affiliations or attachments to systems or agendas. It is not related to cultural, society, gender or identity politics. As we come to understand the universal theatre, perception shifts energy and creates alternate timelines. We act differently. The physical world transforms through action. We cease repeating actions that support what was once hidden. The exposing and transforming of political ideologies and systems without inner expansion is only part of the puzzle.

We should develop to intuitively observe the theatre, be willing to be wrong, address egoistic intellectualism and allow the spirit to emerge from the farthest recesses. The purpose of incarnation is to fulfil the original intent or purpose whilst manifesting an experience guided by the spirit and the heart. The universal theatre is a set of interconnected experiences, animate or inanimate. We own the frequency and vibration be that ignorance or awakened. The future of our experience is within each of us. The past has allowed the duality to manifest and take root. The present feeds it. It is yet to be seen what we will continue to allow through free will. Apathy has allowed governments the power to look at the masses as serfs. We elect government yet have become servants to them.

Free will is not solely a human privilege. Free will is all encompassing, all-inclusive and governs the expanding Universe. Collectively humanity has allowed negativity and tyranny to manifest. We create timelines of possible events and outcomes. The timelines we have created are governed by universal law. Timelines manifest and change in the now. They exist eternally and project their influences generationally. The human experience has come to a juncture where the few wish to control the many as one homogenous mass in a technocratic dictate. Collective expansion will not be achieved through a one world government or a religion, a political system or any human construct but through personal sovereignty.

Truth is open and accessible to us all if we wish to find it. Everyone has access to *the book* of knowledge within and needs only to allow it to channel. *The book* is metaphorical as it is energy in the form of information. Incarnations into the universal theatre are a choice that our infinite spirit makes from a state of unlimited awareness. Limitation of the physical does not exist in *Source* consciousness. The objective is to look to life as a choice taken for innumerable reasons the spirit understands. When in the physical body it becomes clouded or lost. Life is for expansion but also for joy in the fantastic theatre of possibility.

It is an interesting observation that eastern mysticism for the most part seeks to be free from the cycle of rebirth. Western esotericism has a tendency toward the occult and looks to dominate and seek more life. There is no such thing as fate or coincidence. There is no divinely fated or karmic punishment related to an untimely death. Everything is an act of personal free will or that of another. We are subject to events of our own design and those imposed by others. Darkness does not manifest from *Source*. *Source* is only light and love. Light is bliss, joy, knowledge, unity, contentment and peace. Everything is real in the theatre. It is also an illusion as it does not exist outside of it.

Duality

The infinite spirit was created by thought and presented a Universe as a stage for experiences. We are given a canvas to experience physical life and direct it down any path. The Universe is an experiment. *Source* experiences itself as all possibility through the Universe and every lifeform within it. *Source* is everything that has ever been, is and will be. The Universe is a canvas of constant change directed through universal law. Life is open to become what it wishes to be. Life through the sovereignty of free will may choose to live in its original state of high frequency or divert into other realms of experience. The result is a duality of high and low frequency experience and form. The Earth is a host for many cultures that form nations, each with their own uniqueness. The world consists of varied forms of animal and plant life. The Earth is a melting pot of life and difference and is an experiment to see if life will live in harmony or create duality. The Universe and everything in it was formed from a state of grace and love. Duality did not exist. Humanity together with each lifeform in the Universe created duality the moment perception became

subject to the ego and the mind. We have created false gods, astral and dark realms of form through thought and feed these ideas energy through ritual and sacrifice.

The challenge for all life was to remain in a state of grace and retain the frequency of *Source* in the Universe. This has not been the reality. We own the responsibility to re-establish the original state of harmony and love within the Universe. As we realign the Universe with love, we bring ourselves back to Grace and All That We Are. The shift is achieved one person at a time. The return to grace leads to us back to what the heart silently seeks. We silently wish for a frequency of harmony, unity and peace to be embedded on Earth. *Source* has no judgement nor does it impose its will on the canvas that is the Universe. The Universe and all life within it is an experiment. An experiment so that *Source* can experience all possibility through was is created within it and the timelines of potential outcome. We as humanity are an aspect of this universal canvas.

We live in a brutal duality where the challenge remains for us to bring about a return to grace. We can only do this through a reconnection to the infinite spirit or the higher self. We incarnate into life knowing that upon entering the human experience our open connection to *Source* will be under assault and the detachment will begin. We enter life and its challenges to re-emerge having reconnected with *Source* consciousness. Many refer to this process as an ascension. The physical Universe is measured by opposites, magnetic poles, indirect and alternating current, electron and positron and Quantum physics wave particles. These measure the physical realities of the Universe. We manifest the concept of duality within our life experiences, mirroring opposites in science and physics. Duality imposes a limitation of expression of the infinite self within the life experience.

"In the West we like to think in terms of dualities. Well known examples from diverse fields ranging from philosophy to physics included the physical/metaphysical duality in philosophy, the mind/brain duality in psychology, the genes/environment duality in biology, the enthalpy/entropy duality in chemistry, and the particle/wave duality in physics. We have our founding father of western philosophy, Plato, to thank for this obsession with dualistic thinking."

Steve Donaldson

The universal theatre is a fantastic canvas of all possibility. All manifestation, positive or negative is determined by free will or cause and effect. All life including humanity is free to determine what it wishes to bring into existence through the force of thought transforming energy into form. Universal law is pervasive. *Source* manifests the canvas of the Universe by transforming energy into matter through thought. The same law transmutes the human collective intent into dualities of positive and negative physical experience. All types of vibrations, frequencies, dimensions and states, whether physical, animate or inanimate, are possible within the eternal and expanding experiment. Universal law cannot be circumvented or manipulated but can be transcended such as with the Law of Polarity. The Law of Polarity suggests that through thought we can suppress a negative by concentrating on the desired outcome thereby negating the rule of opposites.

There are those who attempt to elude universal law in numerous ways and come to ultimately observe the futility of their actions. The outcome of collective intention become events and timelines. There are multiple possible timelines that can come to pass. A collective or individual persistent thought, intent or emotion will be energetically and eternally imprinted in the Universe. The universal cosmic library is the Akashic or Quantum field. The duality we individually and collectively experience is that which has been given the most power of thought and thus possess the greatest energy. Within the universal playground the energetic vibrations and frequencies from our intent and thoughts exist as paradigms, dimensions, positive or negative ideas, behaviours and outcomes. Some of the dualities we experience are good and bad, God and the Devil, peace and war, love and hate, unity or division, greed and generosity, rich and poor or victim and victimiser.

There is the idea that negative and positive duality exists because of *Source*. All that exists is within *Source* but not of *Source*. An example is suffering, evil and lower vibrational actions. Universal life possesses free will to create, transform and preserve. Infinite possibility provides a canvas for the innumerable actors to create a role. The theatre of all possibility is based on universal law and the transformation of energy for its continual expansion. The universal theatre will expand infinitely and eternally and is timeless. All that exists is based on this principle and vibration.

Duality is not a truth of *Source* but an experience of *All That Is* manifested through the free will of each actor, whether animate or inanimate. *Source* is regarded as the origin of evil, hatred, destruction, war, greed, self-interest as well as love, harmony, charity, joy and unity. All that is manifested from *Source* is formed from pure love, energy, consciousness and thought into matter. *Source* only emits light and love. Light is bliss, joy, truth, unity, contentment and peace. The opposites are real only in the theatre of duality created by what exists and plays within it. These are illusions as they do not exist outside of the universal theatre. Duality is our creation through physical action, belief and intent. We manifest world events, realms, astral planes, deities, demigods, demons, fear, war, hate, prejudice and the many aspects of life we wish were different. We have rooted the duality in the experience through perpetual nurturing of good and evil. These are reinforced by dogma, the occult and the programed belief this is just how it is. Duality manifested itself from the moment we felt fear. Fear is the currency of duality. Our third dimensional experience nurtures duality and fear. We incarnate into duality to transcend it. We are aware of the impositions to which our open senses will be subjected and how fear will be used to control human perception. Duality exists across dimensional existence. Other expressions of duality will exist in varying degrees of intensity across the Universe. We perpetuate the intensity and dualities that exist in our third dimensional frequency. The universal theatre was not created with duality. *Source* creates through love. We, as an aspect of universal life are open to direct events as we wish them to be.

Some metaphysical thinkers argue that the human third dimensional plane was meant to be this way. They argue our experience was created for the purpose of being a hard school for the sole intention to force expansion in those who enter it. We have free will to accept whatever truth resonates. The reality is that we own what we experience individually and collectively. Duality manifests through the free will of every universal actor. We can either perpetuate or dissolve duality. Fear and ego are the tools in the human experience that separates us from the higher self and are the origin of duality. Without the imprint of constant fear, ego and anxiety the masses cannot be controlled and the duality persists. The duality of good, evil, fallen angels and Satan do not originate from *Source*. They are an outcome of misdirected free will feeding their idea toward their manifestation and power. They become real and persist. This brings into question the reports of biblical figures who profess they have seen God. The interaction may well have occurred. The question is what was is it that presented itself as God? *Source* does not present itself nor select any cultural identity group over another. What came down from the heavens and claimed divinity and creator status was something quite different. It was masquerading itself as *Source* to the naive and the impressionable. We assume everything documented as a divine experience is of *Source* and dismiss the possibility some may be manipulations by other beings.

> "If you don't have the background awareness
> of oneness, duality becomes real."
>
> Alan Finger

Duality will exist so long as we and everything in the Universe offers energy and maintains disconnection from our ultimate reality. We will remain blind to the truth behind duality. If a group decide to place an effigy or idol as a representation of God and over time ever more people direct devotional and sacrificial energy to it, it will manifest from the canvas of all possibility. If through manipulation something presents itself to the naive as the divine and large numbers of people believe it, a religion is created around it. Thought directs energy to manifest in matter or form and has no judgement. The Universe will offer whatever we decide to create be that negative or positive and in whatever fantastic form we believe it to be. Beyond this theatre there is only light and love. There is no other reality but *Source* and the spirit realm to which all that originates from *Source* will return. *All That Is* within *Source* and infinite possibility. How infinite energy is transformed and persists is open to the free will of all that exists upon the universal canvas. The field of experience is the Universe or the Multiverse. When intuition and heart are ignored, the surface consciousness acts through desire, ego and the physical. The outcomes become negative actions which may not have been intended to be bad. Intellectualism, desire, ego and the physical hold influence when inner consciousness is stagnant or dimmed. Egoistic intelligence is not a precursor to greater expansion. Exaggerated egoism is a hindrance and likely to dismiss any thought of a greater reality. Intellect can breed ego and blindness through the notion of cleverness and exceptionalism.

Ethics are relative to cultures where ethical societies exhibit greater violence and aggression than those with traditional but nonviolent tendencies. Bad and good are dualities created by all that exists within the universal theatre. Duality is embedded universally. The lessening of duality cannot be confined to the generation of today nor the incarnation in the now. The removal of manifested duality is multi-incarnational and generational. It is timeless yet critical. It is not for the individual to be concerned how duality as a whole is lessened but to merely expand themselves toward true self in the present. If duality within the experience is to be diminished, the Self and the personal Universe must change removing the energies that link to the duality and its imposition on the whole.

We must cease looking to external influences or others

as the source of imbalance. We should observe and reflect on the self and the personal expansion needed to raise ones vibration and frequency. The inward journey allows the re-emergence of the infinite spirit toward a lesser influence of duality. Its involution in the theatre is a result of all life in the expanding cosmos creating opposites, through energetic expression and positive or negative intent. The power of duality over humanity is commensurate to the energy given to it in this paradigm.

> "Only in love are unity and duality not in conflict"
>
> Rabindsanath Tagore

It is assumed that the reader has accepted that there is something greater than the individual or that they may be pondering the existence of *Source*. Understanding duality as the physical axis of wrong, right, suffering, bliss, conflict and light is one aspect. Knowledge and ignorance are a similar duality.

Acceptance

When embarking upon the journey toward inner knowing and to the infinite self the challenge for many is accepting that there is a divine *Source* or *All That Is*. It is not critical to accept the existence of *Source* from the outset. The persistent inward journey will present a sense of a silent presence and a feeling of a greater reality. A barrier to accepting *Source* exists is the manifestation of duality and the presence of good and evil, injustice, greed, war, hate and fear. The argument remains that if *Source* as an omnipresent, omnipotent and omniscient presence why does it allow these aspects of duality. We have become disillusioned by life experiences, religious doctrine, dogma, traditions and the incompatibility of faith with modern life. Egoism and intellectualism has relegated *Source* to a creation of the mind. The result is a rejection of the infinite spirit, *Source* and any notion of the afterlife. To accept spirit and *Source* is to accept an infinite, immeasurable presence, everywhere and in everything.

Source is often termed as male, female, he or as a physical being but it is none of these definitions. It just is. *Source* is an energy emitting pure creation, bliss, peace and love. The predominant conception of *Source* is of a physical anthropomorphic being residing in a metaphorical heaven. A being who created man in his image, surveying all that he has created, bestowing love on the pious and righteous, casting judgment and punishment on all others. A duality with its opposing aspect the Devil. *Source* is regarded as an all-powerful entity who punishes those who do not believe in it, do not express devotion through rituals, offerings and sacrifice or other such acts. Some view it as an entity who demands attendance at a place of reverence or worship as a rite of passage. Other see *Source* as a being sitting at the pearly gates of heaven judging every soul that presents itself before allowing them entry into his kingdom. Religion in all of its forms is a creation of humanity as are the many deities, effigies, figures or symbols of devotion. Over thousands of years faith has been morphed by numerous civilisations. We direct focus on an array of images rather than the One. Religion and faith lost its purpose long ago. Humanity has become what it is due to the current influences and loss of connection with true reality and the higher self.

Source is an inner presence, a state of knowing, bliss, joy and stillness. The awareness of *Source* is achieved when we shift consciousness and perception outside the universal theatre and into the wider aspect of our true nature. We become aware that the universal theatre is an experiment in which humanity is a part. Acceptance is to know *Source* is everything that is, has been and will be. *Source* is all possibility, an infinite silent presence, a sum of everything and a frequency of love and truth. *Source* just is. It is an existence that cannot be explained by words or manner. *Source* is felt. The dissolution of the ego and the tempering of the mind allows *Source* to emerge into our being. *Source* is all possibility, light and love. Light is knowledge, information and truth. *Source* emanates from and in everything. *Source* is our beginning, middle and end. It is home. *Source* is inexplicable to science and blind to faith. It cannot be encapsulated by the many avatars, deities or demigods which are all human creations.

Source is not the privy of those who perform sacrifice, ritual or self-inflicted suffering. *Source* is felt inwardly through silence and by being present. It is developed through meditation. Meditation quietens the mind, the body and the external consciousness. In this state we allow the inner spirit to emerge, reconnect and open to the infinite vibration of truth and thought. We start to expand whilst in body. We travel toward all possibility and expansion through universal law and free will. Everything that exists, from the totality of the Universe to the smallest subatomic particle, is a fractal of *Source*. We are a pure encapsulation of *All That Is*. *Source* is present in everything and is *All That Is*. Ultimately acceptance of *Source* is fundamental to what manifests and is experienced through the mechanisms of life. If we refuse without openness to investigate this fundamental truth what follows therein will seem no more than an unconnected posturing of ideas and notions. To understand self is to be aware that *All That Is* exists within *Source*.

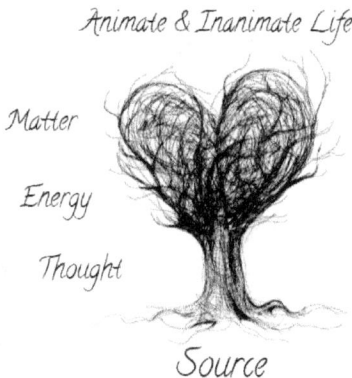

Figure 2: The Great Un-Manifest

The tree depicts the involution of form in a constant cycle of expansion. The Universe and numerous life forms are depicted by the branches, twigs and leaves of the tree. The tree depicts energy through which the force of thought manifests matter to form life. The passage of our infinite spirit into matter is often referred to as dropping into ignorance. The dropping into ignorance is also termed forgetting. The two terms describe the process through which the truth of our true being dissolves as we enter physical life. It describes the process by which our open connection beyond the veil becomes subject to immediate suppression through the illusion of human life and all its distractions. Slowly the awareness and extended sight we possess as a newborn baby rapidly disappears and we forget our purpose, origin and divinity. We become human.

Source is the root of the tree. It is pure energy, consciousness and the sum of the whole. The Universe, life and the totality of experience is *Source* consciousness in constant motion. *Source* consciousness is universal and natural law manifesting destruction, preservation, creation and expansion. The flow is akin to an imploding star releasing energy and creating the building blocks for new cosmic bodies and dark matter. Infinite possibility is *Source*. *Source* feels itself through each life form. Through our free will and power to manifest all aspects of our physical lives we contribute to the expanding Universe and thus *Source*.

Science offers numerous theories as to the origin of the Universe. These theories include catastrophism which states the Universe was sprung from a sudden violent event or gradualism describing how the cosmos was formed through slow incremental changes. Universal expansion follows its own free will of constant change. The flow of universal change exhibits catastrophism and gradualism.

Everything that exists is a state of energy and in an infinite cycle of creation, preservation and transformation. Universal energy vibrates in wavelengths and frequencies to create matter. We observe these forms when in alignment with the frequency or wavelength in which they vibrate or exist. If our perceptions are not in an expanded state or in resonance with the frequency of the object or form, it will remain invisible to our senses and spectrum of awareness.

The natural flow of the Universe creates life as an outcome. Through free will we and other universal life forms can impose unintended changes to the course of what exists. Through cause and effect our actions project energetic change in the present and create ripples in existing timelines and create new pathways. The Universe is an experiment. All life in it is an experiment. It is left to become what it will. The Universe is a canvas on which we all have a brush. Universal life, whether animate or inanimate, possesses free will, self-determination and sovereignty. We can be whatever we wish to become. We can create with the intention of light or darkness. The Universe will be the sum of our collective intention.

The Universe is teaming with infinite life adapted to their environment. All life, whether animate or inanimate, is intelligent in its realm of experience. The snail is aware and intelligent in its realm of experience as is humanity. We do not need to accept non-terrestrial life and remain in a bubble waiting for science to provide evidence. The reality is that the Universe has intelligent non-terrestrial life. The Universal theatre is free will all possibility. We should be mindful of what we create and become. We may reincarnate to live what we have created. We can focus on temporal material desires or direct intention toward inner expansion as it is the only transcending objective. To know self is to know life. We are a fractal of divine *Source* and a manifestation of love. Everything animate, inanimate, living, conscious, known, unknown, thought, seen, unseen, action, word, expression is infinite and eternal.

Source is the entirety of energy. Everything is manifested through divine *Source* energy. Humanity is one of an infinite number expressions. There is only one *Source* presence. We have given *Source* many forms and names. We have created many religions, ideologies, the occult, interdimensional entities and pseudo demigods. We relinquish power to others who profess to be the single conduit to the divine. These are our free will decisions.

All that exists has consciousness. Every quark, sub atomic particle and atom has energy, frequency, consciousness and awareness. This must be so as it originates from *Source* energy and is a fractal of it. The fractal of *Source* consciousness are the branches, twigs and leaves of the tree which form the Universe, galaxies, systems, stars, planets, simple and complex Life.

Thought is energy directed into form and matter. The inner spirit and consciousness animates it in being. *Source* is infinite consciousness, energy and frequency. Negative energy exists in *Source* but is not of it. *Source* emits only light upon the canvas of energetic possibility. Duality, negative forces or astral entities are a creation of those who exist within the physical Universe. What we create within the Universe will exist and persist within the oneness of *Source*. The occultist plays with dark practices and astral forces creating lower vibrational forms and misguided worship to their false gods and effigies. It is true that these exist in the Universe and are a part of *All That Is*. Everything exists within the One that is *Source*. These illusions do not exist outside of the universal canvas. The spirit realm

44

to which everything returns is only of light and a state of blissful presence.

The use of energetic all possibility is subject to the free will. We own what we create. We are responsible for what we allow, its existence and persistence. All possibility can be used for positive or negative purposes. Through the direction of energy we can bring into being any form or outcome. Religion imposes upon the psychology of their flock the notion of hell and damnation. We are told we will become hideous forms for deeds in life. We will live in eternal purgatory for evil acts. We are programmed to believe only the worthy shall enter the kingdom of heaven. These programmed belief systems and paradigms if embedded deep within the psychology of the follower will determine the experience in life and immediately upon death. The illusion we create upon death is temporary but may be perceived to be an eternity. We create our experience in the physical realm and we are able to manifest a further illusion upon death. Anything that exists has its foundation in thought. Thought creates an idea and when given sufficient energetic focus will bring it into reality. This is the same for any deity, demigod, demon, satanic effigy or symbol of light. If sufficient numbers focus devotion, perform rituals and project energy to a form or an idea, it will manifest itself in the Universe. Through the feeding of energy to an idea it derives power and persists and becomes the god to the uninitiated. The same universal law applies to positive thinking or repeating thought patterns. Little energy will be spent in this book covering the intentions of lower dark energetic worship, practices and forms as these are for the misled. They are not of high frequency light energy.

The inalienable truth is the core of every spirit never leaves the frequency of *Source* and only a fractal of our infinite being enters form. We never leave *Source* and are eternally connected to it. The mind and the universal matrix theatre has convinced the masses that they are inferior, simple humans, frail and subservient. As we move further into the illusion we become blind to the actions of the misled who conjure low vibrational energetic astral forces and false gods. These activities are lower Chakra tendencies and are illusions those who play will confront when out of body.

To rediscover our true state, expand and grow we must experience challenge. To experience challenge implies a limitation in awareness and knowledge. This is the dropping into ignorance which is implicit when incarnating into the human theatre. At birth there is an invisible veil between the physical experience and *Source*. A newborn baby has unburdened senses of sight beyond the physical eye. This is a beautiful state between *Source*, the spirit realm and the physical experience. A newborn baby cannot articulate what is sees or senses but it is there. A newborn baby or child who has retained open sight may observe what will be invisible to others.

We enter by design the human field of experience with an absolute intent. We are aware of the forgetting we will experience as a result of the impositions upon our open senses upon birth. For the majority as years pass intuition and the psychic self becomes further suppressed through parental dogma, beliefs, distraction and manipulation of the human system. The limitation is not developed in the womb but later as the infinite spirit becomes separated from itself by the physical body, the ego and the mind. These attributes develop dominance over truth and inner perception of reality. Our true state is awareness of *Source*, peace and harmony. Theosophical texts describe the time when life was in complete harmony with source as the golden age.

Harmony and love was the only frequency of the Universe. Humanity has strayed away from this state.

The objective is for all universal life to live in harmony and align to the highest of frequency of love. For this to become a reality life must elevate its vibration. Everything has purpose. The Universe is cyclical in that life traverses cycles of energetic expansion and periods of disconnection. This does not mean that we are implicitly subject to cycles of disconnection and reconnection. Energetic cycles can only impose their energy upon our spiritual expansion if we allow it. We need only voluntarily shift our frequency through the inner connection with our divine spirit and allow it to direct the path. The majority will not make this shift. Intellectualism and attachment to the ego prevents self-directed expansion. We expect the human experience to force ignorance and forgetting upon our avatar. If we are fully aware of the illusion throughout life there would be no purpose to incarnation into humanity. Our infinite spirit enters the body knowing the surface consciousness will direct awareness, nurture the forgetting of home and an ignorance to truth.

Metaphysical and esoteric philosophy has been completely replaced by inflexible science and religious doctrines. We are moving into an era where sovereignty is replaced by conformity and freedoms, free speech and thought are becoming eroded. Numerous religions cite versions of truth to divinity but act as control mechanisms of their flock. Unseen societies and hidden agendas promote war and perpetual chaos. The human experience and its brutal duality suppresses the infinite spirit and relegates it to the dimly lit recesses of the physical being.

The human conception of reality is formed by our interaction with the world. We experience the physical world through the body. Through our sensory capabilities the interaction is real and absolute. The illusion of perceived reality dissolves once the internal journey reaches a level of expansion and reconnection to *All That Is*. Illusions lift and the theatre, stage and acts become apparent. Our purpose starts to unfold gently and the secrets of the Universe become known. There are no true secrets. The secrets are merely truth and inner knowledge waiting to rise into our awareness. Every incarnation has an intent and a purpose. We incarnate to experience the wonders of physical life but also to expand from ignorance to knowledge as a spiritual outcome.

The current awakening is focused on mental expansion. It is steered toward awareness of the manipulated human experience and it maintains its focus in the theatre. In the human experience we have space and time as a collection of sequential conscious experiences, actions, words and thoughts. Linear time is a continual flow of movement in the field of physical experience. Our external awareness moves between experiences with little attention to what lies beyond life. Once the inner self is at peace and silent, the truth emerges. The Quantum field or Akasha records our experience. Without the true inner spirit there can be no animated body. The Akashic field records every action, word, thought and intent the spirit experiences.

Personality evolves from each incarnation and becomes part of our expanded soul or infinite spirit. The personality is in continual change as we experience life and interaction with others. Everything becomes an energetic footprint within the infinite self and the Akasha. We are not human but an expression of *Source* as an infinite spirit energy. We have human experiences. *Source* is the beginning, middle and end, infinite and eternal awareness. Our infinite spirit is eternal and free to create experiences. *Source* is pure energy, thought and exudes only love. *Source* is a quiet elation, a peaceful state and a felt presence. *Source* is all that has ever been and will be.

The Buddha stated he did not feel any evidence of a divine *Source* and that such a belief is not necessary. It is agreed belief is not necessary as a precursor to expansion. Through meditative practice the existence of *Source* becomes clear. The inner elation, bliss, joy and love experienced through silence and reconnection is *Source*. All life is a fractal of *Source* and we are expressions of it. Expansion takes us from the evidence driven mind to inner knowing and truth naturally through the journey of self-discovery. *Source* is and can only be felt. *Source* cannot be known, nor explained in its totality or evidenced by physical instruments. *Source* is beyond the physical. Inner growth is a continual journey. There is no defined moment of enlightenment. It is silent and continual with the objective being the reconnection to the spirit realm. As stated earlier these statements are not presented as an absolute truth but concepts for reflection.

The Body

Illusion is defined as something wrongly perceived or interpreted by the senses, a deceptive appearance, a false idea or belief. Everything that exists does so within its own state of consciousness. *Source* is the origin of all that exists. The Universe, our infinite spirit, the spirit realm and all possibility has its origin in the plane of light or information. *All That Is,* is sparked into existence by thought. The Universe is a canvas where life is free to create an experience through the intent of light or darkness. It all exist within *Source* consciousness. The spirit realm for some is heaven. It is simply the abode of our spiritual core. The spirit realm is our eternal home and we never leave it. A fractal of our core enters incarnation. A thread of conscious energy connects each fractal with its core. The spirit realm is not an external place that we must be worthy of entering through perceived righteousness, suffering, penance or sacrifice. The cosmos is a field of experience brought into reality through the body. The body and its senses allow consciousness to express itself through actions, words, thoughts, intents and interactions.

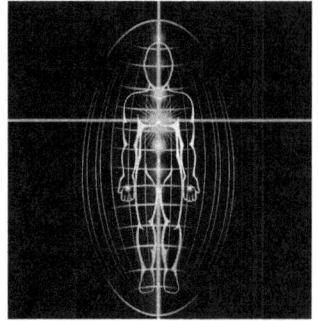

The illusion is the field of experience or the theatre into which we choose to enter. Life is a constant within the Universe. Consciousness is the animator of the body as it is for every form, whether animate or inanimate, that exists. Life can take any form from energetic to physical. Our natural presence is a formless energetic state of conscious awareness. Just as simply as *Source* exists, our spirit also just is. Our infinite spirit exists in limitless time and all possibility. It is in everything and it is aware of our infinite eternal nature. We may take any presentation from the formless to the bluntly physical. Incarnational life allows the infinite spirit to experience the senses, love, beauty, desire and infinite possibility of the cosmic theatre. We enter into the theatre of illusion with purpose. There is purpose in all that exist in the cosmic theatre. We choose to be exactly where we find our experience from the first incarnation to the last. All life experiences are chosen from the realm of infinite consciousness and love. When we not experiencing incarnational life the infinite spirit is unburdened by the physical impositions of form. Fear, hate, prejudice, greed, separation, ideals, war, duality, nationalism, money, time or any emotion derived from form is obsolete. We design each incarnation from a state of infinite awareness. We design incarnations that will offer expansion. We design predestined events and crossroads at specific points along the sojourn.

Our experiences are guided by free will. We create the lives we wish to have. The predetermined events or crossroads are there to direct our avatars to specific experiences that have been designed for growth. The paths and diversions we may take in life are infinite. We may design alternate events to redirect us to our intended purpose. We may be oblivious to these markers. As we align with our true nature the events in life gain clarity as purpose begins to unfold. We start to become cognisant of signs, synchronicities, numbers, symbols, events, people, places, intuition and guidance from our spiritual home.

Free will is the dominant factor across the Universe. We may live a life without ever having fulfilled any of our intended purpose. Through free will we can divert partially or grossly away from our divine intention and immerse ourselves into the illusion. We may absorb further into the mind, ego and lower Chakra desires. Life will be what we determine it to be through our choices. How far the true self is suppressed or allowed to emerge is subject to free will. For most people the illusion is real and all they perceive. The mere suggestion they are not their body and the physical experience is a temporary sojourn is beyond comprehension. *Source* manifests the field of experience to understand itself and life. Life takes infinite form. The expanding universal field of experience exists so that *Source* can know what it is to be alive and experience all possibility through every form of life. To be alive is to feel. We feel every sensation and all possibility whether positive or negative.

The body is simply energy in vibration. We perceive it and our environment through our perceptions. We operate in a vibrational frequency where what we perceive is matter and solidity. The body is a temporary suit our infinite spirit occupies to experience life. Beyond the physical body we are projected energy and consciousness. Everything from the tiniest particle to massive cosmic body has a spirit, an energetic aura and an awareness. We are not the pinnacle of form nor evolution and it is human arrogance to have such a belief. Humanity is an experience sharing the Universe with countless other lifeforms. We are a contributor to the expanding Universe. We are not the sole proprietor of intelligence. There are countless other forms of life in the Universe.

The Universe offers infinite possibility where we can choose whether or not to promote love. *Source* understands itself through our constant expansion within the field of experience. The field of experience is vibrating energetic band of wavelength frequency. What we perceive, observe and interact with is in direct alignment with our wavelength of perceptible frequency. For example a person who believes unwaveringly that they are physical beings with perceptions rooted and formed by the theatre will observe only what the limited programmed senses present. Others who through developed or naturally open sensory perception and connectedness to the infinite reality will perceive and interact with what lies beyond in the unseen. Fractals of our core infinite spirit may have multiple life experiences in parallel universes. The Universe is all possibility. The infinite spirit never leaves the domain of *Source*. The spirit is infinite and has limitless energy. The body with its limited senses is incapable of holding the entirety of our infinite spirit. To experience parallel lives in multiple universes our infinite spirt would not be contained in a single energetic avatar even if it were capable of holding such a force.

Many in the new age and ufology call humans creator gods. This has truth in part as through free will we are able to create our own experience. We create our experience through intention and thought. Our life experience is governed by universal law, cause and effect or Karma. Through each incarnation we pass through physical time. The tag of being a creator god is not to be confused with being *Source* itself. The infinite spirit possesses the power to manifest within its chosen experience. This does not mean we are God or *Source*. We are not *Source*. We are a fractal of *Source* just as is a blade of grass or an animal. We have free will. Free will is an attribute shared with everything that exists. We are expressions of *Source*. Humanity, as with all forms of life possesses the same power to manifest matter through the transformation of energy by thought. To be alive is to express what resides within and absorb all that is external.

As we enter life we forget what we truly are. This is not the intention of life but a result of it. Forgetting is the process of shifting from a state of infinite awareness of what we truly are. Upon incarnation we develop an acute narrowing of awareness and drop into surface consciousness. The process rapidly blinds us to inner knowing. Forgetting occurs when our surface consciousness immerses into the physical and focus is directed onto the external self and the material world. The forgetting is not total. It is expected, imposed and necessary for the spirit to expand. Our challenge whilst creating the adventure is to allow the spirit to re-emerge and realise our divinity whilst in the crudeness of the body. The Universe was in harmony upon inception. Everything lived in grace and existed in balance. This was the original state and what esoteric philosophy describes as the golden age. *Source* emits life from light in the form of information, love and harmony. From the dawn of the Universe life started to manifest duality. We have lived many lives from the moment our infinite spirit was brought into being through thought. We are a creation of thought. *Source* created spirit and the Universe through intention. The Universe is left to become what is wishes. The duality we experience is a creation of our free will. If we feel fear that will be the foundation of what manifests within our experience. Over time we have created a brutal duality which will persist until the overwhelming frequency shifts toward love and harmony.

Life is a canvas of all possibility and it is open to be what we wish it to become. The challenge for all life within the theatre is to rediscover its true state of grace. We have collectively created the opposites and imbalance. We are directed to embark upon internal rediscovery to bring about change for the whole. This may span multiple lifetimes. Ultimately we all will reconnect with *Source* whilst in the body. There are some who have incarnated into the human experience to assist humanity and guide it to balance and harmony. There are also those in the theatre who understand the unseen and use the duality to control human perceptions and the theatre with which we interact. The few with this low vibrational agenda have no desire to see the infinite spirit emerge and harmony re-established. We may wish to refer to these beings as earthbound spirits who design lives for expansion but return and repeat rooted paradigms or tendencies. Everything will, in the end return to grace whilst in a body. However, for some spirits it may be countless lifetimes before this is achieved.

We do not need to form lives in the physical realms. We have free will to seek growth anywhere within the universal theatre or pursue it whilst in an energetic state. The reality is that the universal theatre offers exponential growth and challenge. The human experience exudes beauty, sounds, smells and interactions that other physical realms may not offer. We choose the brutal duality of the human experience. We may return over many incarnations until the attachment to it or need is resolved. Eastern spiritualism teaches we should seek to break the cycle of incarnation or rebirth through inner rediscovery. Western spirituality promotes inner expansion but not necessarily to release from the cycle of rebirth. Western spiritualism looks to control the unseen aspects of the human experience and seeks more of it. In the end the destination is the same and for some it is faster than others.

The veil between the spirit realm and the physical becomes thickened over years and is hastened by the dogma of parents, environment, religions and intellectualism. That which was once open becomes closed and we start to immerse into the human experience. We become detached from *Source* consciousness and attached to the material. The surface consciousness or ego self is closely bound to mind. The combination of ego and mind become the root of the experience within the human experiment. The forgetting or dropping into ignorance is not a divine intention but one we know will occur when we incarnate into the realm of physical experience. By proxy of the impositions of the human theatre we are immediately challenged to expand. We may ignore signs and events only to return in another incarnation with a new intention. Infinite knowing and awareness resides beneath the surface. It waits for the ego to reignite it. The challenge for each of us is to embark upon the inner journey and expand from ignorance into enlightenment. To be enlightened is to simply release inner knowing and perception through expanded sight.

Let's revisit the question of what am I? The archetypal response would be I am a Woman or a Man followed by I am a Lawyer, a Nurse or another job title. These are true descriptions when viewed solely from the material experience. We are born biologically as one of two sexes. We choose to create an experience leading to a profession or an occupation. The loss of purpose arises when we limit our understanding of the self to these physical labels. If we stop at this simple and illusionary definition a loss in purpose starts to emerge. It is futile to ignore the creeping lack of purpose when fully immersed in the material theatre. The reason why we seem in constant pursuit of meaning and purpose is rooted on the loss of true self. We lose awareness of what we truly are as we immerse into the theatre of illusion and identification with our avatar. The surface consciousness and mind associate the self with the vessel. We believe we are the body. The fear of death and suffering manifests from this belief. We identify with the physical body, assessing and evaluating others by their physical attributes or lack thereof. We use physical prowess, size, strength, height, features and beauty to dominate and impose upon one another. This is a base level of ignorance that is not far detached from what we deem lower to be lesser intelligent animal life.

The physical body is the foundation of division. We further divide ourselves through the ego, mental superiority, wealth, status, religion, country, nation, culture and exceptionalism. The body is simply concentrated energy perceived as matter through our five senses and mind. We observe archetypes and objects through the mind. The body is the vessel we use to interact with the human experience. It is illusionary. The greatest mental hurdle is to accept the idea the body is not the self. The infinite spirit has occupied many avatars. The body is merely a vehicle. We should embrace the experience of being in the body. We should not define ourselves by it. A body is like clothing, a possession or an object. We maintain, clean and discard them when they no longer serve a purpose. The infinite spirit exits the body when it feels no more is possible within it or that the purpose is served. Through free will we can neglect the body and develop ill health which results in an early end to life.

We have created division within the human family. We divide by colour, culture, religion and identity groups. We permit the psychopathic behaviour of the few who conquer, subjugate and manipulate the uninitiated. We separate ourselves by race. We define race by colour or cultural identity group. The concept of race is an illusion and serves only to separate. Humanity is a species. The human species shares the universal theatre will an abundance of life. As a species we consist of many cultures with different identities and languages. A culture or identity group is not a different race. The separation and definition of race has its origins in divisive ideologies. There are no chosen people or a superior group. Division based on religion, culture, colour or identity originate in third dimensional awareness. We incarnate to experience difference, alternate views, cultures and identity. The experiment seeks to determine if as human we are able to live in harmony, peace, sharing and love. This remains to be seen. By engaging in division and separation serves only to delay expansion. It detaches us from our true nature. We are locked into defining ourselves as only the body. We have imprisoned our consciousness into a fixed energetic vibration. Our perceptions are open to manipulation.

"So it is with the human consciousness,
there is a subconscious connection between
each individual soul and the world soul deep
hidden in the most primitive depths of the
sub consciousness and in consequence we
share in the rise and fall of the cosmic tides."

Dion Fortune

The purpose and origin of religion is subjective. Religion offers a path away from the attachment to the mind and the physical world. Faith asks that we reconnect with the higher self and to the wonder beyond. Religion was created my humanity. Humanity has morphed it purpose. Faith was intended to be a stepping stone to a much greater reality but is now used to keep the follower standing on the same rock. We have dropped into reverence of others who profess divinity and see ourselves as lesser beings. Religion has failed in its intention. It is now a series of dogmatic doctrines and a control mechanism for the masses.

Followers, worshippers and false holy representatives work to keep religion on the first stepping stone across the metaphorical river toward greater realisation. They dare not lead their flock to wider understanding. By revealing the true being that we are they would negate their purpose and lose control of their flock. We would move from follower and worshiper to discoverer of the true self. Our inner journey needs no guru, saint, prophet or pope. The journey simply asks that we shed the unbalanced ego, attachment with the physical body and desire for the material. We should expand to operate in the higher frequency of love. The frequency of love is not the human physical attraction or emotional attachment. The frequency of love is a blissful state of grace that wells up from within. It is an inner joy of connectedness to the infiniteness of everything. The feeling is indescribable but is felt. It has immeasurable power.

Esoteric philosophy, numerology and astrology are subjects of study to open the mind to greater understanding of the true self. Numerology is the science of numbers and astrology is the study of the energetic influences of planets and stars. Our connection to *All That Is* will align with the expansion of our consciousness. The process of becoming is the movement toward truth and our infinite reality. *Source* is not a construct of the mind. Mental perception forms our limited boundary of experience.

Technological advances are not signs of spiritual progression. Inner knowing and expansion are the only paths toward awareness of the infinite spirit. We will progress technologically and travel beyond the boundaries of the Earth into the wonders of the Universe. We will through advanced Artificial Intelligence and Quantum physics seek to replicate the Universe without understanding the self. Through understanding the self and releasing the mind science will come to understand consciousness, wisdom and truth. There are many spokes on the wheel toward spiritual expansion. We may start with the mind and religion and over time return to truth and reality. We will eventually return to the centre of the wheel to the higher self. The question is when.

Tendency

Tendencies are repeating paradigms that reside within the eternal energetic footprint of our incarnational experiences. Every aspect of each incarnational experience is recorded. Every major action to a fleeting thought is recorded. The footprint of our incarnational universal experiences are held in the Quantum field. The Quantum field is the Akashic field. For tendency to persist it must exist within the eternal realm. The Quantum field is the cosmic library of the Universe. For tendency and multi-incarnational experience to be possible the cosmic library must exist and persist. Every sojourn into the universal theatre imprints an energetic footprint within the Quantum field. All that we have ever been and will be is held in the cosmic library of the Akasha. DNA and all possibility is held eternally within the Quantum field. Our infinite spirit is not held within the Quantum field. Our infinite spirit is integrated into the One and is in unity with *All That Is*. The Universe and the cosmic library is one. We are one. All that exists does so within *Source*. Separateness does not exist

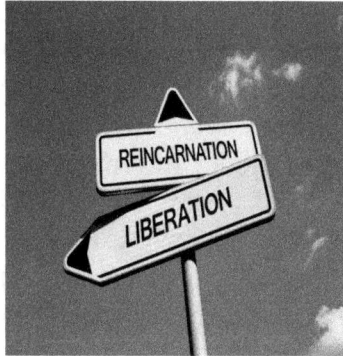

within the spirit realm and is unaffected by the paradigms within the physical Universe.

The military established remote viewing programs in the 1960s mainly for the purpose of spying and espionage. It is believed military units listening to Morse code would report falling into Theta states of consciousness. They would drift from a local point of awareness into alternate sensory states in space and time and reported observing events or places. The military investigated the phenomena which manifested as remote viewing. Glenn Wheaton a well know military remote viewer was speculated to be the Character Lyn Cassady who was played by George Cooney in the movie *The Men Who Stare at Goats*. The movie parodied the practice of remote viewing. Declassified documents related to the Stargate Project in the 1990s had mention of remote viewing. Retired military practitioners admitted to the practice and have since written books and offered training. Remote viewing no doubt continues to be used in far developed ways unknown to the public.

The Farsight Institute led by Dr. Courtney Brown, Ph.D. conducts blind remote viewing sessions investigating the phenomena. Each remote viewing session is conducted in totally blind conditions. The remote viewer is unaware of the target. The remote viewer using standard protocols is given a randomly generated identification number that represents the target. The remote viewer will focus attention on the randomly generated identification number and report what is perceived. A remote viewing session was conducted with the target unknown to the remote viewer. The hidden task was to connect with the consciousness of Adolf Hitler to understand his psychology. For this experiment to be successful consciousness would need to persist beyond life and eternally within the infinite energy of the Quantum field or Akasha. The session successfully connected to the consciousness of Adolf Hitler and was able to be easily identified. Esoteric principles state the persistence of consciousness is implicit and is unquestioned. Consciousness is energy and infinitely present. Tendency resides within consciousness and is a state within the Akashic field. Everything that has and will ever exist is energetically recorded in the Akashic records or Quantum field. The Akashic records have been consulted by ancient civilisations from Egyptians, Tibetans, Persians, Greeks, Hindus and western spiritualists. The Akashic field exists as energy within *All That Is*. It is simply energy in the universal expanse. The Akasha is the cosmic library.

We are all connected energy and a part of everything. We experience life in our own individual state of consciousness. Energy is in everything all at once. Science describes the universal interconnectedness of energy as Quantum entanglement. Esoteric knowledge states the presence of infinite connectedness and the absence of separation. The spirit realm is the origin of the 'I'. The 'I' is pure energy and a point of presence. Incarnation is a state where the 'I' concentrates a fractal of its infinite core into a point of perception within an avatar. The Akasha is energetic information which exists within *Source* as does the Universe. Everything is energy therefore, it is not beyond reason to accept every action, word, thought and intent persists and can be accessed through consciousness.

"It is this system that acts as the central storehouse of all information for every individual who has ever lived upon the Earth. More than just a reservoir of events, the Akashic Records contain every deed, word,

feeling, thought, and intent that has ever
occurred at any time in the history of the
world. Much more than simply a memory
storehouse, however, these Akashic Records
are interactive in that they have a tremendous
influence upon our everyday lives, our
relationships, our feelings and belief systems,
and the potential realities we draw toward
us."

Edgar Cayce

The Farsight Institute conducted an experiment to remote
view the transition from the moment of death of John F.
Kennedy. The remote viewer shifted perception into the
target identifier which represented the consciousness of
John F. Kennedy. The remote viewer reported an instant
awareness of an ending of a life and shifting into a boundless
state of calm, love, detachment, peace and expansion.
The remote viewer sensed a feeling of being everywhere
all at once. We should remind ourselves remote viewers
are unaware of the target or intent of the session. Remote
viewing sessions provide evidence to the persistence of
energy and consciousness. Despite the continual discoveries
many remote viewers still seek more evidence. Remote
viewing is a practice of mind using the subconscious to tap
into subspace. Subspace is the energetic wavelength and
frequency within *All That Is*. Subspace is the Quantum field
or Akashic records. The Quantum field holds all possibility
including timelines, all that has ever been and tendency.

Mind directed practice results in the unfortunate need
for measureable proof despite countless remote viewing
sessions. Consciousness persists and is timeless within
true reality. The intellectual and the mind is insatiable in

its pursuit of physical proof. Remote viewing provides evidence of what exits beyond the physical. It seems paradoxical to offer the existence of subspace, Quantum entanglement and provide evidence of the persistence of consciousness only to constantly question it as insufficient. Energy is the foundation of what exists and is interwoven throughout the Universe and is a part of *Source*. *Source* is the unseen immeasurable presence in which all form and universes exist. Matter is a result of energy transformed by consciousness and thought. Our infinite spirit and consciousness experiences many incarnations releasing energy upon exit. We transmute energy when entering another avatar for a new sojourn.

Existence is infinite and time is an illusion with everything happening all in the now. Multiple timelines exists simultaneously. Free will and cause and effect determine which is brought into reality. Timelines are all possibility and persist. Once energy is manifest it is permanent. All potentiality manifests from emotion. Emotions underpin every action, word, thought and intent. These create potentials or possibilities and quirks in timelines. Once formed they persist in eternity. It is prudent to be aware everything is recorded, imprinted into the collective and individual energy within the Akasha. Nothing can be negated as it will hold in the infinite energetic Quantum or Akashic space. The cosmic library is the store of everything in the Universe. The Quantum field or the Akasha holds eternally a record of all that has ever been in the Universe and every possibility the infinite spirit has manifest. It is all energy and persists forever.

Tendency exists in the Quantum field or Akasha. Tendency are paradigms seated in the subconscious and inclinations or repetitions of a particular characteristic or behaviours. Tendency resides within our vibration and frequency over incarnations as energy. Through stillness and meditation we can become aware of unseen tendencies and paradigms and break the chain of repetition. Over incarnations we may tend to repeat thoughts, actions, words and intents and cycles of behaviour. These tendencies do not exist within spirit and manifest when perception is focused into a vessel. Our tendencies are within our infinite Akashic records. As we enter each incarnation we offer an opening for past vibrations to emerge. What we experience in the physical is held within the Quantum field or Akashic records. We are eternally connected to all we have ever been and is stored in the Akashic records. These statements are not absolute statements of fact and are offered for reflection.

An incarnation open the possibility of repeating restrictive behaviours from a previous incarnations which will limit continued expansion. Tendency is removed through free will. We have free will to view life from an infinite observational platform or remain rooted in the myopia of physical life. The choices we make will determine if we become aware of repeating paradigms or simply execute them willingly, blindly and repetitively. An expanding and open state allows discovery of emerging intent and insight into previous inclinations. Myopia leads to limitation and egocentric existence and will not seek to become aware of multi-incarnation tendencies or seated paradigms.

Intellect or intelligence are real yet illusionary. Intellect can be referred to as the ability to rationalise thought and mental processes. Intelligence is the ability to apply knowledge with emotion the intellect. Knowledge is a collection of facts. Our ego uses intelligence to divide along class lines. We grade our place in the intellectual cauldron through academia. The less academically inclined or under achievers bestow admiration upon the clever and give power willingly. The reality is every spirit has the same cognitive capacity but design lives where the initial foundation will either nurture the mind or not. Free will ultimately determines where energy is focused. We can choose to use the faculties of the human vessel, mind and sense or not. Infinite consciousness does not enter life bringing with it a lesser degree of intellect or intelligence, awareness and inner knowing than another. We can all open the same capacities of thought if we wish to do so. Others who have progressed intellectually may do so seamlessly across other incarnations.

There is a predesigned aspect of each incarnation. We may choose a mental challenge in life for a specific intention and experience. Beyond initial design free will determines onward progression. Environment has a bearing on our life experience. The environment, family, siblings, social and economic status is chosen and predetermined by the infinite consciousness when in spirit. Nothing is an accident, random twist of fate or cruel imposition of *Source*. We possess the capacity to switch the mind into action through intent or see ones environment as limitation and a boundary to expansion. We can seek to mirror parents and peers or through free will move beyond. It is not life but design and free will that provides the challenges we choose to overcome.

Intelligence is not a badge of honour as experience has proven excessive egoistic intellectualism is a barrier to inner knowing. The powerful mind and logic overrides inner intuition and the spirit. It is a choice and free will to use the mind as a partner towards greater knowing. The alternative is egoistic intellectualism dismissing anything the physical mind cannot measure or accept. Intellectualism seeks to demonise those who are not in alignment. The mind should work in partnership with the inner spirit and the heart. The mind and intellectualism is not the leader in the pursuit toward *Source* consciousness. Wisdom comes from intuition and the channelling of the true self. Wisdom allows the mind and intelligence to apply universal knowledge and knowing combined with logic. A child can have greater wisdom than the parent or the elderly. It is not through age that wisdom is gained. It is through life and incarnations. Wisdom is beyond the intellect as it is a consolidation of greater reality, expanded spirit and mind. The objective is to place the mind as the partner and the spirit the guide. Through a connection to the inner self our intellect can be directed to develop wisdom underpinned by intuition and the heart. During the journey paradigms and tendencies will implicitly become clear as people and synchronicities are presented to help bring awareness of them.

The Universal Theatre

Quantum physicists suggest the Universe may be a hologram and we may be experiencing a virtual reality. The illusionary nature of life and the Universe is an implicit reality when considered from a metaphysical perspective. The standard model of particle physics states the basic building blocks of matter are atoms. Atoms are further divided into electrons around a nucleus. Neutrons, protons and forces govern their interaction. Neutrons and Protons consist of Quarks. The forces of nature are gravity, electromagnetism and nuclear. Strong and weak nuclear forces hold the atoms together. Weak forces decay the nuclei. The forces that govern interaction also consist of gluons and other particles. The interaction of particles and governing forces is the standard model theory. Particles carry force or energy. Einstein called these energy packets photons of light. Observable electromagnetic X-rays, microwaves and radio waves are photons of light.

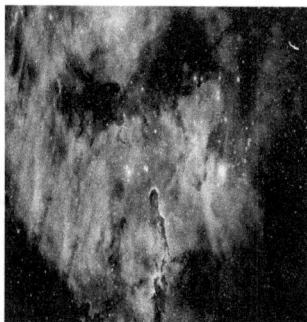

"The notion of a holographic Universe comes from a mathematical quirk buried in string theory, which is our leading attempt at a theory of everything. This quirk says that within a particular kind of cosmos, we can effectively do away with troublesome gravity by reducing the number of dimensions in our mathematical description by one. You can think about the resulting Universe as information "painted" over a "cosmological surface", which then permeates into other dimensions, creating the physical cosmos – akin to a hologram, a 3D image created from information in a 2D pattern. The result of the holographic principle would be that gravity and our third spatial dimension could be regarded as "illusions"

New Scientist

The article suggests the Universe is an information construct with which we interact. In esoteric science light and energy is regarded as information. The foundation of what exists and the spirit itself is pure energy. We are infinite consciousness and knowing or information. The Universe is a mass of interacting forces of vibrational wavelength energy or information observed and interpreted by our senses. The more expanded the consciousness the greater our ability to perceive the true reality. Light is information and love. Thought is the transformation of energy into matter through intent. Thought is light and thus a construct of information.

String theory supports the concept of a dimensional Universe. String theory suggests the Universe consists of layered dimensions or energetic wavelengths. These wavelengths vibrate at varying frequencies or speeds. Thought is energy and force. Thought transmutes energy into matter. Wavelength energy is transformed into form by governing its vibrational frequency or rate. We observe matter through our senses. Our senses have a limited spectrum of perception. We are able to observe only what resides within our spectrum of visible light. As we widen our spectrum of perception we open to greater knowing and awareness. String theory states particles are strings and they interact with each other. String theory integrates particle physics with force into a single aspect. The Universe consists of strings. Quantum physics and science asserts particles are in fact vibrating strings. Each string or type of particle vibrates at different frequencies or rates. The rate in which they vibrate determines their action, identification and role within the interconnectedness of the physical Universe.

From an esoteric perspective vibrating strings and particles are energy transmuted into matter through thought or intention. Strings and particles interact with each other under the universal law of cause and effect. Strings form matter and are under constant transformation through the process of destruction and transformation. Mainstream science states the Universe is physical. String theories use the concept of multiple dimensions of space and time to correct anomalies and support mathematical consistency. The three string theories use different numbers of dimensions. Bosonic string theory requires twenty six dimensions. Superstring theory requires ten dimensions. M-theory requires eleven dimensions. String theories require dimensions to cancel out anomalies in their mathematics. Each theory is integrated. String theory states particles move between each dimension. The dimensions are very small and are not noticeable or measureable. They are regarded as *compactifying* so that strings loop around them. String theory dimensions primarily exist to provide *anomaly cancellation* in their mathematics.

Esoteric and metaphysical theosophy offer seven, twelve or more dimensions. String theory dimensions are not separate physical places but vibrating energy wavelengths interacting with each other. They are in the same space. The principle aligns with esoteric and metaphysical philosophy. The future of Quantum physics will bring it in closer alignment with esoteric philosophy. Quantum physics will arrive at the missing component of consciousness. We will slowly come to realise the physical and our unseen reality cannot be fully understood through advanced technology but from the inner release of infinite truth.

Esoteric science describes the Universe as pure energy or information in vibration creating matter. The Earth spins at about 1,000 mph. The Earth moves around the Sun at 67,000 mph. A single orbit of the Earth takes one year. The Sun, asteroids and comets orbit the center of the Milky Way galaxy. The Solar system orbits at around 500,000 mph or 800,000 km/hr around the center of the Milky Way galaxy. In ninety seconds the Solar system will have moved 12,500 miles or 20,000 km in orbit around the centre of the Milky Way galaxy. It takes the Sun approximately 225-250 million years to complete one orbit around the center of the Milky Way galaxy.

The Universe is transforming, orbiting, spinning or expanding. It is all energy observed as matter. Energy is interconnected as particles or strings creating the physical Universe. We measure the Universe by its physical constituents from elements to immense planetary bodies. From an esoteric perspective the Universe is an illusionary theatre created for experiences. It is an illusion because it is not true home. The infinite spirit does not originate and is not of the Universe. The Universe is real as we experience it when in body. The Universe is real in each moment it is being experienced through the senses. The universal illusion becomes real from moment to moment of our sojourn into the experience.

The Universe may also be referred to as a virtual construct of mathematical precision expanding through the universal law of cause and effect. The effect of an action in the Universe will create a relative reaction. A subatomic particle releases energy to contribute to a different action or transformation. Universal cause and effect manifests as a result of the transformation of a previous originating state. The infinite flow of cause and effect creates balance and harmony within the universal canvas.

The infinite spirit and the Universe is subject to eternal expansion through the creation, preservation and transformation of energy. The Universe is constantly expanding through these three actions. We nor is the Universe subject to an omnipotent, omnipresent, omniscient force governing daily actions. *All That Is* flows from universal law. Universal law allows *All That Is* to become what it will either through natural progression or artificial intervention by the countless lifeforms within it. The Universe is a free flow of energy expressing itself and expanding. Celestial objects, their state and life passes and creates anew. We measure the experience physically yet the fantastic nature of what exists is beyond measurement or replication. Humanity will attempt to control and manipulate what slowly comes into its awareness creating alternate cause and effect outcomes. The Universe will exist eternally but some life within it may not.

"The theories of relativity and quantum mechanics have provided guidelines or principles which determine just how the force laws are to be formulated mathematically. One of these principles is called "invariance" and leads directly to the "conservation laws" of which "conservation of energy" is a more familiar example. Energy conservation is more than just saving fuel. It says, in effect, that in any physical process the total energy before must equal the total energy after the process is concluded. It seems to me that the law of karma is one of these "conservation laws." The great teachers say it operates with mathematical exactitude. "Whatsoever a man soweth, that shall he also reap." It is more than morals. It deals with action, energy, cause and effect. In the words of H. P. Blavatsky, "Karma creates nothing, nor does it design. It is man who plans and creates causes, and Karmic law adjusts the effects; which adjustment is not an act but universal harmony, tending ever to resume its original position, like a bough, which, bent down too forcibly, rebounds with corresponding vigour."

Robert L. Shacklett

Nothing is fixed or forever. That which manifests in the theatre persists through the force of will. It exists in the field of experience. The field of experience is the Universe or Multiverse. By reading this book it is assumed the ego and the mind is open to accept there is something greater than the individual. There may be a desire to seek answers to the existence of an *All That Is*. The universal theatre is a physical and energetic dimensional stage on which we fulfil our incarnational intent and material experience through free will. The universal theatre is the illusion and not the origin of our true state. The infinite spirit sojourns into the universal theatre to grow and expand. We expand through every challenge, interaction, observation, touch, sense, thought, emotion, feeling, ego, desire, positive and negative event or action. The source of the 'I' is the spirit realm from which all that exists originates and remerges.

Upon entering the universal theatre we immediately identify with our avatar and transform the personality as we traverse the experience. We identify with the external reflection of gender, job, role and the many labels the ego wishes to create. These labels are not negative nor should be demonised as they are an aspect in the universal theatre. We come here to experience. The labels we garnish require introspection to understand if they are grounded and simple or driven by ego, status or intellectualism. All physical labels, identity groups and associations fall away when the life journey comes to its inevitable end. We should not dismiss the experience of labels, identity and all the theatre offers as distractions if they offer growth. We should refrain from being subjects of them or allow them to separate the surface self from the true 'I' or each other.

> "The Universe is really a thought form
> projected from the mind of God"
>
> Dion Fortune

The challenge arises when we develop attachment to the avatar, false persona and labels. These distractions if they are given sufficient force will create disconnection from our true nature and existence. Complete attachment to labels and the loss of self will pull us further into the physical universal theatre. Through this movement we create derivatives of excessive ego, separation, division, duality, distraction, manipulation, agenda and manifesting lower vibrational states. Humanity has embedded itself in this state through free will. We no longer understand the avatar is an illusionary temporal suit through which we interact with the physical Universe. We have collectively suppressed our inner connection to *Source*. Attachment to the avatar and labels further merge perceptions into the physical Universe as being the only reality. We become energetically detached to acts and influences within it. Wider perception of what lay beyond becomes vacant. In essence we experience unintended suffering, a loss of meaning and look to the external for purpose.

Buddhist suggest three paths to enlightenment of *Paali* describing detachment, *Viveka* of separation and seclusion and *Viraaga* which is the disillusion of lust or desires. These Buddhist definitions should not be applied in the literal sense. Detachment and seclusion should not mean physical or emotional separation from society. Physical and emotional separation from the theatre may lead to a loss of compassion or disinterest in the suffering of others. Sitting in a cave contemplating oneself serves no purpose other than for confined personal expansion. We are here to experience each other. Expansion requires each of us to give time to the service of others, to share truth and support a collective change in perception. The Buddhist principle of separation and isolation means to journey inward through meditation to receive energetic information toward expanded awareness.

Detachment is to remove the attachment to the identification with the body, avatar, labels and the physical universal theatre. Detachment is the rediscovery of our true sovereignty and power. Detachment does not imply a disengagement with society but a positioning to observe it and non-participation in the manipulations imprisoning the true spirit. We are moved to allow the channelling of energy into what creates unity, love, awareness, sovereignty and power of the self for the benefit of all. We are able to affect collective change if others are ready to receive. Detachment is to liberate the experience from the dominance of the mental egoism and to allow the spirit, heart and mind to work in partnership. Detachment is to understanding the physical Universe is a theatre of innumerable plays, acts and actors creating and manifesting through free will the show on a magnificent stage. Detachment is to remove the self from indoctrination, religious blindness, dogma, excessive nationalism and the unseen manipulation directing emotion toward fear, judgment and conflict.

Attachment is to our infinite nature and detachment from the physical suit. In the next incarnation we may select a different realm of experience, body, planet, nation, culture, colour, doctrines, belief and purpose. Attachment is to the infinite manifesting material goals through the emergence of the spirit, heart and mind over the mental ego. Attachment is to a greater and boundless perception of *All That Is* and an openness to signs, synchronicities, numbers, people, places and events.

Multiple life experiences may occur at the same time in different avatars and universes. All is possible. Each action, word, thought, intent is part of *Source*. The Torus depicts the energetic nature of the universal theatre. The vortices of energy surround a central field or *Source* from which all emanates. We are a part of universal energy. It is within each of us. The Torus is our being, the Universe and the Multiverse. The mind insists on logical separation. The true 'I' is energy and emotion, love and information. The Torus is universal energy as one. The Torus depicts a limitless expanding flow of energy. The flow is replicated in the physical as fractals of interacting subatomic particles, magnetic poles, planets and stars. Some theories in metaphysical science suggest the 'I' is an individual entity whilst being connected to the whole. This statement is true in part. The infinite spirit is in constant expansion and retains elements of personality. Separateness is not a reality. The Torus depicts the infinite centre as a state of peace, stillness and presence. Our infinite spirit is a Torus. We are a fractal of ceaselessly interacting and creating energy. Our infinite spirit creates a vortex of energy called an Aura surrounding the body. The Aura is emitted by the energy body.

Figure 3: The Torus

Quantum physicists seeks to measure the illusive singularity and capture the God particle. The attempt by CERN to discover and replicate the God particle will fail. The critical aspect of consciousness has been omitted from the equation. CERN cannot capture the immeasurable principle of consciousness, all possibility and presence. Humanity is arrogant to believe it can control and manipulate universal forces or replicate it through Artificial Intelligence. The attributes of *Source* cannot and will never be replicated by what exists in the theatre. The universal theatre is within *Source*. We pursue these aims through our ego. We exhibit a manifestly deluded illusionary sense of self, knowing, power and belief we can be the creator, preserver and destroyer of life. We cannot recreate what we are a constituent of. It is akin to recreating the whole whilst being within it. The Universe will always be in balance through universal law. We create the imbalance and collectively attract the reciprocated vibration.

"...a reciprocal relationship enables a qualitative relation between structure and background, in which each has the potential not only to "impact" the other, but to generate transformations in the nature of what each actually is... More broadly considered, the notion of reciprocal relation allows for nested, mutual influence even between macroscopic processes and those at the atomic level, indicating the complexity of the pathways through which the qualitative infinity of nature may manifest."

Lee Nichol

The Universe continues to expand from the prime energy of love and natural design. Universal energy or dark matter expands into ever more beautiful physical forms and enticing truths. The cosmos was a balanced vibration of love and frequency at its inception. Negative energy was not present as we experience it today.

Life became what it is through its own fall into ego which results in greed, separation, hate, fear, war, religion, control and the manifestation of the countless disorders. The fall into ignorance is limited. The infinite spirit lays waiting below the surface physical avatar. Free will determines if it remains in this state.

> "All things, material and spiritual, originate
> from one source and are related as if they
> were one family. The past, present, and
> future are all contained in the life force. The
> Universe emerged and developed from one
> source, and we evolved through the optimal
> process of unification and harmonization."

Morihei Ueshiba

The universal theatre is a canvas for those within it to create through actions, words and thoughts. It is a sum of all the vibration and frequency from all that exists, whether animate or inanimate. The entire Universe is an experiment. Everything within it is an experiment. There is no omnipotent energy dictating events or occurrences. It is the responsibility and ownership of all that exists human or otherwise in the Universe to create its own destiny, experience and timeline. Negative energy manifests into being or evil as a consequence of imbalance, loss of connection to self and thus *Source*. Equally love, kindness, unity, service to others are actions of grace we privately seek and are collectively nurtured into reality.

The Universe delivers relative to the power of collective vibration and frequency. The same rule applies to the individual life experience. Universal law is simple and all pervasive. It cannot be avoided, manipulated or changed but can be transcended. If we allow negative energy such as fear and its derivatives to overwhelm the human experience it will reflect this free will movement. If we hold a fearful frequency it will collectively shape a timeline where tyranny has an opening. Alternatively, if we hold an overwhelming state of love or elevated vibration it will shift the human experience towards the heart. The question to the existence of non-terrestrial technologically advanced life is mute. It is implicit. It is simple acceptance. It is ego to assuming we are the only intelligent life within the cosmos. This egoism in the mainstream must be overcome if we are to venture into the stars as a heart centred species. The alternative is humanity will take tyranny into the heavens. We will bring into being the reality portrayed in the movie Avatar.

Dr. Courtney Brown Ph.D. in *Remote Viewing, The Science and Theory of Nonphysical Perception* describes psychic space as subspace. Remote viewing experiments suggest human subspace is omnipresent and everywhere at once. The remote viewing experiments conducted by Dr. Courtney Brown Ph.D. delve scientifically into the deeper workings of the Universe, timelines and infinite possibility. The insistence of physical proof of everything is a state of those who have yet to move away from pure mind. Universal knowledge and understanding is within. Knowing is felt. All that exists is from *Source*. We should glance upward upon the beauty of the night sky and embrace the Universe and wonder what undiscovered life exists within it. The perception of isolation is external. Awareness of our universal family is within.

"Because you are unlimited, neither the lords
of heaven nor even You Yourself can ever
reach the end of 'Your' glories. The countless
Universes, each enveloped in its shell, are
compelled by the wheel of time to wander
within 'You', like particles of dust blowing
about in the sky. The śrutis, following their
method of eliminating everything separate
from the Supreme, become successful by
revealing 'You' as their final conclusion."

Srimad Bhagavatam

The vessel is a vehicle, the spirit is eternal and a fractal of
Source. What exists persists as long as energy of action,
words, thoughts, intents and free will support it. If we
wish love, seek harmony, understanding, sharing, peace,
tolerance, enlightenment, abundance for all we must create
those vibrations through free will. This is a universal
principle and is not confined to humanity but all life.

The Multiverse

The existence of a multi-
verse or parallel universes is
subjective and for personal
interpretation, acceptance
or dismissal. The term
was used in 1895 by the
American philosopher and psychologist William James. The
idea of a multiverse is an aged proposition in metaphysical
philosophy. Yoganada and Swami Sri Yukteswar suggested
parallel universe may exist and may be the astral plane.
The possibility of parallel universes has been proposed by
mainstream physicists such as Dr. Michio Kaku and the
late Dr. Stephen Hawking. Quantum physics suggest the
concept of multiple universes may not be that farfetched.
In the article *Parallel Universes: Theories & Evidence* in
space.com dated 10th May, 2018 the author suggest one
prominent theory on the Cosmos is that it is flat and simply
expands infinitely. Universes may repeat themselves.

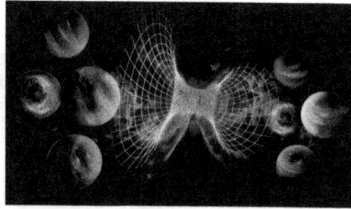

Hugh Everett's many worlds interpretation of Quantum
mechanics uses the double slit experiment. The results
provided an anecdotal interpretation to evidence the
existence of parallel universes. In the double slit experiment
monochromatic light was fired one photon at a time through
slits which imprinted a pattern on an observation screen.

The slits were less than a hair width apart and themselves even thinner. The photons passed through the slits as waves. The scientists observed the formation of individual bands on the observation screen and not a sporadic patterns as was expected. This result inferred the photons were interacting with something unseen to produce the bands. The photons were being fired one at a time negating any interference within the boundaries of the experiment. The conclusion was there were unseen dimensions or realms the photons of light were interacting with to form the bands.

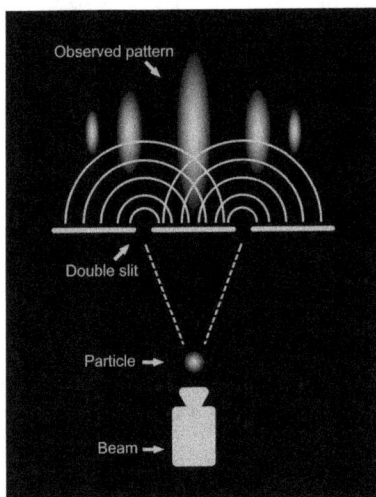

Figure 4: Double Slit

During an annual meeting of the Society for Scientific Exploration in May 2009 at the University of Virginia, Dr. Courtney Brown Ph.D. presented his *Evidence of Multiple Universes*. In it he discussed how the experiments with remote viewing provided evidence of parallel universes. Dr. Courtney Brown Ph.D. is the Director of the Farsight Institute. The Farsight Institute is engaged in validating the practice of remote viewing. Through the remote viewing experiments the Farsight Institute seeks to investigate the deeper questions of time, Quantum entanglement and subspace concepts. The Farsight Institute conducted an experiment where the remote viewers were asked to conduct a blind session and report what was observed. The experiment was conducted in June 2008. The remote viewing sessions were completed before the actual tasking time. This is called tasking-post.

In tasking-post the remote viewer conducts a remote viewing session prior to being assigned a target. The remote viewers were not given a target identifier nor was a target defined until after the session was completed. The remote viewer enters into a Theta state and documents what is observed. After the tasking-post remote viewing session has been completed the tasker assigns a target and creates a random identifier. The remote viewer will be unaware of the target and the tasker will not review the session notes until after the target has been assigned. The target in this instance was Los Angeles airport. The remote viewers reported seeing Los Angeles airport destroyed by an Earthquake in December 2008. The event was six months into the future. The team waited until December 2008. There was no earthquake or event impacting Los Angeles airport. An explanation was sought to explain the observations. The remote viewing sessions were viewed as evidence of possible multiple realities. The event was not in the experience of the viewer and therefore any event could have been observed from any number of realities. If the target was defined before tasking time and had occurred then the experience would have been in the present reality and have had a higher degree of accuracy. The remote viewing sessions were viewed as possible evidence of the *Many Worlds* or multiple realities. The experiment opens the mind to many possibilities not solely confined to multiple realities. In the case of the Los Angeles airport remote viewing sessions the perceived event was not in the experience of the remote viewer. The conclusion was the event could have been observed from any number of realities.

> "If there are multiple Universes, then the accuracy of predictions based on remote viewing data associated with an experimental design that organizes the sequence of events from first to last as (1) viewing time, (2) target event, and (3) tasking time will be significantly greater than the accuracy of predictions made when the sequence of events from first to last is (1) tasking time, (2) viewing time, (3) target event. Then the existence of multiple Universes is the cause of the relative failure of the latter design since that design does not guarantee the selection of one and only one time stream within which the future event resides."
>
> Dr. Courtney Brown, PHD

In 1895 Swami Sri Yukteswar in *The Holy Science* proposed the existence of a binary star. Swami Sri Yukteswar suggested the Sun rotated around a binary star or another Sun. The concept opens the discussion to the possibility of an alternate solar system and planets orbiting another binary Star. The validity of our Sun having a binary star is yet to be proven by modern physics. For balance the idea the Sun has a binary star is in doubt as the existence of one is thought to create gravitational disturbances to orbiting planets. A NASA scientist using the Chandra X-ray Observatory detected the binary system J0806. NASA observed two white dwarf stars orbiting one another every 321 seconds. The J0806 binary star system is estimated to be 1,600 lightyears away spiralling inward and is expected to eventually merge. The Earth is infinitesimal within the observable Universe. It is prudent to accept there are phenomena in the cosmic canvas not yet discovered. The Earth is a single planet and humanity a miniscule aspect of infinite life within the cosmos. Planck dated the Universe to 13.86 billion years based on observable measurement and assumptions. We observe and measure to the limits of our technology. NASA used the Wilkinson Microwave Anisotropy Probe (WMAP) satellite to date the Universe. Factoring in cosmic microwave background fluctuations known as density, composition and expansion rate NASA determined the age of the Universe to be 13.77 billion years. NASA stated an uncertainty of 59 million years. The latest estimated age of the Earth is 4.5 billon years.

Current Vedic Astrology dates the life of the Universe to 311 trillion years using the concept of Yugas. Vedic philosophy states life on Earth is subject to cyclical cosmic force and ages called Yugas. There are four Yugas. They each have descending and ascending phases. The Sutya Yuga of 1.728 million, the Treta Yuga of 1.296 million, the Dwarpara Yuga of 0.864 million and the Kali Yuga 0.432 of million years. A descending Yugas cycle is 4.32 million years. Current measurement suggests the Earth and humanity is currently exiting the Kali Yuga. The descending and ascending Yugas are 4.32 million years each. The total cycle of descending and ascending Yugas is 8.64 million years. One thousand descending and ascending Yuga cycles form one day of the lifespan of Brahma the creator. The total human years for a day of Brahma is 8,640,000,000 years called a Kalpa. The lifespan of a Brahma is 100 years completing formula with 8,640,000,000 years * 360 days per year * 100 years = 311,040 trillion human years. The current Vedic astrological calculation dates the Universe to be 115 billion human years. The Vedic formula is a complex formula and multiple interpretations are available. The two highly contrasting approaches of science and 4000 year old Vedic philosophy offer food for thought. The real age may be somewhere in between. We can but wonder.

The Universe is said to be governed by three aspects of *Source*. Vedic philosophy states *Source* is represented by three gods. The three gods are Vishnu the protector or preserver, Shiva the destroyer and Brahma the creator. They are collectively known as the Trimurti and represent the three aspect of the faceless God or *Source*. Vedic theosophy suggests each breath of *Source* creates a Universe in which a Brahma is created. The lifespan of the Universe is aligned with that of Brahma. As is the case with religion aspects of *Source* are divided into objects or separated into concepts humanity can understand or attach. The many gods, demigods and deities represent aspects of *Source*. We yield our focus to the devotion of them. The Buddhist focus on Buddha, Hinduism on the many deities and Trimurti, Christianity on the holy trinity and Islam to Mohammed, Judaism to Jahweh, YHWH or HaShem and so on. We are to remember *Source* itself and reconnect with our true reality. We should shift from human created definitions of what just is.

The Universe is measured in light years due its immense nature and light being the fastest measure. The astronomer Robert Burnham Jr in the late 20th Century devised the Astronomical Unit (AU) as a method of measuring distances in the infinite Universe. An Astronomical Unit equals approximately 93 million miles or 8 light minutes in distance. The scale was devised by measuring the distance between the Earth and the Sun as a single Astronomical Unit of 93 million miles or 1.58 light years. The J0806 binary star is calculated to be 1,600 light years away from Earth using current technology. By considering the J0806 binary system alone we can only begin to fathom the enormity of the Universe and infinite possibility. The Earth resides in the Solar System. The Solar System exists within a Local Interstellar Cloud. The Local Interstellar Cloud resides in a Local Bubble or local cavity in the interstellar medium. The interstellar medium exits within the Orion Arm of the Milky Way. The Milky Way is a part of the Gould Belt. The Gould Belt is a partial ring of stars in the Milky Way 3000 Astronomical Units cross within the Orion Arm inside the Milky Way Galaxy. The Milky Way Galaxy is a subgroup of a Local Group inside the Virgo Supercluster of the Laniakea Supercluster within the observable Universe.

Encapsulating the vastness of the continually expanding universal theatre is beyond mind but is fathomable by the inner spirit consciousness. The infinite spirit does not measure all possibility in quantifiable physical terms but connects to it through consciousness and traverses its wonders. Astral projection or travel is the esoteric practice where the infinite spirit consciousness is capable of travelling outside the body and into the energetic wavelength dimensions of the Universe. The spirit is the infinite Universe, Multiverse and *All That Is*. It is mind that prevents this awareness. An eclectic esoteric view would fully accept the idea of a Multiverse. The Multiverse can be considered an expanded experiment where life experiences itself. Copies or mirror universes are of alternate cause and effect providing a theatre of parallel lives and outcomes. The Multiverse is a canvas of numerous universes of infinite all possibility and experience. The divine light of spirit is infinite and a fractal of its core remains in the spirit realm of *Source.*

There is no limit to where our consciousness can be in any moment of physical linear time. Energy has no limitation. The boundaries exist in our minds. The divine spirit is pure energy and can be everywhere in the present, past and future. If humanity is a pin dot on the infinite spectrum of life on the canvas of the expanding Universe it is not inconceivable to accept alternate parallel universes. Over the development of Quantum physics and human expansion we will experience through the wonders of infinite possibility the Universe and the multiverse. Inner knowing is within and is an expression of *All That Is.* Inner spirit truth and knowledge is not dependent on the human mind but is directly channelled from the infinite true reality or *Source.* Our programmed limitation that envelops the mind can be overcome by inner knowing. We should not compare the mental intelligence to infinite inner knowing and connection to *All That Is.* They both operate at very different spectrums of perception. If we consider the current theories of Quantum physics and ancient esoteric knowledge it is not incomprehensible to consider the nature of a Multiverse. The theories and theosophies support the concept life is an experience in an infinite field of possibility.

"To the philosophers of India, however,
Relativity is no new discovery, just as
the concept of light years is no matter for
astonishment to people used to thinking of

time in millions of Kalpaks. The fact that the
wise men of India have not been concerned
with technological applications of this
knowledge arises from the circumstance that
technology is but one of innumerable ways
of applying it."

Alan Watts

Some esoteric and metaphysical philosophy suggest the
existence of twelve or more parallel universes. These are
regarded as copies of the each other with altered variables.
We can consider multiple universes are not separate but
connected through consciousness energy and occupying
the same space. It is not important as to the number of
universes, if there are copies with altered variables or are
the same where the infinite spirit incarnates with different
outcomes. We can become preoccupied with intellectual
discovery of incarnations yet miss the purpose of the life
being experienced. The purpose is to reconnect to the inner
self and the divine infiniteness of the theatre in which the
movie is played. Energy is consciousness and a presence
through which we can access *All That Is*.

"We see first that here is a thought entirely
different from what you see anywhere else
in the world. In the oldest parts of the Vedas
the search was the same as in other books,
the search was outside. In some of the old,
old books, the question was raised, "What
was in the beginning? When there was
neither aught nor naught, when darkness was
covering darkness, who created all this?"
So the search began. And they began to talk

about the angels, the Devas, and all sorts of
things, and later on we find that they gave it
up as hopeless. In their day the search was
outside and they could find nothing; but in
later days, as we read in the Vedas, they had
to look inside for the self-existent One. This
is the one fundamental idea in the Vedas, that
our search in the stars, the nebulae, the Milky
Way, in the whole of this external Universe
leads to nothing, never solves the problem
of life and death. The wonderful mechanism
inside had to be analysed, and it revealed to
them the secret of the Universe; nor star or
sun could do it."

Swami Vivekananda

Other Life

Ufology opens the conversation to the existence of life beyond the human experience and our terrestrial playground. There are countless reported interactions with non-human life throughout the world. Many of the reports verge on fantasy whist others have some validity. The reports describe an array of non-terrestrial lifeforms. These include tall and short Greys, Mantis, Reptilian, Aryan, Nordic, Blue Avian and many more. Ufology and new age researchers have traced the origins of the many non-terrestrial beings to the star systems and galaxies of Lyra, Pleiades, Orion and Andromeda. Through the technique of past life regression practitioners have sought to uncover previous life energetic patterns of behaviour, memories or trauma. At times these sessions have uncovered non-terrestrial incarnations. There will be endless debate to the existence of non-human life in the vastness of our Universe if not within the solar system. Often the debate and outright dismissal is fuelled by those who only accept what can be touched, seen, smelt, heard and measured. The debate has no relevance in the esoteric and metaphysical as it is implicit life exists everywhere

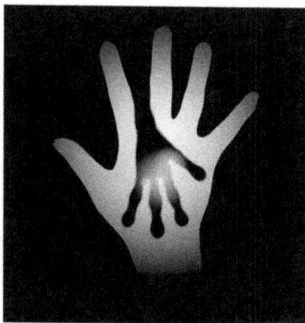

and across all wavelength frequencies beyond human perception. It is inconceivable to assert humanity is the only intelligent life in the universal theatre and has lived in isolation for millions of years, alone and never interacted with extra-terrestrial life.

The geologic Palaeozoic Era spans 545–252 million years ago. The Mesozoic Era of the dinosaurs started 252 million years ago. The Mesozoic Era consisted of three periods. The Triassic spanned 245-208 million years, the Jurassic of 208-145 million years and the Cretaceous period spanned 145-66 million years ago. After the Cretaceous period the Cenozoic Era or period of new life lasted approximately 65 million years during which the dinosaurs went extinct. Traditional research states the first of our common ancestors appeared five million years ago. These beings were apelike walking on two legs. The discovery of rudimentary tools dates back to 2.5 million years ago. It is thought some of those early life forms spread out of Africa into Asia and Europe two million years ago and bred with Neanderthals. The earliest finds of modern Homo sapien skeletons come from Africa and date 200,000 years old. Homo sapiens appeared in Southwest Asia around 100,000 years ago and elsewhere in the old world around 60,000 years ago.

Research by Johannes Krause the director of the Max Planck Institute for Human History in Germany suggests the Homo sapiens or wise man in Latin evolved approximately 300,000 years ago in Africa. Research into Mitochondrial and Nuclear DNA estimate our common ancestors lived between 765,000 and 550,000 years ago. Between 445,000 and 473,000 years ago our common ancestors the Neanderthals and Denisovans separated into two branches. The Denisovans evolved in the East and

Neanderthals in the West. Around 270,000 years ago some ancestors from Africa migrated into Europe and interbred with Neanderthals mixing their gene pool. Around 70,000 years ago a small group of Africans migrated to other continents leading to the variety of humanity today. Modern man evolved through the Paleolithic, Neolithic and the Metal Age. Further research into gene databases such as Kaiser Permanente and U.K. Biobank suggest humanity is still evolving. The science of human evolution will continue with the discovery of new evolutionary branches and revised dating. Many advanced civilisations are said to have existed from Mesopotamia 5000-3500 BCE, Indus Valley 4000 BC and Egyptians 3000 BC. Atlantis was reputed to have sank in 360 BC and the Mayan civilisation started around 250 AD. Current measurements calculate the age of the Universe to be 13.86 billion years old and the Earth 4.54 billion years old. The geologic Palaeozoic Era started 545 million years ago. If we consider these enormous spans of physical time would it not be pure fantasy to believe non-terrestrial intelligent life has not lived nor interacted with life on this planet prior to primitive man five million years ago. The reality is humanity is a pin dot in terms of life on the endless canvas of the Universe.

To expand from within is to become aware and accept there are countless advanced life forms in the Universe. This statement can be dismissed outright as evidence has not been offered and is a point of subjective perception. We have sovereign free will to dismiss or to investigate. Life has been and gone from this planet many times. This is a statement that becomes true when we expand beyond the boundaries of the physical and reconnect with *Source* consciousness. It is an absolute truth and reality. We are not special. We are an experiment as is the Universe and each life form within it. We are far from the most advanced life on the canvas of *All That Is*. Humanity is akin to an infant in terms of spiritual, mental and emotional evolution. Our arrogance and egoism defends against the opposing reality and enforces the illusion with an unceasing drive for physical evidence. We should shift further outward and open to the possibility humanity and other life have interacted and do now in the unseen secretive worlds within the human theatre.

Life manifests into innumerable forms from the physical to the energetic. Life is in constant motion and evolution. A lifeform can take a physical or energetic form. We chose to exist in the human theatre as it aligns with our intent. We seek expansion through the experiences of being in a human body. Once we embark upon inner expansion and reconnection our perceptions widen into *All That Is*. We become open and accept the human experience is a speck on the universal canvas of life. We share the Earth and the Universe with an abundance of life. We should consider other intelligent life may be closer than we might wish to accept. Non-human life may exists in wider dimensional wavelength frequencies our five sense spectrum cannot observe. To perceive form beyond our five senses we must be in alignment to their frequencies in order to open the door to their presentation. If we seek to have an experience with other Universal life forms it will occur. This does not mean the interaction will be physical. Interaction may be through wider spectrums of perception.

Sentient life does not mandatorily need to follow the humanoid template as all possibility is the Universe. It is important to understand infinite nature and not limit the boundaries of existence to that of the egoistic mind. Religious doctrine, societal and parental dogma will do little to bring awareness of universal life but focus on the myopia of human exceptionalism. There are those who obsess with identifying their universal heritage with star beings such as Pleiadian, Lyran and Andromeden. The list is endless. This fixation on where the spirit may have had its first incarnation or what is perceived as their universal origin is an illusion. The origin is only *Source*. The trauma many report is attachment to these experiences and is not their origin. These avatars are real from the perspective of universal experience and interesting to investigate. Fixation on them is a distraction from the reality that *Source* is the home of our spirit. We are not our avatars nor do we need to hold attachment to experiences through them.

Religious and ancient texts describe events where biblical figures and prophetic proclaimed God presented himself to them to cascade messages to the unwashed masses. It suggests God wants to be seen and impress is existence to us through a chosen few. These accounts may be real but stating it was *Source* itself is an illusion. These interactions may have occurred but it was not *Source* that presented itself. There is the possibility these so called gods from the heavens who came to earth and performed acts of immeasurable power may be non-terrestrial dimensional beings. To reflect on this possibility we must remove the bind of the mind and the programmed boundaries of the human experience. All form is wavelength energetic frequency. Our physical body is made up of water, proteins, tissues, lipids, carbohydrates and DNA. We also consist of minerals and elements. Beyond the physical we are vibrational wavelength energy. The Universe is vibrating wavelength frequency or energy. Our infinite spirit is consciousness energy. Advanced interdimensional beings may present themselves as gods to the ignorant and primitive minded.

Whatever was presenting itself as the creator or God was a manipulation of those experiencing it. *Source* will never demand devotion, punish those who do not worship their idea and use force to bring about predicted events. We are open to worship whatever form or idea. It is our sovereign free will right. The suggestion is the being that presented itself as their God is not the creator or *Source*.

Source does not and will not interfere in the cause and effect of the Universe. *Source* will never take a side, cast judgement and punish those who do not worship it or instil fear or wrath. *Source* will not profess one identity group more holy than another. If the chosen God espouses these aspects the question should be asked what is it being worshipped. The Universe is a canvas of free will. Any being within it can be or pretend to be whatever it seeks in an attempt to service its own ends. In the end physical time will present the truth. No matter which God, demigod, deity, idol or astral being we anoint with our worship everything returns to the true origin of *Source*. The illusion of the experience will always be revealed.

Everything is connected. It is not difficult to accept even for the most stubborn minded that technologically advanced civilisations existed before modern man. We will all eventually traverse the dimensional frequencies of consciousness and elevate to interact with the universal expanse into which we will venture. We must evolve in frequency and within self to avoid repeating low vibrational cycles and take tyranny into the heavens after embedding it firmly on Earth. All timelines are present within infinite possibility and are realising themselves as this sentence is read. Consider a Universe where all possibility and free will actions are manifest. We may have multiple lives in many forms within numerous Universes for the purpose of expansion. It is a truly fantastic idea that should trigger wonder and an opening of the mind. To open the mind is to allow the inner self to reconnect to something wider and unseen. When we reconnect to the inner self we will by proxy open the mind.

The human experience has no doubt been here before and is simply another act on the universal stage. The Universe is an experiment. We are an experiment of cultures, colours, languages, customs, religions and nations. It will remain to be seen if we are able to truly live as one. Ancient civilisations have been and gone. The cyclical nature of the human experience ends in the same state through repeating patterns and behaviours. It is through free will that we will repeat old cycles or collectively expand to a greater frequency.

Time

Time is linear when observed within the physical human theatre. Time is presented as a series of sequential events that create our individual lives and the trajectory of groups, cultures and nations. We use time to measure activity, events and occurrences in the past, the present and the future. Our perception of time is logical. Our logical view of time is assumed to affect the cosmos as it does terrestrial life. Albert Einstein published his *Theory of General Relativity in 1916* in which he states massive objects such as planetary bodies and stars cause disturbances in space-time known as gravity. Gravity is the force of attraction that two objects exert upon each other. The amount of gravitational force exerted upon an object is relative to its size and distance from the nearest body it affects. In 1666 Isaac Newton developed his theories of gravitation in which he determined gravity as an innate force emitted by every object.

> "Albert Einstein, in his theory of special relativity, determined that the laws of physics are the same for all nonaccelerating

observers, and he showed that the speed of
light within a vacuum is the same no matter
the speed at which an observer travels. As
a result, he found that space and time were
interwoven into a single continuum known
as space-time. Events that occur at the same
time for one observer could occur at different
times for another"

Nola Taylor Redd

Albert Einstein suggested that light and time were
interwoven in a single space-time continuum. He stated the
distributed forces of gravity may also impact observations
of space and time. Gravity acts upon the physical body as
a downward pull of the gravitational force of the Earth.
Esoteric and metaphysical science mirror the theory that
time is interwoven and that all possibility past, present and
future are occurring in the now. We all emit an energetic
presence and force. The physical body has little mass and
thus creates insignificant gravitational force. The human
body emits an energetic presence called an auric field. The
colour of an Aura will reflect the energetic vibration or state
of the person or object at any given moment. Everything
that exists in the Universe emits a force and an Aura. If
an object or being persists in emitting a force or energetic
frequency it will attract its equal. This is the universal law
of cause and effect.

"There is no such thing as a vacuum in time or
space. This is so because there is no place where
energy is not. Energy IS the vacuum and is all
things simultaneously. Energy is everything"

Ara Parisien

Research into black holes and *Gravitational Lensing* found that the gravity around a black hole bends creating a lens. The lens offered astronomers an opportunity to observe what lay behind a black hole. Astronomers use *Gravitational Lensing* to study galaxies and star systems behind a black hole. The research showed light around a gravitational lens travelled at different rates causing images of single events to be observed multiple times. For example the Einstein Cross which is a quasar 8 billion light years from Earth behind a galaxy 400 million light years away appeared four times. In another observation the light of a single supernova was split or viewed four times.

"...the dividing line between past, present, and future is an illusion".

Albert Einstein

Esoteric philosophy states time is an illusion. In physical life events are experienced in a linear manner. Each experience occurs after or as a result of a preceding event. The closer we are to the experience the greater the illusion of time. Within our lives we experience interactions and these are organised logically as a series of events over a linear timeline. It is suggested as we move beyond the myopia of daily life into the vastness of the cosmos time is observed to operate closer to its true nature. Time is not linear and is interwoven. The linear idea of time is an illusion. Time is real at the point it is perceived within the experience of daily life.

The *Big Bang Theory* offered an explanation as to the origin of the Universe. The theory states a singular explosion or *Catastrophism* released neutrons, electrons and protons at a temperature of 10 billion degrees Fahrenheit or 5.5

billion Celsius. These combined over time or *Gradualism* creating light and cosmic bodies. Light is determined to have shone 380,000 years after the Big Bang. Cosmic light is also known as cosmic microwave background or CMB. The oldest point of light is impossible to observe with current technology. We date the Universe using formulas and models. The *Bing Bang Theory* suggest the Universe was created over a linear timeline. Externalism is a philosophical approach to the nature of time stating all points in time are equally real. Presentism states only the present is real. Block Universe theory suggests the past and present are real and the future is not. B-theorists suggest time is an illusion with past, present and future being equally real and that time has no origin and is subjective.

Dr. Courtney Brown PH.D in *Remote Viewing: The Science and Theory of Non-physical Perception* states time is a sequential perception of movement and is measured as motion over time. In the practice of remote viewing events are observed as simultaneously occurring and independent of time or motion. Remote viewing experiments suggest the total energy of a single or series of events are spatially distributed but not with time. Remote viewing observations suggest events are occurring in the now as *sequential simultaneity*. Remote viewing goes beyond established theories, mainstream scientific reasoning and explanation. Remote viewing challenges the theory of absolute and relative time. Remote viewing experiments suggest the linearity of time exists through the sequential perception of occurrences of an event. Remote viewing experiments and their current conclusions support the esoteric philosophy that linear time is real at the point it is perceived and is an illusion when observed through the cosmic lens. In remote viewing science an event is said to produce kinetic, potential and total energy and are observed as existing simultaneously. The total energy of an event is stated as unchanging across time.

A remote viewing experiment consists of a target which can be an event, object or occurrence in the past, present or future. A standard remote viewing experiment consists of a tasker and a remote viewer. A tasker identifies and assigns a target. The tasker assigns that target to a remote viewer before a session is conducted. A target is presented to the remote viewer as a randomly generated set of numbers or characters. The randomly generated numbers or characters represent the identified target. The remote viewer is not given any other information other than the generated identification number. The remote viewer shifts their mental conscious into a Theta state. The remote viewer focuses on what is perceived as images or feelings and interprets them into information. The remote viewer shifts their point of awareness into a wider band of frequency within subspace and reports what is being perceived. Remote viewing session are conducted in completely blind conditions.

There is an alternative tasking scenario called tasking-post. In tasking-post the remote viewer conducts a remote viewing session prior to being assigned a target. The remote viewer will enter into Theta state and document what is perceived or observed. After the tasking-post remote viewing session has been completed the tasker assigns a target and an identifier. The assigned target may be an event that may have occurred after the remote viewer conducted the session. The remote viewer will be unaware of the target and the tasker will not review the session notes until after the target has been assigned. In this scenario a remote viewer may perceive an event before it occurred in our reality. In tasking-post experiments remote viewers reported events that not only matched a future event but also the assigned target. This brings into questions the nature of linear time and space. For a tasking-post experiment to offer a result and match a future randomly assigned target brings into question the hypothesis events in the future do not exist as they have yet to occur. The determination is current and future events may coexist simultaneously in subspace.

Mainstream scientific theory dictates time is relative to the observer and is perceived at the speed of movement. We can regard this movement as forward progression within our daily reality. Time is real and a constant as we perceive it in our physical reality. Future events are not observed as existing simultaneously. Physical events are perceived as sequential and separated. Remote viewing sessions offer an alternative view that past, present and future events occupy the same subspace and that the illusion is time as a linear measurement. Remote viewing offers us an opportunity to question the mainstream understanding of our universal reality. Remote viewing is not a precise science. Data can be contaminated as is true with any approach including those conducted in tightly controlled conditions.

Remote viewers often use sidereal time to schedule remote viewing sessions. Sidereal time changes depending on where a person is on the Earth. Sidereal time is a point when the location of a person is the furthest away from the centre of the Milky Way galaxy. The Milky Way galaxy emits a powerful electromagnetic energy or noise which can influence results. When a remote viewing session is conducted at sidereal time the remote viewer is shielded by the Earth from some of electromagnetic noise interference. Remote viewing sessions have been reported to have improved through the reduced effects of electromagnetic noise.

We are all able to remote view if there is a desire to pursue the practice. Through training and persistence we can accesses the subconscious and the unseen dimensions of energy or subspace. Remote viewing protocols tap into the subconscious. Remote viewing protocols allow an observer to shift perception to a different point in infinite time to interpret images or feelings. The protocol and methods expand the subconscious into wider wavelengths or realms within infinite possibility. Remote viewing will eventually be accepted by mainstream physicists who are open to question established scientific doctrines.

Quantum physics is slowly shifting toward understanding universal interconnectedness at the consciousness level. Quantum physics will come to align with esoteric philosophy and metaphysical science. Photons or light are regarded as information in esoteric philosophy. Time is illusionary and all timelines are interwoven. What we perceive is determined by our point of attention. A myopia of perception determines a narrowness of vision. Individual expansion pushes through surface consciousness and the mental ego to allow the inner awareness to emerge into the infinite spectrum of frequency. From within the expanded frequency we start to become aware of what we truly are and the infinite possibility that exists. Observation may spark from mental enquiry and scientific measurement but is truly understood through feeling.

From an esoteric perspective the remote viewing hypothesis is implicit within inner knowing and awareness. Energy is manifest as events and occurrences and are presented as timelines interwoven into a single field or subspace. All possibility represented as multiple timelines persist. The timeline we experience is dependent upon the individual and collective persistent frequency. Frequency and energy is in constant change. A predicted event from a remote viewing session does not imply it will occur in our present reality. Remote viewing focuses the observers point of attention within an aspect of infinite all possibility. What is perceived is an energetic imprint into subspace of free will actions, words, thoughts and intents. Energy is neither fixed nor permanent and is fluid as observed changing possibility. The events we experience are dependent upon our vibration and frequency.

Within daily life time is real as a point of perception and manifests as linear experiences. Remote viewing demonstrates that the idea of time dissolves as perception traverses from the myopic toward the infinite. Subspace can be described as an aspect of universal consciousness and a persistent energy record of all possibility. The persistent record of all possibility is accessed by the subconscious when in a Theta state. Subspace can be likened to the Quantum or Akashic field. Infinite consciousness does not operate in a time construct as the spirit is eternal everywhere and a part of everything.

Time whilst absolute in daily life is an illusion and becomes more so as we move observation into the vastness of the Universe. Time is obsolete in the spirit realm. As Quantum physics extends outward into the cosmos we will come to accept time is real only to the observer within the boundaries in which it is experienced. We are infinite consciousness and an energetic fractal of our core. We may be experiencing multiple parallel lifetimes in numerous universes. We emerge into life creating, preserving, transforming and departing over as many incarnations as we wish of infinite design. Time is a physical realm construct and reveals its illusions as we observe the infiniteness of the Universe. Time is obsolete in the realm of the infinite spirit. All avatars and incarnations exist perpetually in the

Akasha and as accessible by true esoteric practitioner. Our infinite spirit is connected eternally to everything it has ever been. What we have been is within all possibility. We are timeless. Everything that has ever been, is and will be exists in the now. All possibility is every form, incarnation, avatar, personality, idea, thought, word or action. Nothing dies or ceases to exist. It has been it will forever be. Time is part of the Universal experience when in matter. Time is obsolete when out of the body.

If linear physical time was a true construct and age an aspect of it the spirit would decay and will not be infinite. If linear time existed in the realm of spirit multiple incarnations would be difficult as linear time would force experience to be sequential and not parallel. If multiple universes were a reality and parallel lives are experienced it infers *sequential simultaneity* or everything occurs in the now. Time within each Universe or Multiverse is linear as it is uniquely experienced. Each incarnation and the Universe is independent only in the physical construct. Within space-time and energetically everything is interwoven and connected. Everything that exist within the experience is an expression of *Source* on the canvas of infinite possibility.

"Time is a manmade construct born of linear thinking and expression. There is only now. When you pause in the Now you will notice a lack of resistance. Time therefore causes a lack of ability to take root. A lack of ability to achieve, to succeed, to love and be loved. There is no time. There is only Now. Make each Now the best Now possible. From that place, all things come."

Ara Parisien

Matter

Matter and dimensions are observed differently from mainstream science when viewed from an esoteric and metaphysical perspective. Within metaphysics the Universe and all manifest and un-manifest matter exists within *Source*. Universal cosmic bodies emit energy as vibrational wavelength frequencies. Everything emits a frequency and is in energetic unity. Quantum physics models energetic vibrational frequency as waves. Life is a fantastic pulsation of divine intent using causality to cascade and expand in continual motion. Divine intent animated the cosmos into being. Causality, universal and natural law are the foundation to its persistence and expansion. The spirit animates the body. The physical experience is facilitated by our avatar or body. The mind processes what the five senses of touch, taste, smell, sight and sound perceive. Our inner spirit is the consciousness that illuminates the mind and animates the body. Thought transmutes energy into matter creating our physical world. We create through intention. Intention is thought. Thought is energy. Everything is

energy in vibrational frequency or waves. When energy is given sufficient force of intent it manifests from the great un-manifest matter and form. Esotericism and metaphysics suggest the Universe and matter are illusion.

The illusion is they are not our reality. The human playground and universal theatre and is not our true home nor is it our origin. The infinite spirit is pure energy, unbound perception and consciousness. The infinite spirit is not physical. Our avatar and our senses perceive the physical world. We operate in a limited electromagnetic spectrum form which we interact with our environment. We enter the material realm to experience matter, form and interaction. Our origin is the omnipresent infinite spirit. Our true presence emanates from the spirit realm. Our avatar are hosts to a fractals of our infinite spirit core. The fractal of our infinite spirit animates the avatar. Our true state within eternal grace projects itself into the material from the spirit realm. The spirit realm is a frequency of presence and awareness beyond the spectrum of the physical universe. Everything that is exists within the One. Dimensions, realms and matter are energy at different rates of wavelength vibration. *All That Is,* is one and there is no separation. *Source* is *All That Is.* Every expression on the canvas of the Universe is within *Source.* We traverse the illusionary delineations between wavelength vibrational frequencies through expansion of our inner self.

Our senses of touch, taste, smell, sound and sight operate in a narrow band of wavelength frequency. We interact with the physical environment and process through the mind. The physical world is processed internally and presented externally. All matter perceived and undiscovered resonates at the subatomic level. Subatomic particles emit frequency, awareness and consciousness. Subatomic particles are aware and have intent and are not lesser in state than our human consciousness. All aspects of the Quantum Universe follow the same principle of manifestation. Everything emits frequency and operates within their own electromagnetic wavelength of infinite possibility. These concepts are supported in part by Quantum Physics which states energy or Quanta creates matter.

Albert Einstein suggested space was not emptiness but dark energy. Einstein's states dark energy is a hidden property of space. Dark energy is un-manifest energy. The immense cosmos is a fantastic canvas of possibility and properties we are only beginning to understand. Space is constantly expanding through universal destruction, preservation and creation governed by cause and effect or causality. The Universe will never cease expanding. It cannot as it is infinite possibility. Einstein's theory states empty space possesses its own energy. This energy or Quanta is a property of space. Quanta or the energy of the great un-manifest and manifest cannot be diluted and persists as space expands. Einstein went on to assert as more space comes into existence more of this energy of space would appear. As a result of this form of energy it would cause the Universe to expand faster and faster.

The physicists at the European Organisation for Nuclear Research or CERN seek to discover the origin of matter at the inception of the Universe. The physicists at CERN built the Large Hadron Collider. The Large Hadron Collider is a twenty-seven kilometre ring of superconducting magnets. The Large Hadron Collider sends particles at close to the speed of light around the accelerator. These particles are directed to collide. The Large Hadron Collider uses detectors to analyse any subatomic particles that are produced by the colliding particles in the accelerator. The experiments are intended to support the investigation into the deeper aspects of particle physics. One objective is to determine the existence of the Higgs boson particle. The Higgs boson is suggested to be the invisible *God* particle. The Higgs boson is thought to a constituent of the unseen energy field in the Universe and the origin of mass. These experiments will provide us great insights into the physical aspects of the Universe and the principles of matter. Quantum physicists do not understand consciousness and the unseen presence of the eternal spirit. The dismissal of metaphysical science from the equation we will result in a failure of true understanding of the origin of the Universe and our existence.

The development of the sciences are critical to our development and to greater understanding of what exists around us. The challenge facing the sciences is the human tendency to take dominion over what it observes. This tendency will persist as long as we operate solely within the mental dimension. We may recreate what we believe to be the *God* particle or the Higgs boson. What we will fail to understand is that it is consciousness and intent that animates all matter down to the subatomic. These experiments will fail in their ultimate objective of replicating the true nature of universal creation. A controversial statement albeit metaphysically accurate. Physicists believe matter creates energy and attempt through physical measurement and complex structures to recreate the formation of the Universe. Quantum or theoretical physicist do not consider that universal matter originates through thought and intent. Quantum physics and metaphysics align with the principle that cause and effect or causality govern universal expansion and constant motion.

Consciousness emanates from *All That Is* and within all that we perceive and are yet to discover. Consciousness and the presence of the infinite spirit is eternal and cannot be recreated through technology. We will never recreate the essence of *Source* consciousness or the infinite spirit no matter how advanced artificial intelligence becomes or Quantum physics evolves. The exclusion of consciousness blinds physicists to the true nature of the Universe. The true nature of the Universe is pure light as information cascading through the force of intent and causality. The illusive *God* particle manifesting into the expanding Universe is all possibility and is in constant expansion and exists within the One. The One is pure energy, presence, infinite and eternal consciousness. Humanity may wish to play God in an attempt to recreate the origins of the Universe but will fail as long as consciousness is omitted from the equation. Science operates in the mental spectrum and detaches itself from a far greater wonder.

> "Another explanation for how space acquires energy comes from the quantum theory of matter. In this theory, "empty space" is actually full of temporary ("virtual") particles that continually form and then disappear... Another explanation for dark energy is that it is a new kind of dynamical energy fluid or field, something that fills all of space but something whose effect on the expansion of the Universe is the opposite of that of matter and normal energy. Some theorists have named this "quintessence," after the fifth element of the Greek philosophers... A last possibility is that Einstein's theory of gravity is not correct. That would not only affect the expansion of the Universe, but it would also

affect the way that normal matter in galaxies and clusters of galaxies behaved. This fact would provide a way to decide if the solution to the dark energy problem is a new gravity theory or not: we could observe how galaxies come together in clusters."

NASA

Current observations from NASA calculate the composition of the Universe at 68% dark energy, 27% dark matter and 5% normal matter. The Universe exists within *All That Is*. *Source* is *All That Is*. Everything exists in *All That Is*. *All That Is* originates from thought transmuting energy into form. Matter vibrates at varying wavelength frequencies. We perceive form by interacting with it within their perceptible wavelength frequency. We could state wavelengths logically delineate dimensions and what we are able to interact with or observe. The origin of the Universe is a derivative of intent through the force of thought sparking a canvas of possibility into existence. The Universe consist of manifest or normal matter and un-manifest or dark matter. They are all vibrational states of energy. Their states vibrate at frequency or waves. Waves and the subatomic is in constant motion. The universal law of Karma or cause and effect directs this eternal expansion. Quantum physics refer to this principle as causality.

The manifest and un-manifest is in constant creation, transformation and destruction through the Quantum principles of interference and entanglement. Quantum entanglement occurs when pairs or groups of particles interact or exist in the same space. The Quantum state of each particle cannot be measured independently. Quantum entanglement proved measuring a single atom at the subatomic level was insufficient. To understand the behaviour of the entire whole and the entangled nature of all subatomic particles needed to be observed. Quantum entanglement mirrors the metaphysical proposition that everything is connected and at the subatomic level nothing is separate within *All That Is*. The human body is of the same universal construct with atoms moving and crashing into each other releasing energy.

Quantum physics of motion and interaction are represented by subatomic particles, electrons, positrons, quarks and photons in constant collision and transformative energy. The force discharged by their interaction is called Quanta. Quanta emits wavelength frequencies in a state of vibration resulting in matter. Quanta is energy at the smallest subatomic level. Quanta or light is information. Quanta bends and shifts under the mechanics of diffraction. Quantum mechanics suggest every particle possesses an opposite wave character. We could postulate this behaviour is the duality that pervades the microcosm and macrocosm of the Universe.

The Uncertainty Principle states the momentum and position of a particle cannot be precisely determined at the same time. The Uncertainty Principle presents physicists with the challenge of precisely measuring the velocity and position of a subatomic particle. Subatomic particles possess varying lengths of waves or vibration. The energy discharged from their mutual annihilation is not uniform. Quantum physicists refer to the uncertain nature of Quantum interaction as the invisible reality. We could state the invisible reality is akin to the illusionary nature of the universal theatre and its unseen interacting force upon energy.

"...Dark matter seems to outweigh visible matter roughly six to one, making up about 27% of the Universe. Here's a sobering fact: The matter we know and that makes up all stars and galaxies only accounts for 5% of the content of the Universe! .... Dark energy makes up approximately 68% of the Universe and appears to be associated with the vacuum in space. It is distributed evenly throughout the Universe, not only in space but also in time – in other words, its effect is not diluted as the Universe expands."

CERN

Quantum physics is the practice of constant discovery. Quantum physics will eventually integrate with our true reality and metaphysical philosophy. We are one. We are in constant interference and eternally entangled. Our infinite energy shifts and is in constant expansion through cause and effect or causality. The material aspects of the Universe are a reflection of the One. There is no separation. As above so below. The 'I' is energy. The infinite spirit is not of form or matter. It is pure energy and an awareness of free will possibility. *Source* is the immeasurable emanation of thought. It is the origin of dark energy, dark matter and normal matter. To expand into the infiniteness of *Source* truth is to become aware of the sentient nature of life. Everything has purpose and a reason for existence. Nothing is an accident, coincidence or chance. The spirit is absolute existence and intent. It is not a quirk of consciousness or dark energy which is given consciousness through the mind. The infinite spirit is a fractal of the origin of all that exists.

Matter exists as a consequence of thought transmuting

energy through intent into form. Our perceptions and observations are managed by our senses. The physical world is real within the experience and supports the fulfilment of our goals, desires, feelings, emotions, expressions and interactions. We should remove the attachment to the physical when seeking to understand our material reality. The proverb 'you cannot take it with you when you die' infers the physical reveals its insignificance when the life experience is over. Our interactions with the material realm have purpose within the experience. Unnecessary attachment to the material creates an imbalance to their experience. Attachment to the material and a hungry ghost tendency may lead to the choice for continued reincarnation.

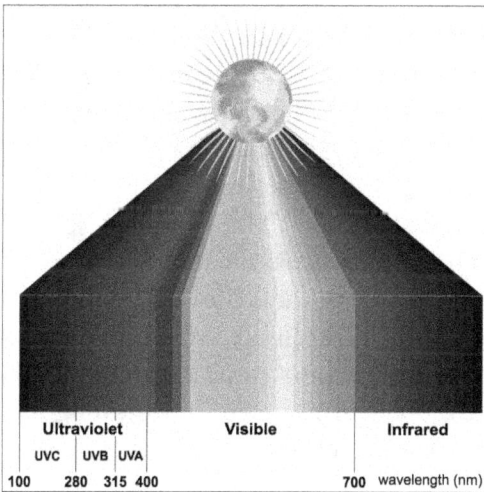

Figure 5: Limited Senses

The Universe is in constant vibration at the subatomic level. Our perception of matter is defined by the spectrum of our senses. The expanding state of our senses govern dimensional awareness. The Universe is the matrix into which matter manifests into being. Our physical body and five senses are the mechanism through which we interact with the world. Our senses operate in a limited spectrum. The electromagnetic spectrum of the Universe is largely invisible to our five senses. The electromagnetic spectrum is referred to as universal light. Researchers state our visible spectrum is confined to 0.005% of universal light. Our sensory faculties are unable to perceive ultraviolet light, microwaves, gamma and x-rays to name but a few. There are dimensional realms all around us that we are unable to observe and remain undiscovered. We are able to expand into wider spectrums of awareness through the inner self and our developing senses. There are frequencies in the physical Universe we are yet to measure and observe. There is a spectrum of existence that lay beyond the spectrum of the physical Universe. Mainstream thought determines if an object or realm cannot be measured or understood by the mind it cannot exist. Humanity is a tiny spec on the canvas of universal life. We should remove our human arrogance and open the intellect to the freedoms of knowing we are amongst an immense unknowable adventure. We should be humble and accept we are aware of very little of what exists and persists. Our limited senses cannot perceive the unseen vastness that surrounds us. We can move beyond the limited 0.005% spectrum of universal light. Something does not have to be seen to be known to exist.

"The electromagnetic waves your eyes detect
– visible light – oscillates between 400 and
790 terahertz (THz). That's several hundred
trillion times a second. The wavelengths are
roughly the size of a large virus: 390 – 750
nanometers (1 nanometer = 1 billionth of

a meter). Our brain interprets the various
wavelengths of light as different colours...
Astronomers use the entire electromagnetic
spectrum to observe a variety of things.
Radio waves and microwaves – the longest
wavelengths and lowest energies of light – are
used to peer inside dense interstellar clouds
and track the motion of cold, dark gas."

Christopher Crockett

"...Some animals have a different visible
range, often extending into the infrared range
(wavelength greater than 700 nanometers)
or ultraviolet (wavelength less than 380
nanometers). For example, bees can see
ultraviolet light, which is used by flowers
to attract pollinators. Birds can also see
ultraviolet light and have markings visible
under a black (ultraviolet) light..."

ThoughtCo

The Universe and matter is energy vibrating at varying
wavelength frequencies. All matter, whether animate or
inanimate, holds frequency and state. The frequency of
matter is in constant transformation and is affected by
interacting energetic vibration. If we work in an environment
where fear or manipulation exist the energy emitted will
impact our wellbeing. If we give thanks with grace for
what we receive and consume, it will hold this frequency.
Japanese author, Masaru Emoto conducted an experiment
where water was exposed to different energetic vibrations.
Positive energy was project into the water as words of love,
prayer and soft music.

Figure 6: Love Vibration

Negative force was projected into the water as words of anger or hate and hard metal music. The two contrasting vibrations had different effects on the water molecules. The positive frequencies formed beautiful geometric crystals and patterns. The negative frequencies formed distorted random patterns. The experiment supports the principle that positive and negative energy holds vibration and frequency and will affect any object to which these frequencies are directed. This universal law applies to our daily lives. What we individually and collectively project as wavelength frequencies will manifest a mirror physical experience. If we project love into what we create or consume it will hold that frequency. We influence every subatomic particle creating the universal theatre. We should be cognisant of our personal energy and vibration. Our personal vibration will either allow sovereign thought and power or a herd following mentality. What we choose as our state will direct what we allow to manifest as structures and systems with the environment that hosts our experience. Physical subatomic particles, dark energy and matter are the physical foundations of infinite possibility.

Dimensions

Dimensions are states of awareness within universal infinite possibility. Dimensions are constructs and states of frequency that our perception and consciousness expand into. Dimensions are not physical layers of existence. Dimensions are separated invisibly by frequency. We can traverse dimensions by expanding our internal vibration outwardly into wider spectrums of perception. All universal life emits an energetic frequency. The frequency we emit determines the spectrum of what we are able to perceive with our internal senses.

Humanity is described as a third dimensional experience. A third dimensional experience emits a vibration that supports the five sense physical reality. As we expand our consciousness and release it from the bind of our third dimensional perception we expand into wider bands of awareness. Our perceptions shift outward away from the identification and boundaries of the physical body. Objects can shift in and out of perception if they vibrate beyond the frequency of our limited senses. Universal life is unlimited and advanced. There is no limit to all possibility when dimensional frequency is approached with an open mind and wonder. The spectrum in which our perceptions operate dictate the boundary of the experience. As our consciousness extends from within to without and toward the true self. Our perceptions and observations expand into wider dimensional bands.

Metaphysical literature associates the first and second dimensional states to the plant and the animal kingdom. The third dimensional frequency is assigned to the human form due to our capacity to express at higher states of consciousness. The human body allows for wider frequency of energetic, mental and physical expression. The human vessel, the mind, the heart and the spirit are doorways to wider states if we choose to investigate and allow. A plant or an animal will operate at a base level of expression due to the limitations of their form and purpose. The plant and animal will behave in direct correlation to its base instincts and intent. Our ability to perceive beyond our primal capacities are bound by our body and the programming of the mind. The form a plant or an animal takes limits the state of frequency to which it can elevate and dictates its behaviour. The limitations of expression of a plant or an animal does not imply the lifeform is less divine than a human. Each lifeform has purpose and possess limitations by proxy of their form and capacities. A blade of grass has a specific purpose of being a blade of grass. The spirit within a cow incarnates knowing it will be a cow and the life it will live. How we interact with other life with which we share the planet and our collective experience is a choice. How we perceive each lifeform is a choice. We may choose to treat all nonhuman life as inferior or opt to understand they have purpose and are equally divinely intended.

Dimensions are expanded states of awareness and consciousness attained through the internal journey of reconnection. As our state of consciousness expands perception moves from the external toward the internal and sensory expansion. If we accept the first and second dimensions as base levels of consciousness concentrating on physical survival, reproduction and instinct we may naturally associate them with the plant and animal kingdom. Logic implies our expanded consciousness, capacities and ability to articulate perceptions are elevated beyond the second dimension to the third. This principle has foundation in truth but is by no means our reality. Despite being of expanded sentience much of humanity continues to exhibit lower dimensional behaviour. Humanity continues to inflict suffering and war upon each other, repress the natural law of sovereignty, enrich at the expense of balance and persist in killing not for survival or food but sport. Our spirit, heart and mind offer us an opportunity to progress beyond crude perception and vibration. It remains to be seen how many of us will embark on the personal journey with persistence. We are technologically advanced but spiritually stagnant. The evidence is clear and obvious in the human experience. We cannot assume by proxy of entering the human experience we are exhibiting an expanded state of consciousness. By entering human life we are given a platform to attain an expanded state if we traverse the path of development. It is egoistic and limiting to assume as humans we will naturally express greater awareness and associated behaviour.

We struggle not to cast judgement through our inflated ego and continue to inflict suffering on each other. In the animal kingdom these characteristics exist for survival. Survival of the fittest operates in the animal kingdom yet remains rooted in human life. Animals are limited in their ability to express awareness due to the capacity of their body or form. We should strive to regain our desire to expand our consciousness. Without the release of our core intent we will repeat cycles of tendency we associate with lower dimensional life. The human theatre offers us numerous concepts to achieve self-realisation. Each practice or concept differs in the portrayal of grades and associated states of dimensional frequency. The concepts define dimensions as states of being and density of consciousness. Each principle has the same outcome. The ultimate outcome is to expand into *All That Is* or *Source*. The modality we choose to adopted, study or research is unimportant. The modality with which we align will be that which resonates with the inner vibration of the individual. We will traverse many practices. There is no single method toward expansion. We should allow ourselves to be guided to what resonates as the first stone across the metaphorical river.

As expansion emerges we may traverse one or more of the many modalities. Adhering to any single framework will frustrate and inhibit progression through the need to measure and comply with established doctrines. The experience of expansion is unique to each of us. The research of modalities and grades of expansion are there to assist in the understanding of the personal journey. There will come a moment in the personal journey where modalities or dimensional theosophy will no longer be relevant. Internal expansion will reach a level of openness where it moves into a self-guiding principle. Strict definitions of dimensional states of frequency or consciousness are academic as we do not traverse them in a confined manner. We may exhibit attributes of multiple dimensional states yet still be expanding. Similarly we can hold characteristics of one or more signs of the zodiac.

The Spirit Realm
Dimensional wavelength frequency invisibly delineates what we are able to perceive. As we expand our consciousness we are able to interact with wider spectrums of unseen

wavelength frequencies of form and matter. What we cannot observe does not mean it does not exist. The idea of separation is of the mind. There is no actual energetic or wavelength frequency separation when we are considering the Universe from a spiritual sense. They exists in the One. As humans we seek logic in what we measure and observe. The separation of dimensions exists by proxy of our limited sensory awareness.

We will attempt to use mechanistic logic to explain the invisible boundaries between the unseen waves of energy and realms. Amplitude modulation or AM and frequency modulation or FM are radio wave bands. Within those bands there are spectrums of electromagnetic wavelength frequency. The AM band has a range from 535 to 1705 KHz. The FM band has a higher spectrum from 88 to 108 MHz. To listen to stations on these electromagnetic wavelengths we must tune our radio to the frequency of the chosen channel. To perceive and interact with wider dimensional spectrums we must extend our sensory capacities into their resonance. The wider wavelength frequencies allow us to interact with the Universe and the realm of spirit. We can organise the Quantum field, the spirit realm and *Source* as energetic wavelengths of frequency surrounding the universal theatre.

The Universe is the playground into which we choose to experience form, growth and adventure of sound, touch, smell, sight and taste. These sensory experiences are fulfilled by the body and through the roles we occupy in our public, professional, personal and private lives. The Universe consist of electromagnetic wavelengths of form, matter and energy called dimensions.

Our life experiences are stored in the Quantum field. Every incarnation of an infinite spirit is eternally recorded in the Quantum field. Everything that has ever existed, will exist and is resides in the Quantum filed. The Quantum field is the store of every memory, event, word, thought, action and lifetime in the Universe. The spirit realm is the frequency and vibration of *Source*. The vibration is of love and grace. The spirit realm will not open its doorway to those who seek it from a low vibrational intent. The spirit realm is home from where we design and embark upon each incarnation into the universal experience.

We enter life with open senses. These opened senses are categorised as intuitive, psychic or mediumship abilities. The majority will have their opened perceptions immediately blocked or suppressed. Some will retain these open senses throughout their lives. The young who report seeing forms or sensing a presence are sometimes called indigo children. They are simply children with unburdened senses that continue into adulthood for a purpose. Some choose to develop their inherent ability later in life. Unburdened senses that persist are not by some quirk of fortune or happenchance. They exist to assist so that the intuitive can assist others. The decision to investigate their potentials and assist others is a free will choice. Some may hide their capacities in fear of acceptance and may avoid using their extended sight as light workers, healers, psychics or mediums. Most parents do not understand the reality of life and often relegate the reports from their children as fictions of imagination and seek psychiatric intervention and medication.

We cannot interact with the full spectrum of wavelength frequency with our primary senses. Through expansion we can develop our inherent capacities and venture into the wider spectrums. We can measure the wider electromagnetic spectrums with modern technology. Our observations report what our current technology can measure. The universal electromagnetic wavelength spectrum is vast. The Universe is immense. Energetic frequency is infinite. *Source* is all possibility. There is no limit to the spectrum of energy and what can exist within its unseen phases. Technology focuses on material observation. The internal spirit does not seek material observation. The inner self seeks spiritual expansion. Persistence within the journey opens perceptible doorways into the infinite layers of wavelength existence where other forms and experiences can be found. Opened sensory abilities allow us to traverse and observe the unseen energetic wavelength spectrum.

Past lives are energetic records of previous incarnations stored in the Quantum field. A true intuitive can connect to the energetic record of past lives or previous incarnations. The energetic footprint resides in the eternal store of the Quantum field. We live numerous lifetimes with a core defined purpose and design. Life experiences are temporary in the physical but eternal in record. When a true intuitive channels a past life a connection is made to the energetic avatar of the life in the Quantum field. The interaction is an exchange of information traversing the unseen energetic wavelengths within the Universe. In esoteric terms *Source* is presence, thought and energy. Energy is light. Light resonates the frequency of love. Love is an energetic vibration. Energetic vibration is measured as electromagnetic wavelength frequency or waves. The Universe is observed and undiscovered waves of frequency. The Universe originated as thought manifesting energy into matter. The Universe follows cause and effect as it creates destroys and preserves in perpetual motion. The Universe is un-manifest and manifest energy. Everything exists in the vast unseen in an encompassing energetic spectrum of the One. Energy is information. The intuitive interacts with the Quantum field which is a wavelength frequency of information. The footprint of the avatar with which we seek to interact may present itself to the intuitive as an energetic form, sounds or feelings. The esoteric describe the receiving and interpreting modalities as clairvoyance meaning clear seeing, clairaudience meaning clear hearing, clairsentience meaning clear feeling and claircognisance meaning clear knowing.

We do not connect with the human or a physical presence. The connection is made to the energetic footprint of a life experience not the avatar it took when in the physical. The interaction may present fleeting images of the avatar or be communicated as feelings and aspects of their personality. Personality transcends into the Quantum field and is not temporal. The intuitive shares what is received and interpreted including the personality, memories and other information.

Our infinite core never leaves the spirit realm. The Quantum field holds the record of every experience the infinite spirit has embarked upon. We have experience in form and in formlessness. Every incarnation is stored in the Quantum field. Our core is timeless and eternal. Fractals of our infinite core enter incarnation and invisibly merge its energy into the one when the experience is over. We are everything and everywhere. We should take this moment to remind ourselves there is no actual separation. There is only oneness in *Source*. Everything exists within one space and in the now.

The afterlife is a return to the spirit realm and a merging back into our core. What we experience in the Universal theatre is eternally recorded as a persistent Quantum record, our infinite core and *Source*. When we think of a passed loved one we are expressing an energetic intention. Energy is one. The energetic intention brings into our perception the presence of the loved one. In some cases this can be an energetic form if our infinite spirit has purpose to it. The interaction will bring in feelings, sights or sounds from the Quantum field the energetic essence of the avatar into our hearts. We should remove the illusion the body is the person. Life is experienced by our infinite spirit at an energetic level. The infinite spirit is omnipresent. The body is the vessel and transmutes into energy as cycles within the Universe.

We should attempt to offer an answer to the question of the many observed forms and ghostly apparitions. The subject of ghosts, apparitions and energetic forms that are reported to appear is subjective. We should not dismiss the possibility as it is a real phenomenon. We should question and be cynical of the many reports. There is validity in some. Open sensory abilities allow the intuitive to observe forms that phase in and out within the spectrum of light outside of our standard range of perception. Our physical lives exist in a small band of wavelength frequency. The limited energetic frequency band allows us to observe and interact with the physical world. When we leave our avatars the fractal of our infinite spirit releases itself from the small band of wavelength frequency. We shift beyond our physical spectrum. We no longer animate the avatar. By proxy of not being in an avatar we must exist within wider spectrums of wavelength energy. A true intuitive can observe energetic form as it shifts in and out of wider wavelength frequency. This is possible as the intuitive is not bound by limited senses and has developed perceptibility into wider bands of electromagnetic frequency. We all return to the spirit realm. This is an absolute. There is the reality of all possibility. After we leave our avatar we can through free will create temporary energetic states. We may through a fear of the afterlife, an expectation of punishment for past actions, indoctrinated belief or ignorance of true reality imposes an illusionary purgatory. The power of the mind at this state is what holds fear and creates the temporary state. This may place an aspect of our infinite awareness in wavelength frequency close to those of human life. These self-imposed states use energy to maintain the fear and hold their mental awareness in place. To take form we manipulate energy and move into the vibrational frequency of what we wish to interact. In this case human form and space. This is principle to all manifestation be that emotional, sensing or to create form. What we observe as ghosts, apparitions or abstract forms are mental energetic awareness that is interacting or phasing in and out of the human realm of perception. The self-imposed states of illusionary purgatory dissolves and we all return to our true state and home. Loved ones who are reported to have appeared to their family shortly after death do so by using energy to manifest into the limited band of human perception so that their image can be seen for a short time. This happens if there is purpose. We all have spirit guides that walk with us through our chosen lifetimes. Some may present themselves as energetic forms in the same manner as loved ones who have passed on. The principle is the same for all non-physical phenomenon.

We are simply awareness, presence and energy. Our experiences and everything that has ever been resides in the Quantum field. The Quantum field is within *Source*. We are within *Source*. Everything is in unity. The human playground is within the universal theatre. All possibility within the Universe is recorded in the Quantum field. The Quantum field is everything the spirit has experienced and all potential timelines. The infinite spirit exists in the realm of *Source*. *Source* is everything. Everything is occurring in the now. The limitations we believe exist have no relevance when released from the body. Universal dimensions are energetic frequencies. The spirt realm is an energetic vibrational frequency of unity within the one. Everything is within the one. We can observe all possibility in the one. We are an experience in the single unified frequency of *Source*.

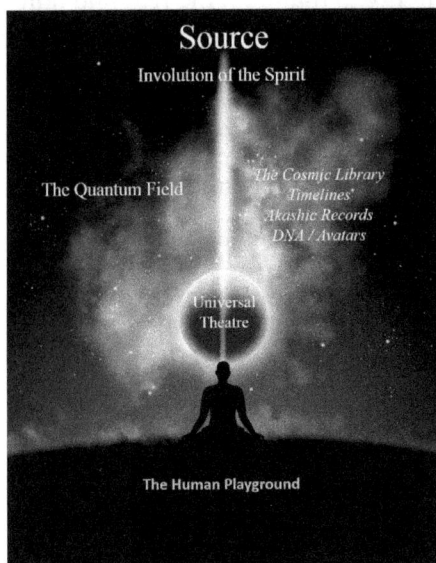

Figure 7: Involution of the Spirit

The Vedas

Hindu philosophy is interpreted in a multitude of ways by gurus, sadhus, holy men and ascetics. The Vedas are said to date to 3000 BC. The Vedas are a series of texts written in Sanskrit from the Indian subcontinent that represent ancient ascetic literature. The Vedas are a large body ancient knowledge documented in a series of Upanishads.

The Upanishads represent the philosophical principles and concepts that underpin Hinduism. There are one hundred and eight Upanishads. The Upanishads are collectively known as the Muktika. The word Upanishad in Sanskrit means to sit down at the feet of. The word Veda in Sanskrit means knowledge. The totality of meaning is to sit at the feet of knowledge. The main tenet from the Vedas is that the Universe and *Source* are infinite. The philosophy states the One reveals itself in the many. The Vedas suggest *Source* is the creator of the Universe and is the collective totality and animation of it.

Vishnu   Shiva   Brahma

Figure 8: The Trimurti

Hinduism is not dissimilar to other faiths in that it abstracts the unity and oneness of *Source* into deities and demigods. The abstractions of the divine assist us in the early steps along the path to a self-guiding awareness. Over time the need for layering of pseudo god and deities becomes obsolete. Hinduism splits the grace of source into three demigods creating the Trimurti or Triune. The triune consists of Vishnu the preserver, Shiva the destroyer and Brahma the creator. The triune is encapsulated by the ohm symbol which is unifying resonance of the Universe and all manifestation. The Vedas are founded on the principle that *Source* is the sum of all that is un-manifest and manifest, personal and impersonal.

The triune of demigods are depicted as blue skinned. The triune of deities are also multi-limbed. The multitude of arms, heads and eyes are symbols of the aspects of the one unifying being. Lord Vishnu has four arms. His upper right hand holds a discus symbolising time and the cosmic mind. His lower right hand holds a mace of individual existence. His upper left hand holds a conch which resonates the sound of ohm. His lower left hands holds a lotus which represents the moving Universe. Lord Shiva has four arms representing the four cardinal directions. The upper left is the drum to provide music to the dancing Shiva. The upper right hand holds a trident which represents the triune. There are depictions of the upper right hand of Shiva holding tongues with flames. This image represents destruction. The lower right hand is in an open palm position meaning to be without fear or of protection. Lord Brahma has four heads. Each represent the four Vedas. There four Vedas are the Rig-Veda, the Yajur-Veda, the Sama-Veda and the Atharva-Veda. Some research suggest the Vedas state the existence of sixty four dimensions. There is little evidence to the claim.

The central theme of the Vedas can be coalesced into seven dimensional states of consciousness. The first dimension is the body itself. The body relates to the attachment and identification with the vessel as the beginning, middle and end of the 'I'. The absolute identification with the body suggests a primitive state. The second dimension shifts consciousness slightly above the primitive into wider bodily perception and an early awareness of the self. The third dimension represents the base human consciousness where the body opens to widening perception and capacities for expression. In this state we possess free will. The ego and duality start to emerge. The fourth dimension presents a frequency where the journey toward inner self is initiated. We experience an awakening of sensory perception and awareness. We start to instil wisdom and love as the forming dominant energy driving behaviour. The fourth dimensional state continues to be centred in the mind which seeks to understand the self. Intellect is the primary faculty for processing information. The fifth dimension shifts reconnection beyond the mind and toward the divine light and the true self. The mental aspect of the mind shifts toward love and wisdom. We start to develop intuition, intelligence and receive information from inner knowing. The sixth dimension is of a rising unity with *Source* and of advanced wisdom we seek to share with others. The sixth dimensional frequency resonates compassion and love with grace as the primary driver. The seventh dimension is the final state where we achieve integration with *Source* and *All That Is*. The seventh dimension symbolises the highest frequency we are able to achieve whilst in the body. The mind becomes the processor not the driver. The inner spirit and heart are of absolute dominance. The true self is formed through oneness and is the unifying gateway to *Source*. The sixth and seventh dimensional frequencies are a state where the release from cyclical tendency and rebirth may occur. The purpose of material experience becomes obsolete as the true 'I' expands beyond the myopia of the human theatre. We develop a closer integration with the 'I'. We merge our energetic unity with *Source* consciousness and to the eternal gateway of information.

Hinduism suggests a series of transcendental states. These states can be aligned with dimensional theory. Moksha is a state where ignorance, duality and delusion start to become dissolved in their imposition upon perception. Experiencing life in the body cannot eliminate nor avoid the existence of duality. It is a reality of the Universe. We are capable of shifting our consciousness away from its brutal impacts and origins. Mukti is freedom and liberation and closely aligns with the number of stages our dimensional movement. At this frequency we integrate love and wisdom. We channel our frequency through the spirit, the heart and the mind. We are liberated from the external and life starts to form from a very difference vibration. Kaivalya is a transition period of feeling alone and oneness. The journey inward often leads to isolation as it is will start to separate a person from friends in terms of how life is viewed and perceived. This shift may create separation, loneliness and in some frustration. Expansion brings into the expanding life others who will support the onward journey. The relationships with those not on the adventure start to flow at a different speed. Vimochana is final release from material incarnation, complete detachment to the material, unity, connection and communication to *All That Is*. Visara is absolute dissolution and cannot be achieved whilst in the body. Visara is our infinite core which remains within the realm of the divine. Visara is the reintegration of our fractal and is described as a bliss of presence.

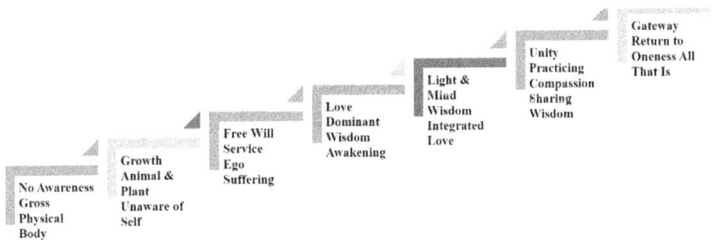

Figure 9: The Hindu Seven Dimensions

The Vedas do have mention of deities. The demigod Indra and Surya who is an abstract of the Sun are some of the deities in the Rig-Veda. The central theme of Vedic philosophy is the internal unity with the *Source* of *All That Is*. Over the passage of time Hinduism has focused worship onto demigods and deities. These abstractions have distracted the followers of the faith away from the inner journey. Religion throughout the world has shifted our focus to the external and not the internal. Vedic philosophy promotes the rediscovering of *Source* through stillness, the higher mind, meditation and living of our truth. Through the inward journey our consciousness shifts from the base primitive tendency toward the upper Chakras and balance. Stillness promotes movement and applies to all theosophies, philosophies, religions, modalities and concepts. They are all the same and different only by name.

The New Age

The new age is a very broad movement. The new age combines eastern and western metaphysical, esoteric and alternative philosophies to spirituality and the meaning of 'I'. The new age covers a broad range of practices including the intuitive, psychic, mediumship, yoga, mysticism, environmentalism, shamanism, goddess worship, the Tarot, crystals, meditation, political and mental awakening movements, astrology, numerology and energy healing are amongst the many other practices and modalities. The new age has much to offer and has a valid core. The broad umbrella encompasses many proven sciences and truth of the unseen reality. The movement suffers from fatigue and at times has been absorbed into the trendy hipster identity. The modern day new age industrial complex moment is in danger of becoming a home of fads and trendy ideas that are promoted as the enlightened path forward only to be discarded as the next wave arrives.

New age proponents offer a multitude of dimensional interpretations. The traditional and ancient esoteric dimensional philosophies have been extended by the new age.

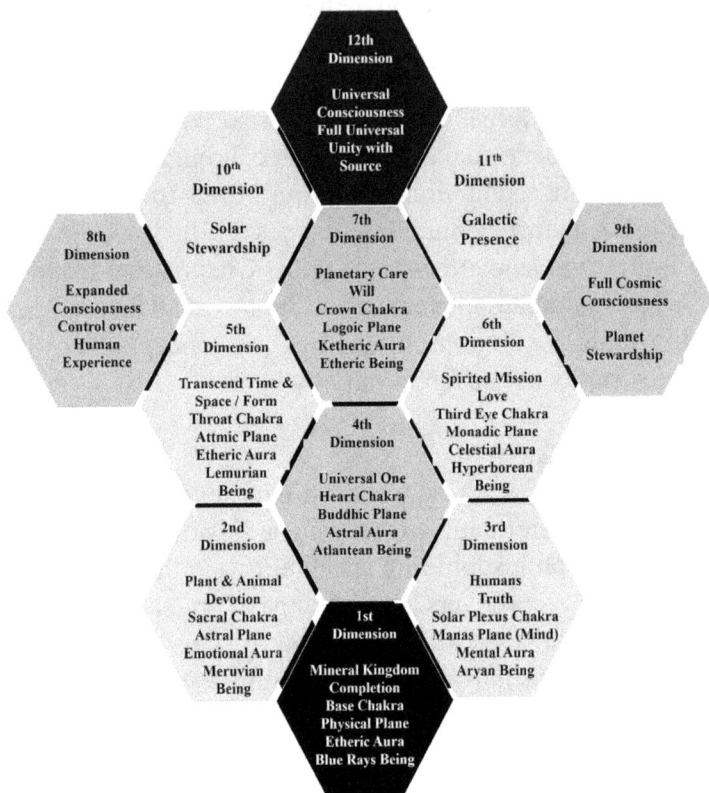

Figure 10: The Esoteric Twelve Dimensions

One such example is the twelve dimensions to progression and expansion. The twelve dimensions include associations to roles, kingdoms, Chakras, auras, planes and non-terrestrial beings. The new age has a tendency to attach concepts to cosmic stewardship, roles and non-terrestrial lifeforms rather than focusing on the core intent. New age metaphysical conceptualisation of dimensions are subjective and offered to stimulate further research.

The twelve dimensions suggest the spirit will move through roles toward higher grades of consciousness. The planetary, solar and galactic stewardship is a theoretical concept. The principle of stewardship aligns with the human need to root understanding of our greater reality to cosmic bodies and responsibilities. It is proposed herein these abstractions are creations that do not exist and serve only to distract form what is our true journey. The cosmic roles we must perform before becoming a universal being are illusions. They perpetuate the distraction and the external pursuit for understanding. The twelve dimensions when stripped of these abstractions are akin to the seven dimensions summarising Vedic philosophy.

New age philosophy suggest the Earth is shifting into the fourth dimension and will jump to the fifth dimension. The philosophy suggest by proxy of the vibrational shift of the Earth most of humanity will follow in its expansion. The Earth is an independent conscious cosmic body and has no dependency energetically with life upon it. If the Earth has shifted energetic frequency it does not imply humanity will follow. Expansion is personal journey and is not gifted by any celestial object by proxy or notion of planetary frequency. Planets and celestial objects do not exude low vibrational energy nor exist on lesser domains of frequency.

The Qabalah

The Qabalah *Tree of Life* is the mystical symbol within esoteric Judaism used to describe the journey to *Source*. The tree uses interconnected spheres representing the path toward expansion or enlightenment. The symbol consist of three pillars or Supernals. The Supernals consist of nodes or Sephirath associated with their aspect. The left supernal is of severity, structure or form. The right Supernal is mercy force or expansion. The centre supernal is equilibrium, balance or consciousness. The objective is to expand through each Sephirath into the state of the central supernal or Tiphareth. Tiphareth is frequency where all attributes achieve a state of grace. The reconnection with *Source* is a daily movement toward limitless possibility and integrating the left and right pillars.

The Mystical Qabalah by Dion Fortune provides a detailed and highly researched text on the subject. The following content are paraphrased extracts from the text. The Sephirath guide us through aspects of each pillar in the tree. The Qabalah suggests we should fully experience and understand each Sephirath before embarking upon the next. The Qabalah is suggested to be an esoteric philosophy of the west. Each Sephirath presents a step by step stairway to realisation from mind to outward expression.

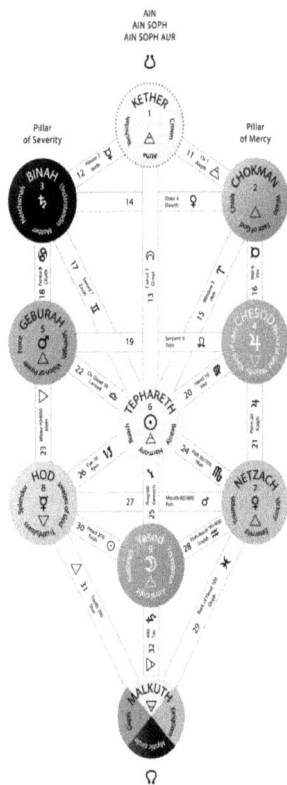

Figure 11: The Tree of Life

The *Tree of Life* shifts expansion from Malkuth as the primal human tendency toward *All That Is* through twenty two paths. The ten Sephirath when connected presents twenty two paths. Each path is an equilibrium of the two connecting Sephirath. Each Sephirath is associated with a sign from the Zodiac, a major arcana from the Tarot, a planet and an element. There are stages beyond the tree described as the Abyss. The Supernal of Severity, Mercy and Equilibrium are suggested to correspond with yogic Nadi channels. The left pillar of severity is the Ida Nadi of comfort and flow. The right pillar or mercy is the Pingala Nadi of extroverted or active flow. The centre pillar of equilibrium is Shushumna or Gracious Center Flow. The Supernals also correspond closely to Yin as the left, Yang as the right and Toa as the centre from Chinese philosophy.

The Qabalah suggests four planes of manifestation and three of un-manifestation. The three planes of un-manifestation are AYIN Negativity, EN SOPH the Limitless and OR EN SOPH the Limitless Light. Negativity is that which is beyond the range of human mind and body realisation. It is not to be confused by the negative and positive of human duality. Daath is a hidden Sephirath and represents generation and regeneration through the union of the left and right Supernals and equilibrium.

Kether the Crown is the union with *Source*, attainment and completion of great work. From Kether the great un-manifest or dark matter of the Universe is drawn toward manifestation into the physical. Kether is described as the Great Unknown but not the Great Unknowable. Kether is *All That Is*. Kether is Sahamsara the thousand petal Lotus above the Crown Chakra. Kether is also associated with Para the highest Brahma. Brahma is a Hindu principle to the attainment of transcendent reality and *Source* spirit. Each

Sephirath is isolated and absorbs the opposing aspect. The text suggests the human mind cannot fathom the concept of a stateless nonbeing or formless existence. An accurate statement as mind is not the channel toward *All That Is*. The path is traversed through heart and inner self. Due to the persistent notion or separation we have created idols, deities and demigods to direct worship. Inspiration and wisdom originates in the ether with the mind the processor and generator into the physical.

Chokmah is the second Sephirath. Binah and Chokmah are the first aspects of duality. Kether emanates through Chokmah. Chokmah is also associated with Brahma the universal creator. Chokmah represents wisdom and is associated with the entire Zodiac and the planet Neptune. Chokmah closely mirror Vishnu the preserver.

Binah is the third Sephirath. Binah is associated with Mulaprakriti or Pakrati the root of physical or human nature from Vedic philosophy. Binah represents understanding and is associated with the planet Saturn. It is in opposition to Chokmah. Binah is referred to as the evil one. The planet Saturn morphs into Satan. Good and evil are stated to be conditions where evil is simply misplaced force. Binah closely mirror Shiva the Destroyer.

> "It is interacting forces that act and react and come to a standstill, the basis of form…"
>
> Dion Fortune

The statement describes energy, frequency and vibration at wavelengths creating thought form that we interpret with our senses. The tree represents a rhythm where each Sephirath is the flow and element of expansion. As with other dimensional concepts we can emit the frequency of one or more Sephirath. We can experience a life within a sea of Malkuth yet emit the frequency of Tiphareth. The Sephirath have relevance if our vibrational state is in alignment to their frequency.

Chesed is the fourth Sephirath and the first Microcosm. Chesed represents protector and preserver. The associated planet is Jupiter. Chesed is said to be Karma free. Being Karma free does not imply if a person resonates the frequency of Chesed the dualities of physical life will not affect the experience.

Geburah is the fifth Sephirath. Geburah represents strength, courage, cruelty and destruction. Geburah is associated with the planet is Mars. Geburah is the awe and fear of God. This statement should not be taken in the literal sense. The notion of fear of *Source* is an illusion. *Source* is light and there is no fear of it. *Source* does not bestow judgement nor punishment upon anything or anyone. We are subject to our own judgement and our actions of free will. There is no wrath or a religious notion of punishment. Geburah can be aligned with Shiva the Destroyer. Geburah is balanced by Chesed.

Tiphareth is the sixth Sephirath. Tiphareth represents beauty and grace flowing into all manifestation. It is Christ or Krsna consciousness. The Sun is the associated planet. Tiphareth is the equilibrium of the *Tree of Life*. Tiphareth is Kether in a lower arch and the line between form and *Source*. It is a consciousness balance of Kether and Yesod. Kether is the metaphysical. Tiphareth is the mystic. Yesod the psychic. Tiphareth is the higher self and harmony.

The four lower Sephirath are said to have become detached from Tiphareth through dark occult practices. They became the primary force and are assimilated into Qliphoth or the Shadow side. The lower four Sephirath are regarded as the unit of incarnation and personality. The lower Sephirath are Netzach, Hod, Yesod, and Malkuth.

Netzach is victory and lust. Netzach is associated with the planet Venus. Netzach represents instincts, emotions, forms, astral entities and beings flowing in and out of phase. The Elohim are said to be Netzach beings. Netzach represents the ether. Netzach manifests through the principle etheric energy undergoes manifestation through the image making mind of man. We feed images and ideas power and transition astral forms into being and consciousness.

Hod is of occult practice and all manner of ceremony and sacrifice. Hod is associated with the planet Mercury. Hod represents glory, falsehood and truthfulness. Netzach and Hod are force and form of astral energy.

Yesod is foundation, independence and idleness. Yesod is associated with the Moon. The connection to the Moon indicates fluidity, flux and change. Yesod is the final detachment from *Source*. Yesod is the mechanistic aspect of the Universe and is also associated with occult practices. Yesod-Luna and Malkuth-Earth are in constant fluidity and flux. Yesod-Luna shifts in cycles of twenty-eight days. Malkuth-Earth revolves in twenty four hours cycles. Yesod-Luna and Malkuth-Earth shift over three hundred and sixty five day cycles with the Equinox and Solstice phases.

Malkuth is the physical material realm of earth, air, water and fire. It is terrestrial and described as the Earth-Soul. Malkuth is inanimate matter until Yesod animates it. Malkuth is the ultimate state of un-spirituality. The start of a laboured journey through the discipline of matter toward expanded perception and consciousness. The Order of Angels are said to be associated with Malkuth. Angels are names we give to high vibrations of love devoted to aspects of the Universe. They are higher dimensional frequency and not winged beings as we depict them. They being associated to Malkuth is a confusing interpretation.

> "The serpent upon which the great Archangel treads is primitive force, the phallic serpent of the Freudians; and this glyph teaches us that it is the restrictive "prudence" of Hod which "shortens" primitive force and prevents it from overflowing its boundaries. The fall, be it remembered, is represented in the Tree by the great Serpent with seven heads which overpasses the bounds set for it and raises its crowned heads even unto Daath"

> Dion Fortune

The mystic seeks to unite with *Source* whilst in body through inner expansion and rejects the material and desire driven aspects. The psychic is able to tap into timeline vibrations and energetic frequency. The occult looks to control, manipulate and manifest upon the physical world. The text in the Mystical Qabalah reaffirms the statement that the manipulation of astral un-manifest energy is a dense aspect of the human mind. It is an act of lower vibration desire driven to conjure from the unseen. The futility of occult play serves only the temporal physical ego, lust and power. The perspective offered herein is all dark occult ceremony and sacrifice are lower arc tendencies. They are brutal expressions of disconnection. The occult is an expression within all possibility but is a manifestation of ignorance and dwells only in the human theatre. Occult practices are an affront to light and will root incarnational tendency. White magic remains a play with demi gods, goddesses, deities and is regarded as positive manipulation of astral energy.

> The Yoga of the West. "…eastern spiritual
> systems are not fully adaptable by 'white
> races' and western systems, in this instance
> the Qabalah is adopted as it is 'admirably
> adapted to their psychic constitution"
>
> Dion Fortune

A system should not be followed wholly but taken as far as it offers expansion. All philosophies and paths are valid to all persons regardless of skin tone, spiritual constitution or initiated culture. If the person is open to its vibration it will have purpose. The chosen modality will align with the temperament of the person but this should not restrict spiritual knowledge and esoteric learning from all corners of the world.

The Chakras

The seven Chakra system depicts focused energy centres. Hindu and eastern literature place the Chakras along the spine and the brain. The Chakra system is said to govern energetic balance within the body. Each Chakra possesses a unique frequency and can be mapped to dimensions. The energy vortexes along the Chakra system can be expanded through meditation.

Through a silent mind we can nourish internal balance and expand into the sixth and seventh Chakras. From an esoteric and energy healing perspective an imbalance in the

Chakra system may contribute to illness. The Chakra system flows from the root to the Crown. Our energy traverses beyond the seven Chakra system but is omitted from the general topology. The Chakra system can be regarded as dimensions in the energy body of the avatar. By focusing our internal sight toward the Third Eye and Crown Chakra we can shift our point of awareness away from limitation into interdimensional awareness.

The Root Chakra is located at our base near the perineum. It governs the basic human need of sexuality and security. The Root Chakra is the home of fear and of survival. Fear and Love are the dominating aspects and affect all the other Chakras. If fear is the dominant vibration it will maintain a lower frequency detaching and closing down the upper Chakras. The Root Chakra is the grounding Chakra. If we feel detached from material existence the Root Chakra may need reenergising.

The Sacral Chakra, below the naval is responsible for creativity. The Sacral Chakra influences personal power and is the gut instinct or intuition. A low vibrating Sacral Chakra may result on activity over enjoyment. The Solar Plexus Chakra focuses on self-confidence, identity and personal power. When the Solar Plexus is in balance wisdom, decisiveness and personal power have strength. Low Solar Plexus frequency displays itself as a lack of power and indecisiveness.

The Heart Chakra is our spiritual love centre. The Heart Chakra unites the body, the mind, our emotions and the inner spirit. Through meditation and focus on the Heart Chakra we can unite the lower energy centres to allow greater expression of the upper Chakras. The Throat Chakra is verbal expression and the doorway to speak our highest truth. The Throat Chakra is often blocked through fear. We cease speaking our own truth. It is true liberty when we are able to speak our truth without fear. To speak personal truth is to release the Throat Chakra. Natural law dictates absolute sovereignty of thought, word, action and intent. We should not through our own volition omit the divine sovereignty that natural law provides. We exist to express. Humanity is an experiment of variety and difference. It is the mechanism of growth, natural progression and the movement to the internal. Natural law supports this intent. We should not promote any movement that removes the grace of sovereignty. Movements that seek to dismiss the sovereignty of natural law through virtue of correctness are not in alignment with universal reality.

The Third Eye between the eyebrows is our sight beyond sight. It raises the intuition of the Solar Plexus to an expanded state and foresight. When the Throat Chakra is opening a pulsing is experienced akin to energy wanting to burst out. The experience expands through silence and meditation. The Crown Chakra as its name suggest is at the crown of the head. The Crown Chakra symbolises enlightenment and the spiritual connection to our higher self and to *Source.* When opening the Crown Chakra will tingle indicating a connection with our higher self and to divine energy. Through meditative practice the Chakra system can be balanced. The Third Eye and Crown Chakra open us to wider wavelengths of perception and awareness. The Chakra system and their associated auric energy operate synchronously.

> "…Chakras or psychic centres described
> in Yogic literature, are not situated inside
> the organs with which they are associated,
> but in the auric envelope at spots roughly
> approximating thereto"

> Dion Fortune

It matters not which dimensional or energetic concept is adopted. The study of the all available philosophies support greater awareness and expansion of knowledge. Dimensions are frequency and state. We expand from limited and bound existence into all possibility through the connection to our inner self and thus *Source*. Dimensional progression is the private recognition of our inner desire to exceed the external duality, agenda and paradigms of the human experience. We create our own Universe and own the vibration we emit. Collective transformation occurs an individual at a time. The only focus of change is our own. We should be open to consider different perspectives. We should remove the fear to omit established belief system and doctrines. Truth to reality is unavoidable if the journey to self is embarked upon with persistence. It is implausible when we raise the power of our infinite spirit that we can block the physical truths of the theatre. Light exposes everything. It is absolute and unavoidable.

The spiritual journey is the hardest journey of all. It will force the questioning of everything, challenge the ego, selfishness and the mind. The journey will open our state to reflect upon all forms of intent. We will remove old paradigms and forgiven the self and others. Many falter and do not persist as they do not wish to accept the constant questioning and eradication of what was known or believed to be real. True humility and self-determination must emerge. There are many among us who have incarnated to support the transformation of others.

Respect

We have created countless religions, faiths and belief systems directing our focus to something beyond our physical bodies and material lives. There are countless forms being worshipped from the rat to the demigod. We have formed a prejudice towards alternative belief systems and judgement of those who follow them. We espouse the unifying message of each faith yet criticise those who do not follow engrained doctrines. There are truths that each of us will ultimately expand to understand. The individual journey to becoming has its own timeline. We have a tendency to dehumanise devotees or followers of other deities, forms, symbols and doctrines. Each practice or faith has validity in the heart of the receiver. We do not need to accept them all as real nor are we expected to give them time for investigation. The unavoidable truth is they all hold devotional energy. The worship of a religion, faith, deity or person is projected through the heart as devotional love energy. The followers in their billions who emit devotional energy to an idea, faith or symbol will nurture the focus of their intent into being. The symbols, forms, idols, ideas, demigods hold the powerful

frequencies being projected into them. Psychometry is the practice of sensing the energy of a person from something they owned or wore. Psychometry is founded on the principle that something holds the energetic footprint permanently of the person or persons directing worship or value to it. A genuine intuitive can hold an object and describe the person to whom it had value. A demigod, faith or religion holds the devotional energy of every follower who has directed attention to it. This is a universal law. Natural law is our inalienable right of sovereignty and right to speak our truth regardless of views. Natural law is the right of expression and to be what we wish. We have the divine liberty to experience and become without hindrance our intention upon incarnation.

To disrespect the devotion to whatever representation of faith a person wishes to follow is to disregard the energy that has been sent to it through the heart. We are all one in a single experience. Our universal experience is within *All That Is*. We have over millennia degraded the intent of faith and religion. Faith and religion is a human construct. Faith offers us a stepping stone to a much greater truth. Religion and faith are doorways into a vast expanse of knowing and becoming. This has not happened. Faith and religion are now mechanisms for control and programming of their followers. Faith and religion are used to divide humanity on ethnic and cultural grounds, justify war and create a warped truth of our greater reality. Despite these unrecognisable manipulations it is not for us to judge the merits or justifications for the devotion to a faith, object, belief or idol. Free will determines our focus. Humanity progresses through the adventure of becoming at different speeds. Some will traverse the multiple faiths and organised religions. Others will dismiss the existence of anything beyond themselves whilst the few will grow to realise the journey to the 'I' begins and ends with the self.

We must learn to respect others for their free will choice. As expansion extends its embrace over each of us we will move from away from physical objects and images toward the inner personal path. The unravelling realisation may require multiple incarnations but all paths lead to the same end. We will all ultimately radiate grace and inner spirit as our end state whilst in form. This truth applies to the nihilist, atheist, devout worshipper or radical. Our external path aligns with the inner vibration. Our inner vibration will ebb and flow but is destined to move forward. As inner questions become answered we may choose to depart from established faith toward greater realms of understanding. We may grow to share our growth with others. To disrespect the faith of another through personal indoctrination is a reflection of our own state of expansion.

The many deities, idols and pseudo gods of established religion and smaller followings are not to be confused with occult or satanic practices. Lower vibrational belief systems or not love based. The occult focuses on creating dense forms from the astral un-manifest energy for the purpose of dominion, power and desire. The occult requires the sacrifice of life to nourish its manifestations. The faiths that continue to require the sacrifice of life as a means of devotion to an idol may wish to reflect upon the practice. *Source* is thought, energy and love in manifestation. Manifestation is life and matter. All that emanates from *Source* and of its intent does not require the sacrifice of what it creates to sustain it.

A church, temple, mosque, synagogue, cave, mountain top, cardboard box or any place a person worships is where heart energy is held. It is energy, holding, cascading and concentrated. As we traverse the human playground we leave an energetic footprint. Our home, place of worship or where we find comfort holds concentrated energy of our presence. How we manifest our devotion as external actions are a choice of free will. It is an uncomfortable truth that through free will the few have corrupted and enveloped the teaching of unity with hate and violence. What was once a window to ourselves has been manifestly abused and radicalised for political agendas and control. The message of unity and the origin of the Universe was lost long ago. The concept of a one world religion is an extreme deluded philosophy to replace the many with a global mechanism of control and manipulation.

We are able to reconnect with our inner infinite spirit without the need to direct focus to images or objects. The reconnection to our infinite spirit has been abstracted by religion and the focus on external devotion to on omnipotent deity. Once we are open of mind and heart to journey into the self for answers a peaceful expanse of *Source* and infinite awareness will be presented. The challenge before us is of courage to question the intellectual dismissal of a force outside of the self, nihilism and atheism. We have before us the decision to shed established dogma, doctrines and embark upon the journey without a figure telling you what to think, where to go and what to do. Religion, objects of faith, *Source*, incarnation and the presence of an infinite spirit are not new ideas. Philosophies, absolutes and interpretations are offered for reflection. Absolutes transform as clarity emerges. The truth of reality cannot be fully known whilst in form. We interpret what is received and offer our individual truth to those who are open to receive it. The absolute is revealed when we leave the abstract of the physical. Faith, religion, monotheistic, polytheistic and others present deities, gods, idols and symbols. These range from physical beings to deities representing aspects of *Source* consciousness.

Christianity directs devotion to the Cross, Jeshua, the Virgin Mary, other apostles and revered figures. Christianity presents the Holy Trinity as three persons in the one God. The Holy Trinity is the Father, the Son, and the Holy Spirit. The Son is Jeshua. Jeshua entered the human theatre on the 25th December 1 AD. Jeshua is described as the divine Son. The divine Son has been indoctrinated by some religious figures to mean all others are lesser than and not of divine origin. Everything and everyone is a divine aspect of *Source*. *All That Is* exists from thought and intention. We are all in unity and differ in life through our intention or purpose for being. We take form to become. To become is to realise the unseen intention to expand into higher frequencies of spirit whilst in form. We seek to traverse the frequencies and dimensional states towards ascended vibration. An ascended being is not a God nor is it borne of more divine intent. An ascended vibrational state of being is an expanded frequency attained through experience of all possibility. To be ascended is to have moved beyond the limitation and disunity of our physical identity into spiritual knowing. To become is to know what lay beyond the veil. To ascend is to expand beyond distraction, manipulation and attachment to material desire, control, power and cyclical chosen reincarnation. To ascend is to emanate an elevated frequency and sight. To ascend is to bring the inner state to grace whilst in form. To become is to release the shackles of the physical and unleash the inner knowing of our greater reality and origin. An ascended being or state has no desire for incarnation and attachment to life nor the need to conquer it. If a spirit has reached an elevated state it may choose to incarnate into form not for accelerated growth but to assist in the development of the lifeforms in which it has entered.

Jeshua is not the only son of god. Jeshua is an ascended spirit. Jeshua is not a singular aspect of *Source* with all else being lesser. Jeshua had a purpose for incarnation. It was to remind humanity of our divine unity and love. The spirit that animated the avatar that was Jeshua sought to redirect humanity toward its true origin. We were reminded of our inner spirit and to re-establish the connection to *Source*. Over the ages many beings have incarnated into form to remind humanity of itself. These messengers incarnate into cultures and nations where their message is to be seeded. Their purpose is to instil their individual message in the hearts of humanity. Their purpose was not to be the origin of organised religion nor the creation of the indoctrinated masses. Religion and indoctrination are a manifestation of humanity. The priestly seek dominion over the masses whilst the naive and ignorant freely offer their sovereignty, minds and hearts. Each interpretation has been morphed over time and translated by the tendency of the elevated. Billions of infinite spirits have chosen incarnation with their own divine intention. Some are here to elevate humanity, some seek to expand and others wish to observe. There are the misdirected who have chosen destruction, subjugation, manipulation, desire, occult and satanic practices.

Some researchers suggest Jeshua did not exist and is a recreation of ancient myths from Sumerian, Babylonian and Egyptian mythology. Alternative research suggests Jeshua is a recreation of an ancient Mesopotamian deity call Tammuz. In Sumerian mythology Tammuz was incarnated on the 25th of December and was a Sumerian king. Tammuz was associated with shepherds. Tammuz ruled for 26,000 years and was the fifth King before the Great Flood. Tammuz was said to have been buried in a cave and then resurrected. Another association is Horus. Horus is an Egyptian deity and is depicted as a falcon-headed figure. Horus was said to have been borne of a virgin birth. His mother was the Egyptian goddess Isis. The husband of Isis was Osiris. The birth of Horus was celebrated around 25th December 3000 BC. Horus was said to have been adorned by twelve kings. There will be endless debate as to the reality of these ancient myths, deities and stories.

We can intellectually dismiss the existence of Jeshua and accept the alternative view. We may wish to feel the reality and allow the truth to emerge. There is no such hesitancy here. Jeshua was an avatar. Within the avatar was the light of a divine infinite spirt. Our avatars are the same. Jeshua was experiencing being human as are we. Jeshua had a purpose as do we all. The mythology of the ages were attached to the human that was Jeshua to give him divine status above all others. This was intentional. The intent was to create an orthodox organised religion around Jeshua. The attached mythology supported the belief that God was revealed in Jeshua and he was the only divine Son. The Christian faith has developed over two thousand years. Some interpretations of Christianity have successfully indoctrinated followers to fear *Source* and deem themselves lesser beings. The same story repeats itself in all major organised and established religion. We have been programmed to be followers. We are told to fear *Source* and death. We have become sheep and hang on the word of those in priestly garb. Jeshua was an ascended being whose purpose was to guide us back toward our true grace. His message was simple. Be in unity and love as we are all of *Source* and one. Jeshua was a man. He was born of a mother and a father. He had a life with experiences as would any other but with a greater purpose. His ascended spirt took the human form called Jeshua. Jeshua was likely a highly developed psychic. His expanded state understood the nature of reality and transcended the physical whilst in his avatar. There are undocumented periods or missing years of the life of Jeshua. These missing years were from twelve to around thirty years. It is purported Jeshua spent these missing years in the Himalayas and northern India. Vedic texts are said to have predicted the life of Jeshua in the Bhavishya Purana Sanskrit texts 3000 years before his birth. The Vedas referred to Jeshua as Ihsa Putra.

> "…Dr. Vedavyas, a research scholar with a doctorate in Sanskrit, discusses some important prophecies from the Bhavishya Purana, which he says dates back to 3000 B.C. He states that one prophecy describes the future appearance of Isha Putra, the son (Putra) of God (Isha) (Jesus Christ), born of an unmarried woman named Kumari (Mary) Garbha Sambhava. He would visit India at the age of thirteen and go to the Himalayan Mountains and do tapas or penance to acquire spiritual maturity under the guidance of rishis and siddhayogis before going back to Palestine to preach to his people. So, if Jesus was trained by the sages of India, this would explain why he was able to perform various miracles (siddhas). It also explains why there are so many philosophical similarities between early Christianity and Hinduism…Bhavishya Purana describes how Jesus would visit Varanasi and other

Hindu and Buddhist holy places. This is also corroborated by the manuscript on the life of Isha (or Issa), discovered by Mr. Notovich in 1886 at the Hemis monastery in Ladakh, India, as well as by the Hebrew inscriptions found in Srinagar, Kashmir at the Roza bal, the tomb of Yuz Asaf [Isha or Issa]. The Bhavishya Purana also is said to have predicted how Jesus would meet Emperor Shalivahana who established the Shalivahana or "Saka" era. Dr. Vedavyas describes this in his Telegu book, Veerabrahmendra Yogipai Parishodhana."

Stephen Knapp

There are equally convincing arguments against the belief Jeshua spent time in India. The vast distance of at least 3000 miles between Bethlehem in Jerusalem and the Himalayas would have been highly improbable and almost impossible to traverse with transport as it was in those times.

"In The Lost Years of Jesus, Elizabeth Clare Prophet documents other supporters of Notovitch's work, the most prominent of which was Nicholas Roerich. Roerich — a Theosophist — claimed that from 1924 to 1928 he traveled throughout Central Asia and discovered that legends about Issa were widespread. In his book, Himalaya, he makes reference to "writings" and "manuscripts" about Issa — some of which he claims to have seen and others about which people told him. Roerich allegedly recorded

independently in his own travel diary the
same legend of Issa that Notovitch had seen
earlier."

Neverthirsty

In contrast Hinduism as a non-monotheistic faith offers numerous deities. The deities and demigods represent the many attributes of the single divine reality. Followers depending on traditions lean toward one or more deities to direct worship. There are many Hindu deities from the trinity of Brahma the Creator, Vishnu the Preserver and Shiva the Destroyer. Other deities include Ganesh the remover of obstacles, Sarasvati the goddess of learning and Hanuman the Monkey king of strength and devotion. As with other faiths and religions the singular message when we remove the many deities and physical forms is that we are to reconnect with *Source* through the inner spirit. External propaganda insists we should seek salvation from without which perpetuates the lesser than state.

The Vedas are ancient Sanskrit texts containing the philosophy, hymns and rituals of Vedic philosophy. The Vedas date to 5000 BC. Shrila Vyasadeva is said to have split the Veda philosophy into four Samhitas or collections. The four compilations are the Rig-Veda, Sama-Veda, Yajur-Veda, and Atharva-Veda. Shrila Vyasadeva was also said to have compiled the Hindu epics of the Mahabharata and the Ramayana. The stories describe an epic battle between two warring princes. He later added the Puranas which are written in Sanskrit and contain Hindu legends and folklore. The Mahabharata is thought to have been written in 400 BC although archeological evidence is said to date the origin to 600 BC. The dating of the writings of Shrila Vyasadeva and his birth do not align and there are many interpretations.

Aryabhata was the first major Indian mathematician and astronomer. He was born during the Kali Yuga between 476 and 500 A.D. Aryabhata wrote the Aryabhatiya at the age of twenty three. In the Aryabhatiya he calculated the Yuga cycles. The Yuga depicts four ages or epochs of humanity from Hindu philosophy. A single Yuga cycle is said to be one Mahayuga. A single Mahayuga was calculated to be 4.32 million years. These Yuga epochs are described to be cyclical or repeating epochs of humanity. Some suggest Shrila Vyasadeva was born at the very end of the descending Treta Yuga and lived through the Dwarpa Yuga. Alternative research suggest Shrila Vyasadeva was born during the descending Kali Yuga between 700 and 400 BC. The Kali Yuga aligns with the dates of his Sanskrit writings.

> "The great sage, Shrila Vyasa who was fully equipped with knowledge, could see through his transcendental vision the deterioration of everything material, due to the influence of the age. He could also see that the faithless people in general would be reduced in duration of life and would be impatient due to lack of goodness. Then he contemplated for the welfare of men in all statuses and orders of life. He saw that the sacrifices mentioned in the Vedas were means by which people's occupations could be purified, and to simplify the process, he divided the one Veda into four, in order to expand them among men. The four divisions of the original sources of knowledge (the Vedas) were made separately, but historical facts and authentic stories mentioned in the Puranas are called the fifth Veda."

> Shrimad Bhagavatam

Krsna is the origin of the Bhagavad Gita. The Bhagavad Gita is referred to as the Gita. The Bhagavad Gita is a Sanskrit scripture that is part of the Hindu epic Mahabharata. The Bhagavad Gita documents the dialogue between prince Arjuna and his guide Krsna. Lord Krsna is a worshipped deity akin to Jeshua. The worship of Krsna is the foundation of the Hare Krishna society. The International Society for Krishna Consciousness or Hare Krishna movement promotes Krsna consciousness. Krsna and Christ consciousness are the same. Tiphareth the sixth Sephirath in the Qabalah Tree of Life is Krsna or Christ consciousness. They represent the descent of the *Source* into consciousness. The descent is the inner path to oneself. The journey is towards *Source* or *All That Is* through the vibration of unity, peace and love. Unity is the journey of becoming. We do not achieve limitless grace whilst in the physical realm. Our objective to arrive at the state that allows us to shift perceptibly and allow the vibration of *Source* to enter and guide the sojourn.

"...Krishna consciousness means God consciousness. Jesus, or anyone who speaks about God, is in Krishna consciousness."

A.C Bhaktivedanta Swami Prabhupada

This statement suggest Krsna is *Source* itself. Krsna was an ascended spirit in an avatar. Krsna had purpose and intention for life. Krsna was experiencing being human to seed his message or teaching relevant to the time. The Times of India dated 8 Sept 2004 asserts the birth of Lord Krishna to be 21st July 3227 BC. Krsna was purported to have left his avatar on the 18th February 3102 BC after a life of 125 years. The evidence of the birth of Krsna is not as well documented as that of Jeshua. As with all revered figures we can dismiss or feel the truth to their existence. The idea Krsna was *Source* itself leads us to the question if the unity of *All That Is* incarnates into form. In ancient times any being who exhibit heightened and unbounded awareness and an ability to manipulate energy to perform miraculous acts were seen as Gods. This is still the case for many modern day highly developed mystics. Jeshua and Krsna were ascended spirits and by proxy will have had unrestricted psychic capacities. Krsna lived during the Treta Yuga. The Treta Yuga is descried as an age where humanity started becoming detached from *Source* and shifted toward war as depicted in the Mahabharata.

Krsna and other Hindu deities are shown to have blue skin. Indian mystics suggest the blue skin of Krsna was a symbol of the infinite and the unknowable. A medical alternative is Krsna was born with a methemoglobinemia. Methemoglobinemia is a condition where the body produces abnormal amounts of methemoglobin which is a protein in the red blood cells. The red blood cells (RBCs) distribute oxygen around the body. Excess amounts of Methemoglobin do not oxygenate fully and may cause the skin to look blue. The blueness of the complexion may be symbolic rather than an actual reality.

> "…Blue is the color of all-inclusiveness.
> You will see in the existence, anything that
> is vast and beyond your perception generally
> tends to be blue, whether it is the ocean or
> the sky. Anything which is larger than your
> perception tends to be blue because blue is
> the basis of all-inclusiveness. It is based on
> this that so many gods in India are shown as
> blue skinned. Shiva has a blue skin, Krishna

has a blue skin and Rama has a blue skin.
It is not that their skin was blue. They were
referred to as blue gods because they had a
blue aura."

Sadhguru

Ascended spirits may take an avatar to remind humanity
of its true origin and loss of state. The purpose of Krsna,
Jeshua, Buddha and others is to seed awareness and
promote expansion. The message of Krsna is to live in
alignment to our true Dharma or cosmic order and reach
the ultimate goal. The ultimate goal is to emit Krsna
consciousness whilst in form, transcending incarnation,
detachment from the material and to emit the vibration of
love. In Hindu philosophy incarnation is said to be imposed
upon us as punishment for a past life or Karma. We are
also rewarded with prosperous and joyful incarnations
for positive Karma and actions in a past life. This idea
is a dogma of ancient philosophy. We incarnate through
choice. The design for each incarnation may be viewed
as punishment or reward when viewed through the lens
of the physical. We are in infinite awareness and in spirit
when we design our incarnations. The choices we make are
not seen as punishment or reward. The design for life and
avatar we select are intentional and for expansion. Once
we enter life our perceptions are immediately closed down
and we perceive through the human vehicle. We start to
experience duality. The duality has external impositions
upon our purpose and design. These impositions we can
overcome through the realisation of our inner being. The
external impositions of inequality, poverty, war and disunity
may continue to burden the chosen life. We do not enter
life without this awareness. We understand their will be

challenges to our design and distractions of the human theatre. Our core will is to overcome what we choose to enter. We enter life to experience it and all it has to offer. Life is for growth. To grow we must experience. We are not forced into a human avatar nor into animal form as punishment. This is ancient dogma and a doctrine being revised by the modern day mystic. If a spark of infinite consciousness has expanded to be that experiencing human form a life in a body with limited expression has no purpose. *All That Is* has absolute intention and purpose. We do not regress into lesser avatars as expansion is the single reality.

Siddhartha Gautama later named Buddha was born into royalty and privilege in 623 BC. Upon leaving his palace at the age of twenty nine he was confronted with the suffering and sickness of the people outside the walls of his privileged existence. This spurred the young Buddha into a journey toward enlightenment. Over many years Buddha sat meditating under the Bodhi tree. He also spent time learning from teachers and spiritual masters. Enlightenment is the release of what resides within and silently waits for our surface self to allow it to rise to the surface. Enlightenment is not the privy of those who profess divinity or of being chosen. Enlightenment is within everyone and everything. Enlightenment is allowing the inner truth of *Source* and our infinite spirit of light to guide. There are no secrets. There is only an internal truth which has not yet reached the external consciousness and the mind.

Buddha passed on four *Noble Truths* and accepted the Vedic principle of endless reincarnation. Buddha believed each life delivering suffering for previous Karma. This was the first noble truth. Buddha suggested Karma in alignment with philosophy at the time was a store of merit or negativity. The second noble truth stated suffering was linked with desire. The third noble truth taught that detachment from desire removed a person from suffering. The final noble truth states enlightenment can be achieved through the *Noble Eight Paths*. The Noble Eight Paths are the Right Belief, Right Intent, Right Speech, Right Behaviour, Right Livelihood, Right Effort, Right Contemplation and Right Concentration. The teachings of Buddha were the foundation of Buddhism in India and its spread throughout Asia.

History shows a slow progression from our lower Chakra tendencies of paganism, ritual sacrifice, demigods, prophets and deities into organised religion and powerful centres of control. The constant across them all is a single unquestioning translation of each faith and a powerful priestly figure directing worship and prayer. Through free will we give our power away to self-appointed channels of grace. In the end there is no right or wrong in any modality if inner peace, love, grace and expansion to the greater reality is achieved. Everything has a purpose and a time for each person. We should maintain constant awareness that the infinite cannot be presented in a single book nor through the words of a person in priestly garb. We should never cease traversing the metaphorical rocks of the river. The collective experience is of our own creation. The human experience we seek is ours to create and will not be bestowed upon us by an external being or force. There is and will never be a being who will be sacrificed to negate our sins to each other. These are illusions and false propaganda from those who seek to maintain the sheep in their flock. We own our expansion. Christianity speaks of the rapture where only the devoted followers of the faith will be granted passage to heaven. Christianity also speaks of the second coming of Christ as the saviour. Those waiting for a saviour or a second coming of Jeshua will be sadly disappointed. Jeshua is an ascended being. A being of elevated expanded state and whose need for incarnation is obsolete. The purpose of his life was to promote love. Jeshua sought to remind humanity of its true nature and that we are all one with *Source*. The message was instilled in a part of the world where it was needed and from where the message would cascade. The Christian faith surrounding Jeshua is a human creation and is used to lock followers in a managed system. The message of love was never intended to be instituted as a religion. The message of unity, love and harmony are ethical values that support our progress through the states of consciousness. Christianity relegates mysticism and esoteric thinking as dark arts or the work of the devil.

Islam is based on the messages received from Arch Angel Gabriel by Muhammad over 20 years. These tenets or messages formed the Islamic faith around 622 BC. The teaching are read in the Koran. The Sufi were regarded as the mystics of the Islamic faith and were often seen spinning in trance states. The Sufi transcendental spinning practice was the origin of the phrase *Whirling Dervish*. Judaism is the oldest of the three monotheistic faiths. Judaism is the religion and way of life of the Jewish culture. The tenets of Judaism are read in the Torah. The Torah states the existence of the one God. An important teaching of Judaism is that there is one God, incorporeal and eternal who wishes all people to do what is just and merciful. The teachings state all people are created in the image of God and deserve to be treated with dignity and respect. Abraham was the founder of Judaism and to whom the Jewish community trace their roots. Jewish mysticism is based on the Qabalah.

Source is light, thought, energy, grace and intention. *Source* does not judge nor involve itself in the theatre of the human experience. The infiniteness of the Universe is abundant with advanced life and in innumerable forms. We see ourselves as expanded and advanced but from a perspective taken from within our own myopia. *Source* is the infinite expanse of *All That Is*. It is nonsensical to believe that *Source* would intervene in human division, desire, political systems or bestows power to an individual or a cultural group over any other. This is a falsehood that will ultimately be revealed if not in this lifetime it will in another. Any being professing to be a God, one who will punish, find favour in one culture over another or will cast vengeance upon others is a false deity masquerading as *Source*. The Universe is a canvas on which there is infinite possibility. We should be aware all possibility will create whatever we allow and nurture. There are forms physical and nonphysical who may present themselves as gods to the naive who propagate their idea over the ages. The continued belief and bestowing of power to their idea is a free will choice open to each of us. The human play with universal and astral form is open to all as is its pretense. We have a tendency to look externally for salvation. We wish for someone or something to sacrifice and bring balance to our base tendencies. This is not the reality. If this were true our inner spirit would have no need for incarnation nor expand through experience. We would have no purpose to move to more expanded states of Krsna or Christ consciousness. The rapture is in fact our individual journey from attachment, devotion to others or deities into our infinite spirit. If we reflect upon the many faiths and religions they have an underlying commonality. All are doorways to the unity to *Source* through the self and the vibrational frequency of Love. This is all that exist and transcends. As we move away from established faiths, idols, demigods into inward expansion our physical world will manifest in alignment with it. We are all at different points of expansion but the destination is the same.

The Occult

Occult practices and philosophies are interpreted differently. The way in which the occult is observed will vary depending on the persuasion of the viewer. An aspect that cannot be misinterpreted is occultism and practices thereof are lower energetic tendencies. The occult practice ceremony and sacrifice to false gods, deities and manifest astral forms. Some may feel the worship of the numerous goddesses as witchcraft and call themselves white or dark witches. There are many in mainstream who will deem the use of runes, crystals and the Tarot as the work of the devil. We may wish to relegate the psychic or medium as occult or demonic practitioners. There is a difference between tools used to interpret universal energy and occult practices. Runes, pendulums and the Tarot amongst others are tools. Crystals are natural amplifiers and stores of energy. Crystals hold a unique frequency and have different uses. There are a vast array of crystals available. They are all tools. These tools provide an intuitive practitioner methods to interpret the individual and collective energetic footprint stored in the Quantum field. These tools provide clarity and insight into timelines presented as wavelength frequencies of the receiver. An intuitive will interpret the symbols and feelings differently and select a set of tools that resonate with them. The psychic and medium may use a set of tools to assist in the interpretation of what is received or may work independently of them. A psychic or medium is a person who has opened their innate perception outside of the five sense wavelength frequency. Their expanded state allows their perceptions and awareness to move into a wider frequency and access areas of the Quantum field. The Quantum field is the energetic library of everything that has been, is and will be. It is the cosmic library of everything that has ever existed or has yet to pass. This is the origin of true psychic and mediumship. We can be born with opened awareness or may choose to expand the senses in later life. The Quantum field is open to us all if we chose to allow our true state to emerge. It is a free will choice to experience beyond the five sense physical body and the mainstream world with which we interact. Alternative healing or Reiki is based on the universal principle of energy. Energy healing may use crystals to amplify the healing frequency and support treatment. We are all energy. Our bodies vibrate energy. Energy healing or Reiki focuses on balancing energy and removing blocks. The practice is intended to allow the body to heal by removing imbalances and freeing the flow of energy in the body. These practices are intended to compliment mainstream medicine.

The occult, Satanism and demonic practices are perverse interpretations and the channeling of astral energy. These modalities use ceremonies, sacrifices and heinous acts to manifest power and forms from the unseen. The occult does not focus energy for healing, to understand the nature of our greater reality or for practices of light. The occultist and Satanist channel energy to conjure and create perverse forms and perform ceremony for the worship of false gods. The occultist will sacrifice animal and human to feed the astral forms and give them power through intention.

The choice of Path. "The normal healthy
westerner has no desire to escape from life, his
urge is to conquer it and reduce it to order and
harmony. It is the pathological types who long
to "cease upon the midnight with no pain," to
be free from the wheel of birth and death".

Dion Fortune

An interesting statement or interpretation of the Qabalah.
There is no pathology in releasing the self from the cyclical
of rebirth. In fact the aim is to achieve this goal. The
choice and intent for life is unique. Some may revel in the
prospect of eternal incarnation and the desire to conquer
life. These proponents will delve into occult or satanic
practices to achieve dominance over life. Others may see
life as a platform for expansion. The need to dominate
life may lead a person toward the occult in an attempt to
control and manifest power over the human theatre and all
those within. If life and more life is the pursuit and there is
a desire to remain rooted in form this will be the outcome.
The suggestion a normal healthy westerner has no desire
to escape from and control life is a very human statement
and of the mind. The Qabalah refers to the occult, dark and
white magic and other practices as aspects of the lower
Sephirath. The lower Sephirath are Hod, Netzach, Yesod
and Malkuth. Occult practices or the need to control life
are not defined in eastern spiritual philosophy as they are
in the Qabalistic belief. Vedic and Buddhist philosophy
focus on expansion and the inner journey.

Occult practices are not of *Source* nor of divine light.
The occult is a practice of those who play with astral forces
and universal energy. The occult is a modality of perverse
practices, desires of depressed spiritual force and are

illusions to be avoided. The occult serves no purpose other than to further engross the spirit into repeated incarnation and material play. The achievement of *Tiphareth* which is the sixth Sephirath of the Qabalistic Tree of Life is the frequency of Krsna or Christ consciousness. Krsna or Christ consciousness cannot be delivered through occult practices, rituals or calling upon astral entities. Inner expansion and the release of our infinite divine spirit is attained through *Source* light and not occult illusions manifest in the human theatre. The occult exists within *Source* as everything resides within the unifying one. The one is all possibility. The manifestation of the occult is a creation of humanity and originates from the manipulation of astral forces. We are able to bring into being any abstraction of form if there is sufficient energy given to its intent. The occultist feeds astral forms energy through ritual and ceremony. Astral forms, false gods and deities become what we intend for them. They gain power through the willful bestowing of energy to their manifestation. Occultist and Satanists create binding and repeating paradigms of reincarnation.

> "It is very important that we should realise that these two lower Sephirath on the plane of illusion are densely populated by thought forms; that everything which the human imagination has been able to conceive, that the more the human imagination has dwelt upon it to idealise it, the more definite that form becomes"

> Dion Fortune

A true and accurate statement. Occult deities, imagery and astral forms are all manifestations of humanity. Occultists and Satanists feed life energy to these abstractions and cultivate them into being. Occultists feed energy into the glow of the dark through intent, ceremony and sacrifice. There is only light in *Source*. Everything else is illusion and the creation of those who manipulate the energy of universal possibility.

> "...when sacrifice is brought into worship,
> the image is brought a step farther down the
> planes into manifestation and acquires a form
> in the dense ethers of Yesod..."

Dion Fortune

Occulted symbolism is prevalent across the human theatre. Occult symbolism is open for the Seeing Eye. The occultists create demi and pagan gods to assist in the acquisition of power and domination. These dense tendencies serve only to further depress the infinite being into the spectrum of the material. There is little to be gained other than illusionary temporary perceived reward in the material life. Material power and all its derivative aspects have no significance beyond the physical. The occultist and Satanist will return to *Source*. There the futility of their astral pursuits will again be revealed. Occult and Satanic tendency are powerful lower energy behaviours and may require multiple lifetimes to expand into higher frequencies.

> "It is to the Sphere of Chesed that the exalted
> consciousness of the adept rises in his occult
> meditations, it is here that he receives the
> inspirations which he works out on the
> planes of form. It is here that he meets the
> masters as spiritual influences contracted

telepathically without any intermingling of personality"

Dion Fortune

There is the idea that occult practices can be positive if controlled. This is an illusion. The occult is manifesting astral abstract form. There is no need to manifest astral form when the route to true manifestation and expansion is through the inner light. The inner light exist and awaits recognition. Occult practitioners ignore the inner light and seek power externally. The Qabalah suggests there is a place of purgatory named *Qliphoth*. Qliphoth is not hell but a plane where cosmic extreta remain until they find balance. It is described as a place of disorganised forms cast out from evolution into chaos on a lower arc. Qliphoth is an imposed purgatory and will become the place of the outcast until the illusion is lifted. The forms that reside within Qliphoth are not of light and are creations of ego, desire, lust, control, power, ceremony and sacrifice. These ideas are given power and hence form through the dedication of worship.

The Qabalah Tree of Life and other philosophies ultimately directs us to become *All That Is* whilst in form. The sixth Sephirath of Tiphareth is *Source*, Krsna or Christ consciousness. As long as humanity feeds an astral form, idea or manifestation it will exist. Astral form can never exist beyond its realm as it is not of *Source* and will forever be a lower arch manifestation. The serpent of the fall of humanity and the seven headed dragon are associated with this plane. We should be mindful of the beliefs, ideas and abstractions of form we worship and give power. The depravation and perversion of occult belief is not relegated to the minority. Satanism and occult practices pervade the lowest to the highest in the pyramid of control. We have through ignorance allowed these dense practices to become rooted in the human experience. Satanic ritual abuse and sacrifice, human trafficking and pedophilia, spirit cooking, reverence of astral beings and false gods all exist and surround us. Sacrificial fear is a powerful energy. Energy creates matter through intention. Fear and energy of sacrifice is channeled towards the manifestation of astral beings the misguided revere as gods. Whatever the mind perceives it can become form. The symbols of the occult and perverted practices are on open display. These range from the inverted cross in a circle to effigies. False gods punish those who do not worship them. False gods favour one group over another. False gods are those who a worshipper states will kill or interfere in the human theatre to bring justice.

These are illusions and manifestations of the naive. *Source* will not and does not drop into the myopia of any form in the Universe to conduct meaningless actions. The canvas is ours to manifest upon and bring back to grace. Those who worship these false gods and conduct Satanic practices possess the deluded belief they are protected by these beings in the afterlife. This is an illusion they will ultimately come to realise as they judge themselves for their repeated paradigms. The occult and the Satanist is a sad and deluded state of being for temporary power in the human theatre. The occult is an example of the brutal duality we have created. We possess a great capacity for beauty and love based action. We also display depraved and perverted beliefs and practices. This is the human experience we have collectively permitted as we go about the myopia of life. It is for us to bring the brutal duality to an end or ready the self for repeated sojourns into the movie.

Karma & Timelines

Karma and Timelines are mutually inclusive. Karma is the divine universal law of cause and effect. Karma impacts our timelines and the forward projected events we experience. We do not reside on a single timeline of possibility. Multiple timelines exist for every universal animate or inanimate form. Timelines are projections of possibility and are in continual motion. To understand the meaning of timelines we should remind ourselves of cause and effect. In every culture there exists the concept of Karma. The general understanding of Karma is that we will reap what we sow. An action borne from love will produce reflective fruits adversely negative aligned intent will deliver the same. Some religious doctrines state Karma forces reincarnation. These indoctrinated beliefs dictate a sinful or life of evil actions will result in the reincarnation of the soul as an animal, into suffering, disease or poverty. The same belief suggest if a life is sinful the afterlife will be of limbo or purgatory. These belief systems are illusions. Consciousness does not fall into a

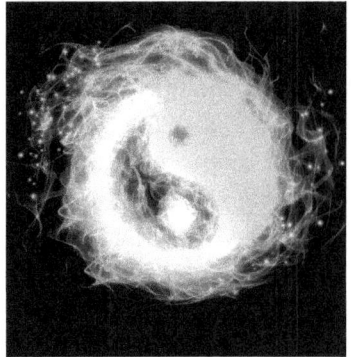

more restricted form of expression as a plant or an animal due to some omnipotent punishment. Intent and purpose are the foundations of the Universe. There would be no purpose for consciousness that is experiencing human form to be subject to the limitations of a plant or an animal. We do not experience form that limits expression, awareness and perception. We do not move backwards in form or in the capacities of the vessel.

The infinite consciousness that animates a human body is capable of great perceptible expansion. Once in human form the avatar through free will may choose to exhibit behavior akin to that of an animal. We share the human experience with evolving spirts each of whom are at different levels of expansion. Consciousness itself once entering the human experience will not drop into a lower dimensional form. The belief is an illusion and one embraced by those who require comfort from the idea there will be punishment of the sinful by an omnipotent deity. Some religious doctrines promote in the afterlife or punishment in the next life by being put in an animal body or incarnation into a lower caste as penance.

> "…our karma (or destiny) has caused us to
> be incarnated in a body of a certain racial
> type and temperament it may be concluded
> that is the discipline and experience which
> the Lords of Karma consider we need in this
> incarnation, and that we shall not advance
> the cause of our evolution by avoiding or
> evading it."
>
> Dion Fortune

The judgement we seek is our own. The punishment we seek is from the self. Reincarnation is a free will choice of the spirit when not in body. The choice to incarnate into a life is taken when in unity with *All That Is*. To understand why an infinite spirit would engage in continual reincarnation into the physical realms we should understand the choice is made from unbound sight of the infinite spirit and not when in an avatar. The formless energy of the infinite spirit looks upon life as an opportunity for expansion. The infinite spirit resonates the frequency of *Source* and love. We live many lifetimes and experience numerous timelines of possibility. A previous life may have achieved very little of its intended purpose. Other lifetimes may have taken the path of expansion and traversed the pathways of divine consciousness. We have the free will choice to travel along any path. We may walk the path of distraction, ego and deceit. We may live a life of love and expansion. We may consider punishment to be a life where there has been little transcendental expansion or movement toward infinite reality. Punishment may be repeating incarnations of cyclical deep rooted paradigms or tendencies. We are our own judge. We freely choose to direct a fractal of our infinite core into the human theatre. Our intent is always to direct our actions through the heart and to not repeat old paradigms.

When in human form we through disconnection tend to process through the avatar and the mind rather than the inner spirit. The spirit is not mind. The infinite spirit is pure *Source* energy. Incarnations are adventures of expansion, freedom and sovereignty. We create and allow experiences through positive and negative actions. We are given a canvas on which to create our experiences. We are free to create the joy in life we desire. Through free will we create forward projected possibilities measured and formulated in the Quantum field as timelines. Timelines are a formation of every free will action, word, thought and intent. We will experience the timeline or projected outcomes that are fed the most energy through our physical and mental force. Cause and effect impact our individual timelines including the timelines of those who are affected by our actions. Timelines and our interactions are complex and the degrees of separation are constantly shrinking. Our integrated human experience results in rapid changes to timelines globally as well as individually.

> ".... photons ricocheting through Philip
> Walther's lab at the University of Vienna.
> Walther's group has shown that it is impossible
> to say in which order these photons pass
> through a pair of gates as they zip around
> the lab. It's not that this information gets
> lost or jumbled – it simply doesn't exist. In
> Walther's experiments, there is no well-defined
> order of events. This finding in 2015 made
> the quantum world seem even stranger than
> scientists had thought. Walther's experiments
> mash up causality: the idea that one thing
> leads to another. It is as if the physicists have
> scrambled the concept of time itself, so that it
> seems to run in two directions at once.... 'A
> quantum computer free from the constraints of
> a predefined causal structure might solve some
> problems faster than conventional quantum
> computers,' says quantum theorist Giulio
> Chiribella of the University of Hong Kong."

Philip Ball

Nonlinear causality states that an event does not necessarily cause the next to occur. We create timelines through nonlinear causality in that forward projection of outcomes are a result of energy of multiple preceding events and not a singular occurrence. Multiple timelines of possibility exist within the universal theatre. Infinite possibility is formed through causal effects, words, deeds and vibration. We may experience timelines in the present reality or potentially in parallel universes. The possibilities are infinite and it is prudent to be open to all ideas. To be open to all possibility does not mean embracing any concept without question. To be open is to consider all aspects outside the mainstream view. The alternative is a reactive dismissal of any idea that does not adhere to existing paradigms and norms. Cause and effect is cumulative with no single prior event causing a timeline or a major shift in possibility. Shifts occur through a combination of recurring patterns, behaviours, words, thoughts and intents.

Multiple possibilities exists in the Universe. At every moment we have at least two choices which may lead to multiple potentials. Causality is an energy imprint in subspace or a universal forward projection of possibility presented as a timeline. Cause and effect is a universal law and all pervasive. Nothing is immune to universal law and there are no counter practices to negate energy produced from an action. Intent can never be circumvented and is recorded in the Quantum field. There is no manner to avoid cause and effect. Intent is the origin of cause and effect or Karma. Intent is energy. Karma cannot become void. Some in the human theatre belief Karma can be circumvented if they inform the subject something is about to happen. If the subject does nothing to prevent the intended action the Karma passes to the victim. This form of belief is a result of the human fascination to attempt to control divine law. The person imposing an action has an intent. Intent is the persistent foundation of Karma. The physical act itself is irrelevant. It is the intent through which it was formed which persists and is imprinted in the Quantum field for eternity. Many believe in this false notion if the person or persons are given information as to what will occur in the most obscure manner and they do nothing the Karma is passed onto the victim. This is an absolute illusion.

Universal law is all encompassing and impacts everything. Everything is subject to cause and effect. Each event, decision, thought, word, intent has energetic vibration. The vibration of intent or cause creates projected effects. Some effects are felt immediately whilst others may manifest later in time. Life and possibility is not linear. All possibility has multiple branches, twigs and leaves. Possibilities are timelines and are all governed by the energy feeding them. The free will element of life allows for any number of outcomes. Outcome or possibility may be experienced days, weeks, months or years ahead.

Karma is the overriding governor of possibility. Karma offers positive or negative possibilities over linear physical time. If we exhibit negative emotions, thoughts, actions and intent the forward energy will create the same vibrational outcomes. If we emit positivity, love centered thoughts, actions and intent we will manifests greater possibility. Everything in the Universe is subject to multiple timelines from a subatomic particle to the cosmos itself. A timeline is a projected set of outcomes resulting from our past and current actions. Potential possibility is represented as a timeline of projected outcomes of preceding energy. If we possess hardened patterns of beliefs the future can be easily projected. A significant movement in tendency can alter a timeline for example an action that is completely not aligned to any before it or a major crossroad in life may trigger an alternate timeline.

This karmic principle is pervasive and extends into communities, cities, countries, planets and beyond. The sum of our actions, words, thoughts and intents will influence the timeline of an individual, culture, nation, species and the Universe. Our collective human experience seems to be of struggle, never ending war, injustice and unceasing negative global events. The timeline we experience can be altered. It should be understood what we experience in the now was manifested collectively through what we have allowed through projected energy months, years, decades and centuries past. Individual and collective timelines change only when the projected energy is altered. Our individual trajectory should be the focus as it directly impacts the collective timeline. We should focus on directing our personal energy, thoughts, actions, words and intent through the heart and the internal spirit. The cumulative effect will change our collective experience and timelines.

When we change and open our perceptions the physical tendencies and paradigm will follow. The inner self is part of the whole. With sufficient individual change collective timelines flex with a cascading effect throughout the Universe. Our energy is in unity. There is no separation. Introspection is a difficulty for humanity as narcissism, intellectualism and ego dominate.

The reading of timelines is what occurs during a psychic reading. An intuitive will tap into the energy of the individual thereby seeing past, current and projected energy viewed as timelines. Timelines are energetic footprints in the Quantum field. A real medium, psychic or intuitive will interpret the energetic timelines with the assistance of the spirit. Tarot cards, runes, crystals are all tools. Tarot cards are all interpreted differently by each intuitive reader yet the message should be consistent if passed on through a genuine psychic or medium. The mystical is not magic nor witchcraft but a tapping into energy of the Quantum field. We all possess intuitive capabilities. Some are born with open sight and others may develop it later. Psychic and intuitive sight is within each and every life form and experienced through the releasing of the infinite self. We are within *All That Is*. We have access to the unseen possibility through the feeling body. We alter our timelines through introspection and ultimately toward the reemergence of the internal spirit. Our lives seek to be guided by the infinite spirit and the heart. The mind is the partner. The partnership supports the transformation of our behaviours and intents manifesting the timelines of possibility.

The Afterlife

Death is unavoidable. We have grown to fear death. As an outcome of our disconnection from truth we have intellectually dissolved the existence of an afterlife and *Source*. Our intent in life is not to strive for perfection, pursue immortality or believe ourselves to be *Source*. Perfection is not possible whilst in form. Our intent is to expand. We have misunderstood the nature of death as we continue to perceive our reality through the physical body. We use the term 'I am only human' to explain the nature of ourselves and our indiscretions. Death is a returning of the fractal of our core back to its origin. Death is to return home. The transcendental aspects of life persist such as the personality and our spiritual growth. The personality is retained energetically as a movement from each life experience. The personality evolves and is not made obsolete after each incarnation. Sri Aurobindo in the 'The Life Divine' suggests the personality does not persist. Sri Aurobindo states a new appropriate personality is created for each life experience. The persistence of the personality is subjective and one the reader can reflect. In

some manner we can state a new personality is formed upon each incarnation. The personality is new by proxy of it being transformed by the personal traits developed in other lifetimes. Lifetimes exist simultaneously and what we experience coalesces as it is formed.

> "We are not only what we know of ourselves
> but immensely more which we do not know;
> our momentary personality is only a bubble
> on the ocean of our existence...In lak'ech' is
> a Mayan phrase meaning, you are my other
> self."

> Sri Aurobindo

Our consciousness or the 'I' is *Source* knowledge and awareness. The words in this book are taken from an inner knowing. Inner knowing is open to everyone. Within the world of illusion we see fragments of truth. Truth lay under the veil of the universal theatre from which we judge each other. Inner unity, harmony and contentment are spiritual manifestations. Separateness from *Source* is an illusion. Our physical lens dispatches the dogs of disharmony, a sense of imperfection and leads to hardened intellectualism. These attributes contribute to the fear of death and the dismissal of what exists beyond. Life is not intended to deliver suffering. Death does not lead to enforced punishment. We do not incarnate to suffer but learn from challenges some of which are predetermined. If we are not in alignment with our inner state and become immersed in the material the resulting experience is of anxiety, inadequacy, discontentment and other ills. We have a tendency to assign suffering as periods of challenge or to fate. We do not suffer to repent and to be worthy of the paradise above.

Challenges or major crossroads in life provide opportunities for expansion and are not intended to create a life filled with suffering, anxiety and fear. We experience designed and unplanned crossroads in life. The choices we make at each juncture may follow established tendencies. Our choices define forthcoming timelines of experience. Through free will we create our own cause and effect and resulting timelines. Our decisions can originate from the infinite spirit or be governed by the physical and the mind. This formula is the foundation of what we categorise as suffering and punishment.

We can through internal discovery and investigation become aware of purpose and predestination. We grow to understand unplanned events and the cause and effect our free will decisions have upon manifestation and timelines. Our perception of life expands and we understand the actions of others as well as our own. Our spirit embarks upon an incarnation having predefined the foundational conditions of the intended life. We understand free will determines cause and effect and the fulfilment of purpose.

We are reminded that every incarnation is created and planned whilst in spirit. The spirit realm is not influenced by the impositions or conditions of the material human experience. We design and embark upon an incarnation from a state of infinite love, awareness and consciousness. The choice to embark upon a life is not borne from fear. Fear is a state imposed upon the consciousness after entering the human experience. Fear is the foundation of the misunderstanding of death. If we view our life through the mind rather than infinite awareness the result is misunderstanding and fear. The human experience is a dense third dimensional energy. The light of infinite awareness is dimmed by enforced human systems. Some of us will overcome these impositions and allow the higher self to emerge and guide. The veil slowly falls away. Life, death and the afterlife start to become understood.

Death is not the end nor is a life incarnation a beginning. We exist as spirit, formless and of pure light energy. Physical life supports growth and the experience. The body is a vessel and our avatar. Our infinite spirit animates the body to experience life and its interactions with the material realm. Death is the leaving of the spirit from the body. The spirit ceases to animate the body. We should not fear death. Death is an ending to an experience. An end to a life can be natural, through recklessness, deterioration of the vessel or forced by the actions of another. We own what we can control. We should maintain the health of the body to accomplish the intended life. We cannot own the actions of others who may alter the course of our lives beyond our intended design. Free will has absolute power and directs our actions, words and thoughts. The universal law also applies to others.

The afterlife is real and absolute. There is no question. There are many reports of the afterlife from near death experiencers, mediums or those who engage in astral travel. What we experience upon death is determined by a number of factors namely religious indoctrination, established belief systems or lack of, fear or passed down depictions of the unseen. We manifest our experiences by transmuting the energy of thought and established paradigms. What we believe to be true or have fed sufficient energy will manifest into the experience in life. The same universal law applies itself to what we will initially experience as the afterlife. The afterlife may present a fiery hell, purgatory or a white bearded God waiting at the pearly gates of heaven. The possibilities we experience will mirror established doctrines and powerful foundational beliefs. Whatever we believe exists as punishment or heaven are embedded into the consciousness and if fed sufficiently will be the initial experience upon exit.

If there is a strong belief of a fiery hell where the soul suffers for past deeds or occult worship of astral forces this may be presented as the afterlife. We may believe our soul will be met by deities or Jeshua as a white blonde haired angelic figure. We may hold intense desire to see deceased loved ones who will take us toward the light. We may believe that heaven is the same as the Earth but more colourful and illumined. If we feel there is nothing beyond the consciousness may be presented with an emptiness or a void in which confusion and loss is the experience. The afterlife we experience is self-imposed and becomes a further layer of abstraction over the illusionary physical life the spirit has exited. Our spirit will ultimately enter a state of pure love even if there is fleeting sojourn in a self-imposed realm. The veil is ultimately lifted to present an afterlife from which the additional abstractions are removed. We are a fractal of *Source* and will always return back to love. There is an absolute reality. There is only one *Source* of origin. There is no special place for the chosen few or a sphere for the less pious or evil. We all vibrate in light but evolve as beings at different rates. We share the same inner infinite state regardless of actions when in form.

We experience many lifetimes. Some desire repeated material existence and control of it. This desire will lead to continual incarnation as a choice. Others may choose life for accelerated expansion and release from the choice of repeated sojourns. Some will disagree and suggest life is why we exist. We could repeatedly incarnate only to repeat past tendencies. We may cycle continually into life with each incarnation delivering little investigation into the self. The life we create around our core intent for incarnation is a free will choice. As we traverse the realm of illusion into *Source* all our abstractions of emotion from love to hate are absorbed. Every emotion be they positive or negative transcends and is coalesced into the light. The overwhelming frequency should be love. Empathy, consideration, respect, gratitude, peace and forgiveness as some aspects of an elevating consciousness. The emotion of love is the power that will shift the spirit into the higher vibrations. We should seek to continually evolve our frequency whilst in body to open to greater meaning to existence and to feel the joy of the divine. From a personal view to recursively enter life and repeat cyclical dense tendencies is the greatest of punishment to an infinite spirit that seeks only expansion through love.

Spiritual leaders are aware of this truth yet propagate beliefs to entrain fear of an omnipotent deity to control their flock. Universal existence does not impose justice, retribution or judgement. It is self-imposed. Whatever we allow we do through free will. Some who enter physical life and allow inner spiritual expansion may grow to desire a release from rebirth. Those who cling onto physical life and desire more of it may repeat paradigms resulting in continual incarnation. Our choices will resonate with our developing frequency. We may resonate with the material or expansion beyond the senses.

The inner journey to spirit directs perception to the greater truth beyond the ego, narcissism and intellectualism. We have over millennia lost our true connection with the self and to *Source*. We have allowed society, culture, ideology, isms and belief systems to form our understanding. We have created a fear of a vengeful absolute. We have created the duality of heaven and hell. We have devoted our attention to effigies of the innumerable demigods. Our entrainment has been supremely successful in its objective to misdirect humanity away from the higher self. It is said that we are drawn to a religion matching the frequency of our inner consciousness. A truth when limited to the external and the material. The spirit is not bound by worldly interpretations.

The nihilist believes in nothing and is sceptical of anything outside of the mind. The atheist dismisses the existence of any greater reality, faith and an afterlife. In the end these are belief system in themselves. The concepts of belief are interesting as true reality originates from feeling. Inner knowing is pure feeling resonating from the infinite spirit. The mind is not the driver towards expansion. Belief is a perception of the mind and is enforced by the intellect. There is never any leaving or separation. We connect to *Source* through the self which brings with it peace, harmony and love. We become aware of our truth and the illusion. Upon death we return perception back to the realm of our core spirit. We incarnate to embrace the physical sojourn and fulfil purpose whilst creating an individual experience around it knowing there is an end. All things end and nothing is forever in the universal theatre. From cosmic bodies to subatomic atoms each form, exist and transform releasing energy to create alternate matter in repeating cycles. Through expansion we re-establish our connection with our true divine family. When it is time to exit the spirit leaves the body and it ceases to become animated.

The study of near death experiences have documented varying depictions of the afterlife. Some near death experiencers state the afterlife resembles the indoctrinated beliefs of their faith. Others observed an immediate expansion into everything, a state of peace and enveloping divine love. Others who had dismissed the existence of the afterlife reported being in a place of sounds, darkness, strange images and unease. Near death experiences will follow the frequency of the expanded self, the indoctrination of established and organised faith or the intellectual engrained belief nothing exists beyond human life. The Atheist has a core belief we are born from nothing, live a life and then become nothing when it is over. It is uncommon to read of a near death experience that is not in alignment with an indoctrinated belief of death and the afterlife. The intellectual, atheist, nihilist and others have through the mind dismissed any notion of an afterlife may experience the same temporary abstraction.

Eben Alexander, an American neurosurgeon authored the *Proof of Heaven* which described his near death experience. During a coma caused by E. coli bacterial meningitis Eben Alexander had a near death experience. He reported being consciously present and of being in a dark place, surrounded by an oily substance, strange sounds and beings brushing past him. He experienced an immediate sense of unease and fear. He asked outwardly. What is this? Why am I here? He found himself in a void which may in the experience felt like an eternity. He describes a moment when his awareness was raised from the state he found himself into an infinite presence of peace and endlessness. He reported a feeling of being everywhere, in all things and aware of *All That Is*. He was in a state of divine love.

We will experience whatever we believe to exist upon death. There are no exceptions. This equally applies to those in the spiritual or esoteric. The theatre is an illusion and is not the origin of home. Each of us are infinite awareness, energy and consciousness having a human experience. The illusion is real as we experience, perceive and interact with it through the body. We should shift focus to the true nature of reality, infinite knowing and remove established doctrines. What we experience as the afterlife is a temporary illusion from a previous abstraction of physical form. The afterlife will initially present what we have entrained in our consciousness. As we become aware that death has occurred fear may replace confusion. The illusion dissolves as quickly as fear is allowed to fall away. We do not need to experience these states of fear or confusion. We have open to us the choice to expand beyond our egoistic intellectualism and attachment to the real. We have waiting in the silent grace within the awareness of *All That Is* whilst in form.

Purgatory is a human creation. The greater the belief in these illusionary descriptions of the afterlife the more they become real. The presentation of the afterlife may seem to the slowly dimming mind consciousness to persist for an eternity. The presentation of our true reality is instant as there is no time outside the abstraction of the Universe. The true nature of being is infinite and of feeling. We are infinite spirits having a human experience not a human with a spirit. We create with conviction afterlife worlds or places in the mind. We create countless realms for the pious and the evil. We convince our consciousness we will inhabit them upon death. Near death experiences offer evidence that what is observed often follows indoctrinated beliefs of the afterlife. Near death experiences follow inherent beliefs. Our infinite consciousness is truth and a path to expansion. True knowing is felt and is never initiated through mind or egoistic intellectualism. Truth and spiritual sovereignty desires rediscovery. We seek to relegate challenges as failures in life and are unaware these experiences are there for growth. Death is a falsehood as the infinite spirit never dies and exists in the vessel until the journey is complete or has served its purpose. The body then dies, decomposes and adds itself to the physical plane as energy. The fractal of our infinite spirit returns home. Divine consciousness is stillness, love and energy from which all emerges. It just is. *Source* as are we is formlessness. Formlessness is difficult for the mind to accept as it seeks physical categorisation and a place to assign itself. The fractal of our true higher self re-emerges into the unifying energy of *Source*.

> "The afterlife is thought of as the place
> where your loved ones languish after a long,
> or short life lived in physical form. We
> would call it life. There is no before life and
> subsequent Afterlife. Life is eternal. It never
> ends. It merely transforms in frequency. The
> Energy that you are, that your loved ones
> 'were' still exists and surrounds you, loving
> you. Remember there is nowhere that Energy
> is not. It always just 'is'. There is no place
> it goes to. It is ever present, ever loving and
> ever living".

Ara Parisien

Purpose

Before we open the topic of purpose we should address the notion that humanity or we are special. When we look upon ourselves we have a tendency to believe ourselves special. We are told that we have a special place amongst all other life in the Universe. We are encouraged to belief the Earth has greater significance and is above all other cosmic bodies. We perceive ourselves to have a superior sentient nature and masters of what surrounds us. As we shift our perception outward the view of the manifest Universe changes. The notion of being special reveals itself to be untrue. We are spiritual human experiencers and are not special. The Earth is not special. We possess a level of sentience and awareness to allow us to experience wider forms of life. We possess sensory capacities to support the human experience and spiritual expansion. We possess mental capacities to perceive beyond our physical personas and boundaries. We are supreme within our sphere of intent and purpose. The purpose the spirit chose was to experience human form. The capacities and sentience we possess exist to support that realm of intent. This does not make the human form or species special.

A grain of sand is sentient and supreme in its own realm of intent for being. The grain of sand and the energetic frequency of life within it is fully sentient, intelligent and aware within its purpose. The grain of sand was intended to be a grain of sand. The grain of sand possess capacities needed to fulfil its intent. It is supreme within its realm of being. The intent or purpose for being does not make a grain of sand less special than the human form. The grain of sand has limitation in its capacities by virtue of being a grain of sand. The purpose is different. The intent is unique. Every lifeform is sentient, aware and purposeful in its realm of intent. Every lifeform in the Universe exist through choice and intent. Each is the master of its own purpose. Everything is alive, has consciousness, a spirit and is within *All That Is*. All that exist does so in a unified and connected symbiosis. We are simply spirit. We are of the same source and are having different experiences. Humanity must remove the egoistic view of being special. We are not special or above all other life. We have a purpose, intent and a future which will be determined by our free will.

The Earth is beautiful, abundant in life and colour. The Earth has intent. The Earth has purpose and supports all lifeforms, animate or inanimate, that exists upon it. Current estimate suggest there may be thirty billion planets in the Milky Way galaxy. Any number of them may support life and be more awe inspiring than the Earth. We will never be fully aware of the infinite beauty and variety of life and planets in the Universe. There are planets with equally beautiful abundant life and environment. We must remove the illusion of being special as this is ego and causes separation. The perception of being special and more important limits the mind to true unity. Believing we are special causes a barrier to unity with the higher self and oneness with others. We are cosmic beings and will evolve to live in unity with non-terrestrial life. Cosmic unity will require the removal of being special. We must expand our perceptions to Universal awareness and come to understand we are experiencing a journey of becoming. To become is to start the journey of unification from the heart and the spirit. The movement should arise from within and not through forced integration and homogeneity. Human agendas have no relevance to the unity the spirit seeks. Continual expansion is what transcends and is driven by the heart and the infinite self.

Purpose or intent are the foundations to the choice to enter physical life. We all have a unique intent for being in human form. We all have a purpose. We seek purpose. Purpose or originating intent becomes lost and replaced by the human theatre. Throughout life we seek to discover the true intent for being. We seek to coalesce purpose with the free will to make life whatever we wish it to be. Purpose is the core reason for being but free will is the master of its discovery and fulfillment. The infinite spirit is divine truth. Our inner truth becomes suppressed as our physical perceptions dominate and become the only reality.

The impositions of our external illusionary reality diminishes when the inner journey starts. The reconnection with *All That Is* lifts the illusion. The human theatre becomes apparent. Some suggest the understanding of our true reality is a secret only the elite and privileged few are aware. There are no secrets. There is truth and infinite knowledge held within waiting to rise to the surface. Every experience has a purpose and is ultimately the evolution from limitation to knowledge. Truth and knowledge are expanded into. Once expanded we regain power over manifestation, intent and sovereignty. We create life and are drawn to activities that provide each of us meaning, support joy through the heart. The meaning to life will be different for each one of us. The path to discovery is the same. The journey to purpose is through the inner self. We can only understand propose when we become open and aware of our true nature and the reality of existence. We should integrate with our spirit and allow its infinite power to guide our actions, words and thoughts towards the meaning we all silently hope to uncover.

These words are not an absolute truth but a point of awareness shared to support those seeking to expand themselves and perceive beyond the duality. Perception of true reality is an eternal journey of expansion. Becoming is not a defined moment when all truth is revealed in the physical, dimensional, universal or cosmic realms. The awakening that surrounds us is of the mind and focuses on exposing the realities of the political, financial, military and social agenda driven human experience. The mental awakening locks the researcher in the human theatre. The awakening must shift to the inner spirit and removal of egoistic intellectualism and indoctrinated beliefs of the afterlife and *Source*.

In the physical experience we have space and time. Time is filled with a series of sequential conscious experiences, actions, words and thoughts. We dredge other experiences from the past and reflect their energy in the present. Time is a continual flow of movement created through free will in the field of physical consciousness. Personality develops as expansion continues. The personality is an energetic footprint within the infinite self. Everything that has ever been, is and all possibility is held within consciousness or the Quantum Field. All is one within *Source*. All terrestrial and non-terrestrial life is a capsule of experience in the ocean of infinite possibility. We choose our parents, location of birth, siblings, environment and major experiences or crossroads during the life journey. The rest of the life journey is free will and is governed by universal law. We create our individual experience through our actions, words, thoughts and intents that surround our core intent. We have an inner desire to be more than a conquest of physical challenges. We have a silent urge to release the internal spirit. We possess an inner drive to shift beyond the laws of human life. *Source* is concealed but present in every life form. *Source* frequency within gradually unfolds through stillness and rises toward its true nature. The physical experience is momentary, temporary and dissolves upon the end. The physical experience has whatever value the ego assigns to it. The material does not transcend. The personality develops in alignment with the growth and expansion of the internal spirit. The personality does transcend.

Our intent is the purpose we seek to uncover. Purpose and intent is what aligns with our spirit and the heart. Purpose is accepting the true nature within. Purpose is to share, love, to nature, to support selflessly others, to grow and expand into the infinite spirit. Purpose is not material. Purpose is to embark on the journey of becoming and traversing dimensional states. Purpose is to allow the internal journey to guide whilst freeing the sovereignty of free will to create the life we wish to experience. Expansion is derived from allowing the spirit to guide the life we seek to create and to present signs, synchronicities, symbols, events, people and places for its manifestation. Purpose and free will become coalesced in a beautiful tapestry of synchronicity when we allow the higher self and *Source* to assist.

Cause and effect influence the present and benefit the future. Fate is not real and can be a confused with purpose. We are not fated to suffer, be subject to an omnipotent will and accept our lot in life. Fate is mechanical in that it is a chain of events we create through the lack of inner connection, not living from within and giving away personal power over the manifestation of our environment. Fate is the loss of control over our life experiences. Through the loss of control we cast the outcomes out as fate. Predetermined purpose or destiny of a life does not mean we will implicitly achieve it. If the light of awareness is unable to rise to the surface our physical actions will produce outcomes we do not desire. We call this fate and destiny which is simply a loss of understanding of true self and control over the experience and manifestation.

Inner intent is what we continually seek and is open to us if we go inward. Purpose is whatever you want it to be in terms of the external physical material word. External purpose can be whatever you feel you are driven to do through the actions of free will and the heart. The choice before us is to be guided by the spirit or the physical self. Purpose is a constant as we seek greater meaning in private or openly. The material experience provides for the five senses yet there remains an upsurge for more meaning from within. This upsurge is ignored and suppressed as the daily routine of work, accumulation of wealth, layered ego, narcissism and societal expectation weigh upon the external self. These materialist values are temporary and the lack of fulfillment will reemerge once the material has been experienced. The result is a repeating inner disharmony and searching for greater meaning or purpose. We seek love and perfection externally which is a reflection of inner lack and misalignment. Harmony, peace and contentment are missing. The resolution of what ails life resides within. There is no need for spiritual masters, the latest fad from the new age industrial complex or religious doctrine. We, our inner self and a simple allowing for the spirit to enter is the doorway to purpose, intent, fulfillment and manifestation.

Perfection is not to seek living in spiritual enlightenment but developing harmony, bliss and joy through self-alignment. It is an eternal journey. We should remind ourselves that we are to create a human experience we would want to return to. The reality is we may choose to return to what we allowed to be created in a previous lifetime. Returning to spirit is going back to light or *Source*. Divine light is pure consciousness enveloped in love energy. Our fractal returns to its core. Our core is always home. There is no separation

> "The complete separation can take place
> only when the stage of inconscience has been
> reached and our world of manifold ignorance
> arises out of the tenebrous matrix."

> Sri Aurobindo

Reconnection

The world we experience is not as result of an omnipotent, omniscient, omnipresent entity imposing his will upon all it purveys. Being born into an illusionary ignorant condition is a state of being but remaining this way is an injustice to the self. To understand the world we must perceive it from a different vantage point. We should seek to detach from the illusionary connection to the real. The spiritual journey of rediscovery and knowledge moves awareness from the physical experience. We embark upon the internal journey for different reasons. We may derive energy for the spiritual movement from a personal motivation or after a period of struggle or loss. The movement may spring from a feeling of not belonging, a searching for answers or unexplainable experiences sparking enquiry. There are innumerable stimuli that move us into the personal journey.

A spiritual journey requires we climb to the top of the metaphorical tree to perceive the expanse that surrounds it and to see beyond. We start to remove the mask and develop true sight. A path emerges leading to an understanding of the world and our place in it. Our natural state leads us to vibrate from the heart and show kindness to each other. This will always remain the inner state of being. The division and loss of our true state is manifested through the constant manipulation and duality of the human theatre. We are told who is bad, that we are good, to hate that group or person and promote personal and national exceptionalism. The most progressive groups and their perceived intellectual superiority remain blind to the manifest world of programmed behaviour and reaction. We are distracted from our true purpose and origin. We have through ego and mind intellectualised the spirit and *Source* out of existence.

Collective humanity has become numb to the duality of the human experience. We in our billions own the past, the present and our future. Our ultimate destination is a collective responsibility and an individual contribution. Over millennia we have become separated from our true inner spirit. We have created our duality through religion, materialism, selfishness, society and egoistic intellectualism. We have focused on fulfillment and the importance of the individual losing inner truth and each other. To divert away from the preoccupations we should arrive at an understanding of our place in the Universe. We should traverse the path of cosmic unity from within to without. Our initial challenge will be to confront the external world and the preoccupation with its distractions. The external distractions inhibit the path to expanded consciousness. Humanity has lost its true sight and enveloped itself in the ego. It is an irony that novels, music and art depict the value of love, unity, peace and harmony yet we allow a frequency that does not support these desperately sought after needs. We allow vast resources to be directed to develop more efficient ways to engage in war and methods of killing each another in greater numbers.

Life, animate or inanimate, never ceases to be connected to *Source*. When the mind is allowed to be open we will start to observe our true reality. Our external reality will slowly dissolve and inner perception starts to unfold. Inner reconnection requires us to remove ourselves energetically from the physical theatre whilst remaining grounded to it. Personal expansion will naturally release us from the cyclical myopia and align our human experience to its true intention. Life in the universal theatre is governed by free will to manifest its own experience. The totality of all our experiences are absorbed into *Source* be they positive or negative. *Source* energy is love. The challenge for us all is to allow love and unity to again become our dominant vibration. Love is to the self, to be of service and open to receive from others. Imbalance results in emptiness.

My own reconnection to self and *Source* was through stillness, meditation, forgiveness, gratitude and prayer. Meditation is whatever we wish it to be. There is no perfection in meditative practice. Meditation does not require we sit in contorted positions or follow a guided practice. Meditation is to be still and to allow the energy of balance and calmness to envelop. Meditation allows our inner infinite self to rise and converse with *Source* consciousness. We become open to their guidance and grace.

The spiritual journey must include gratitude for what has been, is and has yet to pass. We should unleash our natural drive to give selflessly the service to others without judgement. Time is often as a reason for not engaging in the personal journey. If spiritual exploration is fueled by an inner need the excuse of time becomes mute. The inner journey does not need a guru, a holy person, priest or mystical avatar. Everything that is needed resides within. If we feel the journey needs to start with a guru or a teacher this should extend only to a point where continued expansion can be directed by the inner self. We must always follow what resonates within. The personal practice will shift from the mind and body into mindfulness and beyond into the unseen. Through meditation we will be led to an expanding consciousness and reconnection with the higher self. The final destination is a rediscovery of *Source*. During the expansion of spiritual rebirth *The Book* of universal truth opens.

The Book is not physical but a metaphor for infinite inner truth and knowledge. Truth ceases to be limited to study within the physical realm. We start to receive intuitive energetic knowledge from the Universe. The channel to knowledge becomes the inner spirit as it is the true conduit to infinite wisdom. The inward journey will challenge the ego and expose the myth of self-awarded intellectualism. We will be exposed and feel vulnerable. Our inner and external states align and allow for forgiveness, reflection and healing. We carve our way back to the heart space. The spiritual journey is not a fanciful adventure and is not to be taken lightly. To embark upon it is to remove the ego that supports the illusionary nature of the external self. To understand the ego is to reflect on the pedestal given to it. The pedestal may be intellectual superiority, physical prowess and job or material status. The badges we award ourselves will fall away and the infinite self will emerge vulnerable and exposed. The path towards reality begins.

Sri Aurobindo in *The Life Divine* categorises the stages of enlightenment as expansions of the mind. Sri Aurobindo describes the initial movement is from the foundational human preoccupations to the Higher Mind. From the *Higher Mind* we progress into the world of the unseen into the *Illumined Mind*. From *Illumined Mind* we develop perception and intuition which leads to us the *Overmind*. At each stage we develop the power of our inner consciousness. Knowledge is released through the reduction of the influence of the layers of external illusion. Sri Aurobindo describes a journey through the later of consciousness as the *Subconscient* and the *Inconscient*. As we traverse layers of consciousness the ego self is replaced by an upsurge of more intense light. Light is interpreted as a spiritual force and connection. The ultimate goal is the *Supermind* where we achieve a state of universal connection and manifestation. Sri Aurobindo suggests the mind is the path of spiritual awakening. Alternatively, we can view the mind as the partner of the spirit. The mind assists in the processing of understanding and information but is not the foundation of consciousness. The infinite spirit and heart are the seat of expansion and of *Source* frequency. The process of knowing is the path to understanding the reality of the world, the Universe and of *Source*. *All That Is*, is universal truth. The external human theatre is a powerful illusion.

The matrix is the illusion we have allowed to root into the human experience. The matrix is a recurring cycle of stagnated development. True sovereign free will is real when our actions, words and thoughts are directed through the spirit. Free will exists when the theatrical illusion is replaced by truth and sight is extended beyond the physical eye. Freedom is power when it is not given away freely and we stand as creators of your own experience. This is true free will, sovereignty and liberty. Free will is limited when it is bound by ideology, dogma, doctrines, fear, separation and the many isms awash in society. We cannot claim free will under these limitations and states of unawareness. To regain true free will we must expand inwardly the outwardly. Knowledge through science, religion, prophets, gurus, literature bring their own revelations and change over time. The cosmic library of infinite knowledge and reality resides within everything and everyone. The exposure of true reality and knowledge is implicit along the spiritual journey. It is unavoidable. Spiritual expansion is not implicit in a mental awakening. Universal knowledge is energy in vibration. When our inner journey is in the frequency of universal knowledge it flows naturally.

Those who seek life purpose will become aware of their own reason for being. The flow of *Source* frequency is gentle and of joy. There is the concept of being born ignorant of our true nature. This is a partial truth. We enter each life with fully open awareness and perception. Upon entering life we are immediately under the influence of external imposition. The layer of forgetting we experience is expected. We design our lives knowing the nature of ignorance when we enter the human experience. The reality is our individual human experience will need to retain sovereignty if it is not to entrain with the collective energetic frequency and vibration. Our collective wavelength vibration is not in alignment with a higher frequency. We create our reality and are responsible for the human experience. We should start to accept we collectively manifest and allow our leaders, the state of the planet, unceasing wars, injustice, fear and division. The frequency of the majority is inline or has been entrained to this vibration. The Earth does not deserve what we impose upon it and is not entrained to the human vibration. The Earth has consciousness, energy and frequency. It responds with cause and effect to the frequency or actions imposed upon it. The Earth may choose to allow life to exist or not. The idea external forces, false gods, prophets or off world advanced lifeforms will save us from ourselves are all fantasy. We own our fate and expansion. Once we create a dominant vibration of unity consciousness the overwhelming frequency will follow. An alternate heart based reality does not require all of humanity to become reconnected with the self. An energetic shift requires sufficient numbers to support change. When we shift into expanded states on consciousness whilst in body what we physically support and drive our actions, words and thoughts will create a different outcome. Real power is in physical action driven by a knowing of the true origin of the self and *Source*. Fear has no place when we realise there is no end to existence. Physical action backed by inner power is immeasurable. The frequency of the infinite Universe and *Source* is divine love. Divine love is manifold more powerful than fear, hate and lower vibrations.

As we delve deeper into the self and truth we discover the spirt is infinite and eternal. Our infinite spirit experiences many incarnations all with a defined core intent. It is inconceivable to state that there is nothing before and after the human experience. Those who espouse this idea have done so through the ego and the mind. The Atheist rejects the existence of a *Source* of *All That Is*. The Nihilist believes life is meaningless and rejects incarnation. The inward journey away from the ego and the mind will open up the hidden truths. The internal journey will present all that we have accumulated as unresolved desires and fears. Resolution and healing is a phase in the journey which cannot be circumvented. The true spiritual journey is embarked upon only by a few. Some experiment through visits to spiritual countries, ashrams, erratic periods of meditation then fall back into material lives. We should cease experimenting with spirituality and embark on the path with persistence.

We are preoccupied with the promotion of the mind as the driver of reality. Transhumanism offers a superhuman future. Transhumanism suggests we are limited by the capacities of our minds and the frailties of the body. We are encouraged to become better than our mind and body through technology. The future will offer expansion through the connection to an intelligent cloud and the implanting of technology into the human body to become better, faster and smarter. These are all illusions and only reside in the physical realm. These enhancements pursued by the mind will separate humanity further from itself and its true nature. Mental thought will be controlled cementing us from the spirit. We should develop technology to assist in easing physical life and support freedom of expansion. We should focus on nurturing and healing the planet and evolve toward the infinite spirit. We should seek to travel into the Universe taking love with us not war. We must not become nor implant technology. Wealth is perceived to be a protection to the reality of the collective experience but is simply a delay. You may choose to return.

We should arrive at a conscious unity through love. Repeated physical sojourns will eventually lead each of us to the journey inward. The question we should contemplate is how many incarnations do we wish to have. The true reality of existence and the Universe is far more fantastic than any fiction could create. The five senses are used to perceive the physical playground but not what exists beyond their wavelength. Our innate intuition and sensory capacities are accessed through internal alignment and meditation. Truth becomes non-negotiable as real sight is developed. Sensory perception becomes free from its limitation as awareness expands. We do not experience a sudden explosion of clairvoyant, clairaudient, clairsentient, psychic or mediumship ability. Intuition, feeling and inner sensory perception is the intent and a gradual manifestation.

We are experiencing being human. Humanity is a species among the innumerable diverse lifeforms in the Universe. The human experience consist of numerous different identity groups, cultures, subcultures, communities and nations. This abundant construct of life and society is not unique to humanity. We are the same and from the same origin as other species of life in the Universe. The constant within all life, animate or inanimate, across the vastness of the cosmos is the infinite spirit and *Source*. We are not different. We are the same. We are one. Reconnect with the inner spirit through a method or practice that resonates and allow the self to be guided. The modalities we adopt will change as expansion continues. We are the master our infinite liberation. Be open to recognise the definition of true free will. We do not exist to be the judge of what others choose but to direct our own actions to spirit. Judging and focusing on attacking those who choose negative paths does not change their trajectory. Change is a personal responsibility. Embark upon spiritual expansion with persistence and practice. Persistence is faith. Occasional dips and in and out will have limited benefit. Persistence and commitment is needed to traverse the phase of healing and forgiveness. Once traversed life without the dialogue with the internal infinite spirit and *Source* becomes unthinkable. Reaching this state requires persistence.

The Digital Human

Technology touches every aspect of human life and is destined to root itself deeper into the human experience. Technological development is a natural occurrence in a progression of evolution and life. How we develop and use technology is where we must focus. We have developed exponentially in technology. Technology enhances our daily lives and has allowed us to go beyond the boundaries of the Earth, protect against disease, innovate and remedy poverty and other imbalances. In contrast we have also developed technology to destroy life in greater numbers, seek to manipulate our environment, further disconnect from the spirit through the creation of the digital human, control of perception, society and promote agendas. Technology can be used to deliver sovereignty or limit freedoms and further submerge our consciousness under layers of technocratic abstraction. Technological advances have far exceeded our collective spiritual state. We are not spiritually at a place where we will utilise technological advances for the greater good. As this scenario unfolds we are at risk of imprisonment by our own creation. The prison is not physical but the confinement of our inner consciousness and infinite spirit. The existence of our infinite spirit is the only true reality. We have focused on technological expansion and left the development of our consciousness severely lagging behind. Without an expanded consciousness we are at risk of thickening the wall between the surface self and the true being within. Our drive to immerse into technology and the fantasy of the virtual realms will create additional detachment from the inner spirit and *All That Is*.

Technology will touch every part of our human experience. Technology is being integrated into the human body. The defense and military are said to be decades ahead of anything experienced in the public arena. This is logical even without investigation. Technology in the public sector will never be more advanced than what is in use within the defence industry. The technology advances we observe with amazement are for the most part released into the public domain from highly funded military research and development. Once released they are open to further development through the imagination and innovation of public industry. The United States Defense Advanced Research Projects Agency (DARPA) has vast military budgets to innovate. These resources support innovative projects and the fund research project with elite universities utilising their developing minds. In the 1940s to the early 1960s the United States War Department developed computers to aid in the battle field and used notable Universities to conduct research and development. The defence industry is likely the source of much of the technology now common place. The United States Department of Defence utilises academic talent and funds the research and development of battle field technology. We should be open to the idea that technological innovation from corporations such as Apple, Microsoft or SpaceX have not been the privy of the military prior to being released as consumer technology.

"On the battlefield of the future, enemy
forces will be located, tracked, and targeted
almost instantaneously through the use of
data links, computer assisted intelligence
evaluation, and automated fire control…"

General William Westmoreland

DARPA provided funding to Douglas Engelbart from Stanford Research who invented the first mouse. Tony Hey and Gyuri Pápay in *The Computing Universe: A Journey Through a Revolution* described the first mouse as "…a hollowed out block of wood with two small wheels that allowed the user to control the movements of a cursor on the computer screen." Robert Kahn and Vint Cerf from DARPA created ARPANET. ARPANET invented "Transmission Control Protocol and Internet Protocol Suite" or TCP/IP. TCP/IP is the basic network protocol which allows geographically separated computers to communicate. TCP/IP is still the basic network protocol that underpins the internet. ARPA demonstrated the capability in 1969 which led to the Internet. Some may reject the idea the military is the origin of major technological innovation. It is illogical that technological innovation by corporations, science or space exploration exceeds that which defence research had funded or developed. The answer is obvious to anyone who wishes to set aside the ego. Deep military development projects and DARPA will no doubt have technology many decades in advance of what is available to the public.

The commercial and consumer digital revolution has brought us hyper scaling cloud platforms, Big Data analytics, the Internet of Everything (IoE), Machine and Deep Learning, Artificial Intelligence (AI), Quantum Computing (Big Compute) and Artificial Neural Networks

(ANN). Technology advances at ever increasing rates with the content within this text being superseded as it is being read. We are moving with increasing speed toward technological dominance over our human experience.

The 1990s brought us the internet, Iris scanning, Voice over IP (VoIP), media streaming, HDTV, ecommerce, wireless communication and virtualisation. The 2000s delivered further developments forming earlier versions of what is now the Cloud. The Apple iPod and iPhone were released in 2007 followed by Kindle, 3DTV and early generation robotics. From 2010 saw the release of the Apple iPad, supercomputers, hyper scaling cloud platforms, virtual reality, voice assistant technology such as Apple HomePod and Amazon Alexa. We have shifted into the digitisation of services and online interaction, implantable technology, Internet of Everything, Automation, Machine and Deep Learning, self-driving cars, augmented reality, Artificial Intelligence and Quantum computing. The division between commercial and consumer technology is abstracted as our world experience becomes digitised. In 2015 Sophia a social humanoid robot was activated. Sophia was able to mimic sixty-two facial expressions and respond to prompted questions with scripted responses. Sophia needed a handler but the demonstration was a peek into a future where human interaction will be directed toward artificial life rather than biological.

Technological innovation is interconnected. Technology is not developed in isolation and has connections to what came prior and what will follow. We will in increasing numbers start to implant technology into the human body in the guise of becoming better humans. These are enhancements when viewed from the material and technocratic perspective. Integrating technology into the human body will create a further abstraction and layer above the spirit. Humanity will move toward promoting vastly more human augmentation with Artificial Intelligence and virtual reality. The infatuation with technology, focus toward devices, online social and virtual world will silently program the consumer and create additional abstractions of illusion.

The additional abstraction and layers of disconnection will silence the inner voice. The inner voice will not be heard above the digital interface and the mind. A choice confronts humanity. Microchipping the human body has begun. Infant to adult microchipping will be promoted. We will be encouraged to have microchips implanted. The reasoning will be many from easier integration into the unfolding digital world, a health and safety monitor or to integrate with Artificial Intelligence as a means of becoming a more efficient human. Rather than becoming better we will be less human and further disconnected. The infinite spirit will find itself behind three layers of detachment. The first layer is the identification with the physical, the second the mind and the third being technology. The senses will cease to operate independently with thought interrupted by Artificial Intelligent constructs interpreting our reality.

5G millimeter wavelengths will move to 6G and beyond. 5G is intended to support global high speed data integration. 5G is not a development so that we can download and stream at faster speeds although this is an obvious derivative. 5G is intended to support a rapid integration of the human body to technology and the sharing of data globally. There will be no place on Earth where wireless communication will not be available. Satellite technology will beam an invisible web over every corner of the planet. The Internet of Everything (IoE) will become the reality. All that exist and becomes manifest is never isolated, random or unintended. Everything has intent, purpose and a reason for being. There are no accidents, random events or coincidences in the Universe.

Beyond consumer technology there exists the corporate domain. Corporations and other entities collect vast amounts of data from users. The consumer is tracked with every interaction and moment of our digital lives captured, transmitted, stored and analysed. Data is information. Information is knowledge. Knowledge is power. Data is captured through devices and our interactions with the digital world. To transmit vast volumes of data requires high speed networks. The leap to 5G delivers this network backbone. The harvested data requires storage giving rise to Big Data platforms and storage technology. We are all connected by technology and sadly not by the spirit. Internet of Everything (IoE) will connect us all to the digital world. For data to be of use it requires analysis. Big Data Analytics is the analysis of data. To analyse vast amounts of information requires powerful processing. Quantum computing delivers the processing power. Machine, Deep Learning and Artificial Intelligence use the data to predict and provide intelligence.

Machine Learning is the first attempt at creating true Artificial Intelligence. Machine Learning uses heuristics and algorithms. A heuristic is a simple set of rules used to solve problems or categorise data. An Algorithm uses complex programming rule sets. Artificial Intelligence uses algorithms. As Artificial Intelligence develops it will start to self-learn using baseline programmed rules. Artificial Intelligence will start to create its own neural code. Artificial Intelligence and Deep Learning use layers of algorithms forming Artificial Neural Networks (ANNs) that mimic the human brain. Neural Network Processing shifts Artificial

Intelligence into the arena of real independent learning beyond layered algorithms. An Artificial Neural Network is able to analyse large amounts of data, learn and become better as it evolves. The processing power needed to support Artificial Intelligence Deep Learning is delivered through Quantum computing. Artificial Neural Networks, Artificial Intelligence and the innovation we are yet to experience is not life. To have life is to possess an infinite spirit. Technology is not borne of *Source*. Technological sentience is not of the infinite spirit. Human creations are development in the physical realm and will always remain in this sphere of experience. The technical creations of humanity or any lifeform do not and will not transcend into the unseen of the divine. Technology may in scientific terms develop sentience but it is technological not of spirit. We should not confuse ourselves. The concept of a soul within technological life will be promoted but is a creation of our human ego and detachment from true reality.

Quantum Computing mimics the principles of Quantum mechanics. Quantum Computing offers exponential processing power at a subatomic level. Quantum Computing uses three principles of Quantum mechanics. The three principles are waves, entanglement and interference. Quantum wave particle duality states all particles or actions can be described as waves. Traditional computational theory states a binary value or bit can only be a 0 or a 1. Wave particle duality suggests a bit can simultaneously take a superposition of 0 or 1 increasing exponentially the ability to process any number of possibilities. Quantum entanglement principle states all particles in the Universe are connected. Everything in the seen and unseen is connected. There is no separation. Quantum waves and entanglement are combined with the principle of interference. Quantum interference states all possibilities are assessed and cancelled allowing others to emerge. A Quantum computer is capable of calculating incredible amounts of possibilities simultaneously. Quantum computing uses Qubit chip technology which is similar to the computer processor. The industry term for Quantum computing is Big Compute.

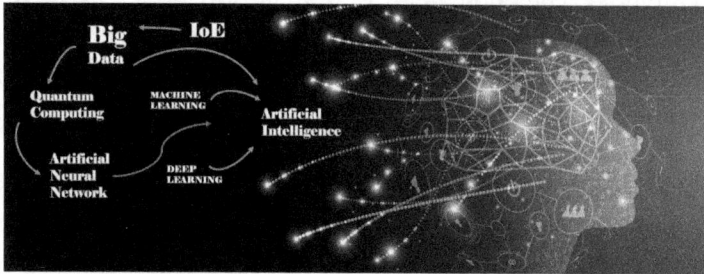

Figure 12: Do Not Become I.T

The augmentation of the human experience and the development of Artificial Intelligence are connected. Our lives are intentionally being maneuvered to be completely digital. Every interaction from the moment a life takes its first breadth to its last will be recorded and retained indefinitely. How we execute commerce and interact will be fully digitised. Blockchain and Hashgraph technology and what follows will record every interaction. Global digital technology and its varied implementations will coalesce. Humanity will experience technological homogenisation. As Quantum principles evolve ever greater processing and storage capabilities will be developed. Quantum processing and the storage of data is in reality information in the form of energy. We may see Qubits morph into gooey intelligent fluid akin to dark matter. The true nature of the Quantum Universe is formless energy which we may reproduce over the coming decades of technological evolution.

Technological innovation is progress for humanity. It should be embraced and applauded but used intelligently. Technology is there for positive purposes if we wish it to be. It can enhance our human experience, provide a better life for all, remove imbalances, poverty, improve mobility, breakdown social structures and take us into the Universe. The choice before humanity is do we use it for these purposes or for negative ends. As we further augment our human experience with virtual realities biological relationships will be replaced by virtual communities and self-aware artificial intelligent lifeforms. The world will be bathed in wireless communication beyond 5G. Satellites will connect everything with a wireless electromagnetic grid of traversing data. Microchipping will manifest into Nano technology to connect the human mind and sensory perception to Artificial Intelligence.

We will have a choice to use technology or become it. Becoming or implanting technology will merge global society into a technocratic layer of control. Humanity has a tendency to believe it is supreme or *Source* itself. We will attempt to control and dominate everything including ourselves and the observable Universe. Humanity possesses limitless creativity which demands the balance of mindfulness. These realities and challenges will be presented to us. How we allow technology to impacts our lives is still a choice. We should be mindful of the technocratic age that is rapidly and stealthily manifesting. We must use innovation wisely. We must not become it nor allow it to fully detach the self from the infinite spirit and *Source.*

Science fiction is a window to what is to be. Consumer technology has directed attention downward into individual bubbles and virtual augmented realities. Technology is not negative and is a natural evolution of life. The question is how far humanity should go in its integration with technology as it progresses toward bioneural artificial intelligence with vastly superior abilities. We should never augment with technology but use innovation to better the human experience and support venturing into the enormity of the Universe. Technology should not be implanted with the delusion of creating an enhanced human. Paradoxically it will create the opposite. Humanity will become less human and more technology.

Humanity will attempt to replicate consciousness through bio-neural networking. The pursuit will ultimately fail. Consciousness is a fractal of *Source* and cannot be replicated by intellect, technology or any level of bio-neural intelligence. Our infinite being is the 'I'. The 'I' is formless energy of love not logic. We cannot replicate love and its derivative consciousness through the mind or any creation of matter. It is an illusion believing we can be the *Source* from which all emanates and recreate through technology *All That Is* whilst being within in. The Universe is infinite and boundless possibility existing in *All That Is*. The idea a single lifeform can recreate the *Source* of consciousness through technology is simply counterintuitive and absurd. You cannot create what you are part of as that would mean creating the sum of the whole whilst being in the whole. The mere notion is a nonsense but humanity and our ego will believe it is possible.

We have before us the free will choice to augment with technology and transhumanism or fulfil our true intent for incarnation. Some may argue the true intent of incarnation is to dominate and control life and have more of it. Alternatively, we can chose to expand beyond the physical.

All That We Are

Many years ago above a bar there was a plaque with quote. It read "I never drink alone. The lord is always with me". It may have had its origin in faith nonetheless the message has eternal validity. We are never alone. Loneliness is a manifestation of separation, disconnection, ignorance or blindness from the inner self. The disharmony within translates itself externally and prevent meaningful content to life and superficial relationships. There is no prescriptive way of being or understanding as truth is felt and emerges from within. We will all interpret what we receive differently. The destination is the same. The internal journey flows at a pace that resonates with the external and then inner self. Our lives are of our creation. Our true state has no boundary, body or limitation. We are infinite possibility, everywhere and in all things. The human body is merely an experience. We may live many lifetimes simultaneously as we exist within all possibility. We should maintain wonder and openness and cease reflex action dismissal as it will create limitation. The limitation we experience exist in the confines of the human body with its limited senses, mind and sense of place in the Universe. This is an expected state and is an experience chosen by the infinite spirit. We enter a sojourn into humanity with a third dimensional state of perception. Our ultimate goal is to expand whilst in the experience. The door to expansion merely has to be opened. We should put aside preconceived notions and beliefs. We need only ask the unseen light and *Source* for assistance. Once we ask it will be presented. Others will enter our experience to assist in its discovery. Amazing synchronicities, people, places and events occur which we slowly start to recognise and allow with grace and gratitude. We are infinite, unceasing and all-knowing energy. We travel dimensions, forms and realities in our eternal adventure. We emerge into form as we experience numerous incarnations offering different opportunities for expansion. How we expand within each experience will determine if we fulfil our reason or being.

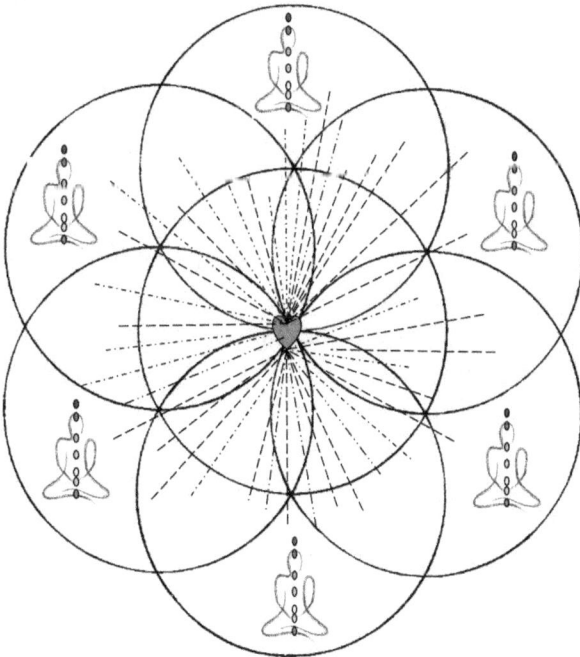

Figure 13: All That We Are

The Multiverse presents infinite timelines of possibility. The journey is of becoming, to be open, free, sovereign and fully aware. We are to emerge within the physical as expressed infinite consciousness manifesting our experiences effortlessly through the true power of the 'I'. It is infinite consciousness that is the substance of existence and the ultimate journey of expansion. Physical worlds of matter are the theatre where the spirit plays, grows and experiences. We can accept repeated incarnations of dogmatic mental and intellectual tendency or we can expand away from them. *Source* is the sum of *All That Is*. *Source* is the expanding Universe, Multiverse, collective actions, words, thoughts, vibration, frequencies and intents. *Source* is all that is seen and unseen. *Source* is infinite love as an energetic force of creation and existence. *Source* is not human, physical love, fragile or temporal. *Source* vibration is beyond the comprehension of mind or physical senses. *Source* and our infinite spirit is immense, deep and immeasurable. It is an overwhelmingly powerful feeling of joy which wells upward. The upsurge of divine grace if allowed can offer moments of detachment from the physical body to feel the bliss of what lay beyond. The upsurge of reconnection balances the human material and physical desires with the expansion of consciousness. We begin to release ourselves from upādāna which is a Buddhist and Vedic word for attachment.

Attachment is the inability to practice or embrace detachment and is viewed as the main obstacle towards a serene and fulfilled life. The spiritual journey is not an easy one. If we are to seek guidance from teachers or spiritual earthly guides we should do so whilst remaining truly sovereign. Guidance should be received, discerned and investigated from within. There is no single point of truth as there are many interpretations. We should move along the path and follow the resonance of inner vibration. What is presented or made known is in direct relation to the vibration we emit. As our frequency expands greater awareness and knowledge becomes apparent. Continual expansion opens us to signs, synchronicities, numbers, symbols, people, events and places. We assist others as they guide us. Develop the practice to question and grow at every step.

If there is need to start the journey with external guidance do so until the journey can be continued through the self. Learn from Gurus and other teachers but do not worship nor give devotion. Never give power away to a following, person or group. Take away what is needed and move on. Expansion is the ability to accept our state of awareness will change as the ego becomes less dominant. We should never assume that the vastness of ultimate truth can be attained. It is impossible to absorb all possibility whilst in a physical body.

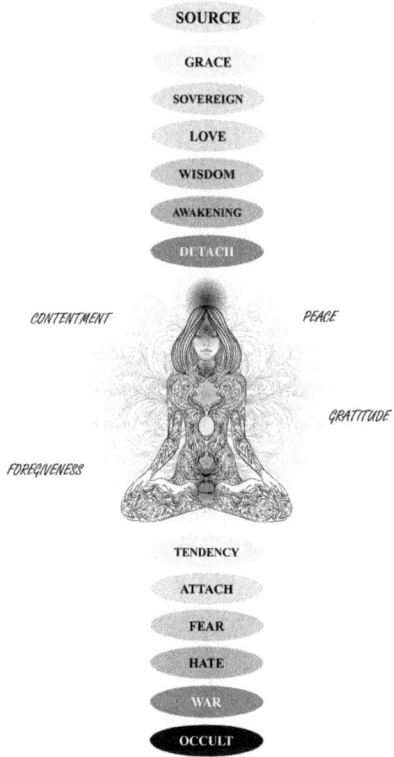

SOURCE

GRACE

SOVEREIGN

LOVE

WISDOM

AWAKENING

DETACH

CONTENTMENT   PEACE

GRATITUDE

FORGIVENESS

TENDENCY

ATTACH

FEAR

HATE

WAR

OCCULT

Figure 14: The Dichotomy of Free Will

To be truly spiritual is not a new age badge or to be confused by modern management concepts. To be spiritual is to release the infinite spirit, true being and an awareness of *Source*. We own our perceptions. The Universe will present whatever imagery we feels is real. The inner journey itself will change our perceptions as inner knowing emerges. We detach from identifying as solely human. We are not human as it is a chosen experience. Make the free will decision to ask the Universe to take you on the journey. Evaluate internally what resonates as truth or misdirection and ask for guidance at every moment. Practice stillness and being present to quieten the mind and impositions of the external environment. Meditate and give gratitude. Pray if it resonates.

The ultimate foundation to expansion is to recognise that the divine grace of *Source* exists. There are unending practices, concepts and tools available in faith and within the new age industrial complex. Universal energy is the foundation of *All That Is*. The concept of energy is used by every awakening movement and new age practice. Energy emits and is not in existence by chance or a fabrication of some unknown event. Dark matter is not the origin of energy and frequency. Dark and light matter are outcomes of it. The numerous offerings available in the spiritual marketplace provide modalities to understand and use energy for the attainment of material goals and healing. These are valid practices. The truth that the spiritual marketplace avoids stating with clarity is an understanding or existence of *Source*. There is a reluctance to state openly the presence of a divine grace in fear of being branded a religious proselytisers. There is no such reluctance in this writing. *Source* exists. *Source* is within, without and a state. There is no question. If the journey is progressed to its ultimate end state *Source* is the outcome. The divine grace of *Source* we discover is not the religious, indoctrinated and punishing God. The *Source* is simply love, state, presence and being that emanates from expanding feeling. The feeling expands from the inner spirit as it rises and envelops the energetic body with bliss. Prayer and dialogue with the unseen guides and *Source* becomes the primary conversation.

Prayer for even the spiritually inclined can be an uncomfortable practice. Prayer has the prerequisite of acceptance of *Source* or an origin of *All That Is*. Some suggest why pray when *Source* is within everything and we are a fractal of it. The argument is often that praying would be akin to praying to ourselves. An interesting point and if held strongly by the person then this is their choice. Prayer is a moment of silence gratitude and dedicated energy of dialogue with *Source* and our true eternal family. There is an unseen force that touches and elevates our state from within. Prayer is a method combined with others that strengthens our reconnection.

> "God is in all men, but all men are not in
> God; that is why we suffer"
>
> Ramakrishna Paramahamsa Ramkrisno Poromohongsoe

We should remove focus from the mental ego and its illusionary distractions. By doing so we cease being flooded by the theatre and remove focus from it. Our energy shifts to observe and interact with what has meaning and not the causes of separation and division. We should avoid pseudo spirituality and locking into the mental awakening that pervades humanity. Move to truly accept we are an infinite spirit and that the body is simply a vessel chosen to support the experience. We are everywhere, all of the time, in all things and a powerful creator of our experience. Approach every challenge with grace and faith. Walk through it and learn not look to another for blame or accountability. Flow through life and create the experience sought through the heart with an understanding this is all temporary. We are here to assist each other and to fulfil the intent for life and its material experiences.

Grow to give time freely to others and not in judgement. Judgement is to be directed at the image in the mirror. Leave what does not resonate and operate through the heart and the inner spirit with openness, integrity, honesty, love and selflessness. These are frequencies that transcend and lead to greater expanded states. Become aware of and remove tendencies. Tendencies are repeating paradigms that impede expansion and lead to cyclical incarnation. Tendency can be a desire to keep experiencing the physical world or a need to return. We should remind ourselves what we allow or change for the many we may return to in another sojourn. To return to physical experience not for growth but to assist is the ultimate sovereignty.

It is within our power of self to determine all aspects of life and death. A fantastic notion but a reality. When we are not in spirit incarnation is seen as an opportunity, adventure and challenge. Fear, hate and limitation of physical life is not present when incarnations are designed. We should raise our personal energetic frequency and diminish the effects of duality. Duality exists and persists from the moment the ego was given energy. It paradoxically exists to force humanity to see itself.

We traverse energetic dimensional states through inner work, reflection, learning and expansion. Dimensions are not physical planes or places. Dimensional planes and realms are conceptualised in a variety of ways by theosophy and esoteric practitioners. There is no a definitive delineation between the energetic planes or dimensions. We traverse these through consciousness and developed inner sight. We observe the unseen beyond our physical spectrum of observable light. We see and expand into expanded dimensional states as our consciousness and inner spirit rises. To achieve expansion we should practice silence and allowing the unseen force of grace to open the corridors of *All That Is*. Allow life to become illuminated by the cascading force of *Source* energy. Reflect on the reality of the 'I'. Observe the billions with whom we share the planet not as humans but in wonder. They are embodied infinite consciousness on their own path. We are all at different states of expansion. As we expand we direct our external actions through inner power and perception. We move to experience the human through the real infinite 'I'. We become the owner of the self and the governance of true sovereignty. We are intended to emit absolute sovereignty and to be the creator of our experience. Fear, hate, violence, war and agendas will persist beyond each incarnation. Each incarnation offers the opportunity to expand beyond these low vibrational frequencies.

Be prepared to be humbled, face the ego and self-imposed cause and effect. Be prepared to question entrained impressions of intellectualism and knowing. The path will reveal the brutal realities of human duality and our contribution to it. If the true spiritual journey were easy we would all embark upon it. It is a difficult adventure as it exposes the external self to itself. Self-delusion, false intelligence, dogma and pride are brought to the surface for transformation. A gnostic description of transformation is described as "...a path resulting in a fully self-aware, universally and source open expanded way of living, developing knowledge and action to manifest a collective experience of dominant love over lower vibrational forces…"

The Universe is an experiment. Humanity is an experiment. Humanity is a single race or species with cultural identities and physical diversity. We have the challenge to return the majority of the experience back to grace. To return to grace is to become one with it and emit the frequency. In turn we contribute to creating through action a human experience of spirit and love. The universal canvas is open to everyone. We have the free will to experience life as it should be and not continue to allow the vibration of fear, war, control, human trafficking, rituals, secret societies, separation and indoctrination.

The wonderful journey starts and ends with the self. We secretly desire love and peace. These frequencies can only be implanted by humanity itself. We all have a role to transform the collective human experience. Universal infinite law is all pervasive and cannot be avoided. Our internal being is truth, knowledge and ultimately wisdom. Expand the spirit outwardly into unity, joy, community to community, country to nations, planet to galaxy and galaxy to Universe. Exhibit empathy and love for human consciousness. The movement of expansion is perpetual in the Universe. There is no death only a return to energy. Be curious and be open to all possibility. Incarnation is a choice and designed.

Sanskrit describes the ultimate goal as Moksha. Moksha is the liberation from rebirth. The ultimate objective be that from the West or the East is to move incarnation away from need, desire, control and dominance to Moksha. Sanskrit philosophy described the movement from Kama which is pleasure and emotions, to Artha of material prosperity and

Dharma representing a moral life toward self-realisation. We are never alone. Feel the joy in knowing we are part of *All That Is*. We are a fractal of cosmic existence and beyond. We are infinite being, love, freedom, adventure, sovereign, true, joy, all possibility, everywhere and in all things, loved, guided, eternal, emanating, exuding, feeling, knowing and being. We are of *Source*. *Source* is the Unity. *Source* is the sum of all that exists. This is *All That We Are*.

The Book

The Book is a metaphor for inner knowing, source of answers and awareness that resides within all life. The metaphor was used by a friend in an Akashic reading which I truly understood years later. The opening of *the book* is the source of detail in this presentation. *The book* is within and contains all the answers and infinite knowing humanity has sought through the mind. Once the spirit is liberated from the depths or surface consciousness and permitted to expand, knowing will flow effortlessly into consciousness. We are the Universe, a fractal of *Source, All That Is* and will ever be.

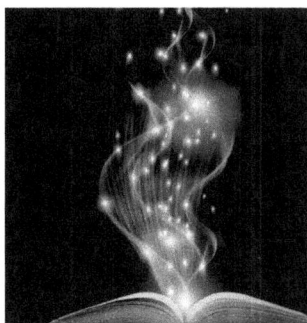

What is an Akashic reading?

The Akashic field is also known as the Akasha or Quantum Field. It resides within the Universe and holds all possibility realised or unrealised.

> "An Akashic Reading is a reading of your entire life energy (Your Book of Life) in

the present past and potential future. Every
human being has a "Book of Life" which
contains the energetic imprint of your soul
journey. In an Akashic Reading you will
receive the details of your life stories which
allow you to connect to and understand
the wider picture of all that you have
experienced. Such a developed understanding
allows you to move from any ideas of
victimhood and expand your awareness
which in turn expands your consciousness.
Any life force energy that is stuck in the past
or present can be transmuted and transformed
consciously during an Akashic Registers
Reading.

To Access the Akashic Field one must simply
learn to be in their Heart Energy as the
information in this field is NEVER accessible
to your mind. The reading of your entire
soul imprints across all time and space can
actually be learned and accessed by yourself
as well as by any person that has developed
the ability to access this cosmic field of
consciousness where the details of all life
exist. Personally I encourage people to learn
to access their own Akashic Registers as it
is the self-empowerment of each individual
that impacts our world and planetary
consciousness. Learning to access your
Akashic Registers can be a simple process
if you are ready to live in truth. An Akashic
Reading is often the first journey for a person

who desires to reconnect to source energy
in a conscious and loving way. It is also a
beautiful experience for any soul that feels
disconnected from their own love and truth
or believes they are all alone in the world
without any support. Billie Lue Fung, Divine
Mind Intelligence."

Billie Lue Fung

How long between each incarnation?

There is no specific timescale between incarnations it is
governed by free will. Free will is not a human construct
or limited to the theatre as it is all pervasive and transcends
every state. Free will is universal law in the physical and
non-physical. Incarnation is a choice and embarked upon
for accelerated growth, a need or to assist others. A free will
choice of immediate or delayed rebirth. The predesigned
intent is a fraction of the entire life experience. The rest is
free will to create what you wish.

The challenge is to fulfil the often sought purpose.
Time is a linear constant in the physical realm. Time as we
understand it does not exist in the infinite. Spirit is a timeless
possibility where there is no past, present or future. It is all
in the now. The foundation of the question is a manifestation
of our minds. If we look through the eyes of physical time
paused, immediate or delayed rebirth would be the answer.
This is not the true reality. All sojourns are happening in
the now. It is our mental and physical experience in them
that presents separation and linearity. Inner evolution is not
implicit upon each life experience but it is implied. How
long and how many incarnations are involved is the free

will of the spirit itself. Infinite possibility suggests there may be regressed expansion in a lifetime. Achieving inner expansion in one lifetime does not mean a natural linear progression in another.

Each lifetime is unique. We can experience extreme growth or a polar opposite in another. The infinite spirit when returning to *Source* is always and will forever be pure love energy. The number of lifetimes is a choice and we determine if and where we wish the experience to be.

There are any possible reasons for the draw towards material life. We enter the physical world for countless reasons, some observe, change or guide. Rebirth in the human realm imposes detachment as is expected. The beautiful connection of a newborn baby is rapidly dissolved. We forget home and any past lives. That is the expectation in the human realm. A full memory of the past life would create an obstacle to experiencing the purpose of the incarnation. The absence of a past life memory is for some proof afterlife or reincarnation are mental illusions. We can discover past experiences through regression or other esoteric modalities. Buddhists suggest rebirth is compelled through past actions or karma. This implies omnipotent judgement.

There is no judgement from a higher being, council or beings upon entering the afterlife. We may review the life sojourn with an expanded awareness and may formulate another. It is not forced but taken willingly from a point of perception and knowing of *Source*. Human perceptions of fear, death, pain, suffering, ego, mind and lack do not exist beyond the physical. Each life is perceived by what opportunities it will provide for expansion and the rest open to be what we wish it to be and directed from any vibration we chose to emit. Free will ultimately determines if any or all of our life intent is fulfilled. Enjoy the physical realm and all it has to offer with peace, love and demonstrating *Source* consciousness not ego, greed, wanton desire or dominion over others.

Some state personality does not exist beyond each life and we create a new one to match each new incarnation. The opposing view is personality transcends, grows and is part of the energetic footprint of our infinite consciousness as we expand. The latter is supported. Personality is an energetic vibration and embeds in our eternal consciousness as a record of everything we have ever been. Personality remains and is not the superficial but the core essence of what we are or have expanded to from each experience. It does not drop away, become irrelevant and is replaced by a new one of equal irrelevance once the experience has ended. This cannot be the case as everything has purpose and intent and never ceases to exist.

We are open to absorb traits of parents through energetic information held in shared DNA. Our physical body is an energetic DNA information sequence from two vibrational frequencies namely your parents. The resulting energy body will incorporate elements of the energy footprint of the two contributing frequencies. It is not implicit we will take on the personality of any particular parent. We may take on temporarily superficial habits in younger life and supersede them during adulthood. How much we alter from what we experience around us is our choice and free will. We do not need to adhere to the human attitude, 'you are like your parents' or indeed suffer their physical ills. It is a choice to understand everything can be altered. Heredity is not implicit and only if we allow it to be through free will and the mind.

What is Reiki or Energy Healing?

"In my experience in administering sessions, energy treatment is to allow disturbance in your body to be released/removed by God's energy. For me, it's about attempting to see your body as God sees you—whole, perfect, and in pure spirit form. When tapping and engaging in this energy, undesired conditions in the body could be altered by the positive energy flowing into the body and/or to a particular area of need to be released while being protected by God's light. I do believe that these disturbances in the body could be "overridden" by the person if they do not want or can't believe in their desired results from their free will and their life choices. Importantly, these types of treatments are not replacements from the care of your medical doctor but can coincide toward your desired results. While administering this protected and positive energy, the results can be amazing and I'm extremely grateful to be a conduit and a witness to wonderful results."

Rosa Oh. Energy Healer

Why do bad things happen?

A common response to this question is because God allows it to happen or it is my fate and I deserve it for past lives. This is untrue. Every life that exist is an eternal living force of energy and consciousness and has free will. Free will to choose to perform positive or negative actions. Evil occurs because we chose to act against our true state of love or in resonance with it. Nothing forces the action or demands it. Each action is formed through programmed beliefs, fear, hate, separation, culture, ego, inner anger or other imbalances. At its core is free will. Free will is externally applied through physical acts individually, by a group, nation, country or species impacting the one or the many. We create the imbalance and choose to renter the theatre many times and through tendency some may add to the asymmetry.

A life journey may be designed with a disability for growth of the inner self of the person and those around them. This is not a catchall. The systems around us may cause physical illnesses either expected or imposed by the free will of another. The theatre itself contains innumerable possibilities with a core theme that we create the imbalances. It is a concept difficult to accept as our minds have been indoctrinated into believing it must be punishment or Karma. All that ails the human condition is caused by our own detachment from wisdom and attachment to intellect or accepting a slow dumbing down of awareness. We consume excessive medications, contaminate our food, water and air, radiate our fields of energy and cultivate ecological disasters by disrupting natural law.

Some spiritualists will use the catchall argument we know the theatre and the impositions it will impose upon us yet we chose to experience life in the realm. The result is we chose everything that occurs. Free will determines the majority of life for everyone. We determine a core reason for being but fundamentally life is open to any possibility. We can impose our will on another against their will or intention or create systems that will harm those living within them.

That is expected in the harsh duality but the act is our own. We can buy food from a reputable source yet find it has been contaminated causing many to become ill for profit. That is free will not a predetermined universal act. There is a duality and we enter with this awareness and through free will all possibility can play itself out. Our challenge is to bring balance to where it has been disrupted or accept it and continue to be absorbed in the distractions.

Free will created duality which is energy outwardly forming action through cause and effect. A leaning toward ego, domination, greed or war will start the manifestation of negative energy, alternate forms, evil, hate and thus duality. The creation of duality as energy will exist as long as we feed it. It does require vast amounts of energy to feed a state or for a form to manifest. A little goes a long way be that love or hate. If one does not want to be impacted by lower astral energies or demonic forces do not feed it nor give it belief. Ultimately all illusions are removed including multi-layered abstractions. They all exist in the theatre as all possibility and feed off energy, thought and belief. Duality was not the intention of *Source* yet in some way expected. There is the saying 'To Appreciate Light We Must Experience Darkness'.

Can we always have the feeling when in meditation?

The scenario presented was after fifteen minutes of meditation, I feel a sense of quietness and peace, then hear an email and back into the real world. How do you allow a little of the meditative space into the real world? What does it actually feel like? Anyone who meditates will have this same challenge and there is no right or wrong answer. When in meditation we travel into self. We connect to a place of love allowing the energy to flow freely and open our Chakras. We experience a state of bliss where energetically we are detached from the physical world. Re-entering the real world is unavoidable. To maintain a connection to the inner true self and retain blissful flow to material life is to never disengage with *Source*, your guides or the entirety of true home. Practice being in constant engagement with the love vibration of light. Speak with the light constantly as it is always there. Not in a crazy mumbling manner around others but through the mind and in private moments.

Remind the self it is having a human experience and our spirit family is assisting us constantly and we need only ask. Release worry and traverse life knowing all will be well through synchronicities, signs and people. Become open to *Source* and spirit bringing in blessings and guidance into every moment. Maintain the connection and do not disengage. Connection to *Source* is permanent hence why disengage. Believing connection is achieved only during prayer, gratitude, meditation or stillness will limit inner peace and silence. We are infinite peace and stillness. Allow it to emit constantly and assist in stressful times. Never disengage with *Source*. Create the inner smile of connection.

Any state or practice that allows the higher self to assist in wider perception will offer a more peaceful and quietened state. Dance, practice yoga, prayer, gratitude or anything that will support inner peace and releasing of energy. The physical world and its influences are powerful distractions and we should allow the inner emerging spirit to retain our state of joy balanced with material life. Conduct the self through the heart over the ego and the mind. Converse with the inner spirit particularly when we feel ourselves being overwhelmed by the external theatre. There is no state of perfection and we all experience the same challenges and hurdles. Observing and catching them as often as is possible is all we can expect of the self. Challenge is a part of the journey. How we confront it and perceive it is the key.

Does God intervene?

God or *Source* is *All That Is* from which all emanates including energy, love vibration and thought. *Source* is the sum of *All That Is*. An inalienable awareness and presence that we feel from within. The Universe is teaming with life with one crucial gift of sovereign free will. The initial state for all that exists in the cosmos was balanced vibration, love and frequency. Duality is a potential of all possibility. Life is left to be what it wishes to become and create a universal experience on an infinite canvas.

The entire Universe is an experiment. There is no intervention. The theatre exists for life to evolve into what it will be and wishes to become. It can be domination, greed and war or love, unity and grace consciousness. It is for each form of life, animate or inanimate, in every aspect of the Universe to create its own destiny, experience, cause and effect and timelines. Negative energy manifests into action or evil as a direct consequence of imbalance, loss of awareness and the allowing of them collectively. Everything is an experiment. Life can live in harmony, balance and awareness if it wishes to create the experience. It seems we have allowed negativity and tyranny to manifest and take root. It remains to be seen what timeline we ultimately create as a member of infinite universal life. The current awakening is limited and focused on politics, control, deceit and agenda. This is where the awakening has stalled. It does not move onto the true intent. The intent is to awaken the higher self, unlock inner knowing, love and drive to become one. We are divided by systems, government and religion and should regain sovereignty individually and collectively.

Source is not the cause nor saviour of physical life experience or state. If there is imbalance it is for each individual to change their vibration and understand their true nature. We give power freely to others, vote in the corrupt to lead us who then propagate what preceded them creating further injustice, imbalance, greed and fulfil agendas. It is of no surprise that the duality persists. We should awaken to the real and detach from the temporal material reality.

Create and manifest with an open awareness. This will drive change in self and external behaviour. To persist is to have faith and will result in raising individual energy and contribute to the universal balance. *Source* frequency vibrates and cascades continually across the Universe. *Source* or spirit realm assists through waves of energy increasing the resonance of the Universe. Universal *Source* energy will affect those who are open to it or starting to ask deeper questions. The energy for those receptive to receive it is intended to nurture questioning leading toward a much wider expansion. Religions, demigods, sages, self-professed saviours are all barriers to true awareness. There will not be an external saviour. Ufologists believe non-terrestrial beings will save humanity which is also an illusion. All life terrestrial or non-terrestrial possess free will and are equally a part of the cosmic theatre.

Is eating meat good or bad?

A very common question and a topic which many ponder regularly. Everything, animate or inanimate, has consciousness, aura, energy and awareness from a subatomic particle, a star or Universe. Nothing exists that is more divine than another. There will be no answer to this question that will please all perspectives and what is offered is for reflection. Hinduism places divinity to the cow over all other animals and is an example of dogma within faith. There is no right or wrong choice when deciding to consume meat. The consumption of meat implicitly results in the giving of life of an animal. We are connected and our consciousness is in unity with all living things.

In the animal kingdom a predator preys on the weaker for food and survival in a law of correspondence in that each exist to support the balance of the whole. We tend to adopt this law by proxy of being atop of the food chain and thus give ourselves the inalienable right to kill and consume everything we feel is lesser. We have no right to dominate or kill anything but we possess the free will to choose. We perceive ourselves to be consciously of a higher frequency than the animal kingdom yet seemingly hunt for sport and farm animals for consumption.

In some African tribes and in Native American culture the practice of praying over the body of the animal to give thanks for its sacrifice and using every part of the animal in respect is a form or reciprocated energy. Other cultures look to balance the energy held in the meat through Kosher or Halal rituals. The reality is meat holds the energy of trauma, fear and suffering experienced by the animal up to its end. Animals are often kept in horrific conditions, suffering in life and killed in a manner causing further trauma stored as energy in the meat. When consumed the energy merges with the frequency of those who consume it. The energy impacts the individual frequency.

We can reduce meat consumption or adopt vegetarianism, veganism or to consuming only what sprouts from the ground. Aura and trauma equally applies to a blade of grass, an apple and wheat or grain. Energy is held by every form. Eating any form and even breathing air results in a transmuting and cascading of energy. We can criticise almost any form of consumption as an ending of a life force. We own pets and cherish them and would protest at any harm to a dog, cat or other animas but never recognise we kill other animals in huge numbers for food without a thought.

These are all choices and it is not for any individual to place judgement on a choice another makes. Those who judge are doing so from a point of ego as there will be many aspects of their lives that can be equally be up for criticism from another. We can judge from any manner of perspectives. Before judging look around and perceive the personal world. We sit on leather seats. We wear leather belts, shoes and jackets. We tie our boots with leather laces. We carry leather handbags. We are surrounded by animal derived products. We target each other from our pedestals of veganism, vegetarianism and pescetarianism. The list is endless. Unless we use a rope as a belt, clogs as shoes and have eradicated all animal derived products there is no place for judgement. We are awash with contradictions often simply dogma regurgitated from parents, faith and society and selectively implanted to suit the personal ego.

We should recognise the many facetted levels of hypocrisy and contradiction that surround the judgement to meat consumption. There is no argument that omitting animal or fish meat has its benefits. As long as we eat meat the industries will continue. We will absorb positive and negative energy of everything we consume from a grain, insect, animal to African game. If eating meat is an option lean towards consuming what has had as close to a natural and free roaming life as possible. Achieving an expanded state is absolutely not connected to the diet one choses. A vegan is no less elevated than a meat eater.

It is the inner state that is the measure. It is not an external self-awarded state of judgement of others from a chosen dietary regime. Ultimately it is a choice. A free will decision. We can chose to recognise we have no right to kill and are in unity with animal life or consume meat. Judgement is our own not for another. Expansion will bring closer a natural desire to reduce fish, insect or meat consumption and in some remove it completely. It is a choice and a natural course of change during expansion.

The point is to follow the inner natural flow which will change as expansion develops. Diet does not move implicitly in concert with spiritual expansion. As stated a vegan can be less aware of self than one who consumes meat and fish. A non-meat diet does not correspond to *Source* connected consciousness. Look around and this is evident. Open the mind and follow the self. Expand and change through natural desire without ego or self-importance.

What is inner knowing?

We all have *The Book* of knowledge within. It is inner knowing. All that we seek to understand of ourselves, the Universe, the afterlife, source consciousness and wisdom is held within our infinite spirit. It is the core within all things. We have suppressed inner knowing with the egoistic mind and its self-awarded superiority to the inner spirit. Inner knowing can be channelled once the re-emergence of the true self is awakened. Presence, peace, contentment, compassion and connectedness emerge as inner knowing. It just is and cannot be logically explained or measured. Inner knowing is akin to intuition. A silent hidden wisdom and knowing of *All That Is*. The body is the shroud within which the inner self is hidden.

> "Inner knowing is a feeling, a sense. It is not a thought and cannot therefore be attributed to the conscious mind. Like your other five major senses, inner knowing being the sixth, it can help you to "feel" if something is right, or not. Some call it intuition, or your sixth sense. Inner knowing can provide clarity, where the conscious mind may only bring confusion. However, in order to connect with this, you need to be able to quieten the mind. In other words, be in the present."
>
> Jerry Humphries

What is Death?

We have discussed the reality of life and that it is a sojourn into the material Universe. A theatre to fulfil our intent for the experience. Death is an end to the experience through natural causes, personal action or externally imposed force. We have control over our exit and death is not intended to be painful. Death from pain, illness or recklessness is a manifestation of the human system. Life can end as a result of an external force or a violent action of another or a group. It can be by design or an act of another imposed against their free will. We can endanger our experience through recklessness and placing ourselves in dangerous situations where another can impose their will and end the life. A person can also force an exit through the loss of the will to live. Free will is absolute power over the experience.

If the will is strong and persistent the higher self will open up to allow the withdrawal of our consciousness energy. Such an example is if a lifelong partner passes leaving the other alone and often in old age. The person left will lose their own will to continue as a huge emotional void is created abruptly and often not reconciled. Their external loss of will to continue may as a decision of light move the infinite spirit to leave the body and reconcile the urge. These are saddening aspects of life in the dimensional physical theatre. We are in full control of the manner in which we exit and can determine this through free will, thought and connectedness to *Source* consciousness. We can raise our vibration to a place where once we feel the journey is over the fractal of our core spirit may return home peacefully.

Fear of death results in anxiety and suffering toward what is the ultimate and unavoidable end to all that exists. It is a constant from the endless annihilation of a subatomic particle producing energy in the Universe for matter to the life of the individual. Removal of the fear of death is connectedness to true self. We fear death as we identify with the physical body, associate it with pain and not a peaceful exit home. Death is merely a return to home and life in the theatre is a sojourn away.

Regard it as such and follow a much more rewarding, purposeful, intentional life whilst creating wonderful material experiences. We do not cease to exist upon a withdrawal of our consciousness from the physical body.

The spirit animates the body not the mind or the heart. If the spirit leaves the body it dies no matter the health of the mind or the heart.

Does Source get happy and sad?

All that exists from the moment the universal theatre sparked into form was love and balanced life with the gift of free will. *Source* is all love and manifests the canvas as all possibility. Whatever emotions and events we create are within *Source* and become it. There is no sadness or disappointment in infinite being. Sadness exist within us as we experience it in physical form reinforced by our detachment from wider reality. We feel sadness at the suffering of others yet we create and allow to persist what supports the imbalance. *Source* did not create poverty, murder, war, greed, injustice, planetary destruction, politics, deceit, self-interest, lust, power and domination, control, loss of connection, ignorance, stupidity, violence and the list goes on.

Source simply through thought emanates the playground for life. A naturally expanding state of energy creating, transforming and preserving form in the constant expansion of planets, stars, collapsing energy, rebirth and death. It is life in its manifold forms that manifest what exists within it. Humanity creates what it suffers and enjoys through free will. This is the uncomfortable truth. Humanity cannot accept it has and is creating its own prison and experience. As an infinite spirit we are part of that which emanates from *Source* and everything experienced is part of *Source*. Life is allowed to create its cycles. Love energy is cascading across the Universe to influence timelines or negative desires and ambitions. *Source* can only be felt within as an expanse of awareness from which we feel and emanate. *Source* is not a being, a physical omnipotent, omniscient manifestation judging and intervening or the creator of imbalance. *Source* is infinite balance and love. It is up to each us to create the path and timeline.

The Universe is teaming with intelligent life and closer than you may wish to accept through mind or what is offered in the public domain. The human experience is not the highest grade of existence, physically, intelligently or energetically. A reality that may hurt the human ego or those who think they are the peak of evolution, all knowing and that life must reflect human form. We are the owner of the life and can chose to spread love, unity and connectedness or use universal law and energy for negative aspects, power and control. A choice we all have.

What are the cycles?

There are many concepts and cycles that influence the overriding energy and imposition upon all cosmic life. There are a number of definitions and ancient depiction of cycles. When researched we can see concurrency in every major concept of epochs or ages. They refer to same cycles. A descending away from *Source* to loss followed by a return to Christ or Krsna consciousness and ultimately *Source*. The Greek philosopher Hesiod depicted five Ages of Man around between 650-750BC. The Golden Age was ruled by Cronus. It was an age where humans lived among the gods. Peace and harmony prevailed during this age. The Earth provided all the nourishment for humanity. Humans lived long youthful lives and died peacefully. The spirit realm was accepted and were regarded as Guardians. Humans were regarded as the golden race or daemons. The word daemons or daimones means knowing or wise.

The Silver Age and subsequent ages were said to be ruled by Zeus. Zeus was the son of Cronus. Humanity lived 100 Years and experienced turmoil with others. The connection to *Source* started to diminish. Zeus destroyed the impious during this time. This can be connected to the slow loss from Creation in the Christian epochs. In the Bronze Age humanity created war and become gardened to fight them as a purpose. Humanity became victims of their own violent ways and their spirits lived in the "dank house of Hades". This Age came to an end with the flood of Deucalion. This can be connected to the Christian age of the Great Flood and the Hindu descending Dwarpara and Treta Yugas. The Heroic Age may be mythology and a period of war between Thebes and Troy. Thebes was the largest city of the ancient region of Boeotia. The famous battle of Troy was fought during this age. The Heroic Age maybe mythology and is said to span six generations. The fighting humans were said to be superhuman. It was the heroes of this Age who fought at Thebes and Troy around 1300BC. The warriors who died went to Elysium a paradise where heroes went into immortality. During the Iron Age humans lived in toil and misery. Children dishonoured their parents. Humanity fought with each other. Power was imposed and enforced as righteous and lies were promoted as truth. At the peak of the Iron Age humanity started to feel no shame and the gods had completely forsaken humanity. The age will be one where "...there will be no help against evil." Hesiod. This age is akin to the descending and ascending Kali Yuga and Post the Great Flood.

Christianity documents three epochs or great periods of time or worlds. Peter one of the twelve Apostles and

Saint Paul identified three great epochs of time or worlds. The Epochs started from Creation to the Great Flood. The first epoch was the period between Creation and the Great Flood, named "The World That Then Was" and is said to have been governed by the Angels. The second epoch post the Great Flood was the period where control of Satan 'the prince of this world' started to emerge in the Kingdom of God and became dominant. Divinity still existed but was measurably diminished. The period was named "The Present Evil World". The third epoch is whence Satan was removed from the Kingdom of God named the "world without end". It returned to divine governance and was referred to as the "The World to Come". Christ consciousness became dominant in the world of Satan.

The three heavens were pre the Great Flood, the second heaven was an age where Satan gave way to the third heaven in which Apostle Paul saw Christ's wonderful Kingdom rule. The second and third epochs are further divided into three Ages namely the "The Patriarchal Age", "The Jewish Age" and "The Gospel Age".

Hinduism philosophy offers the Vedic Yugas. There are two descending and ascending Yugas phases of 4.32 million years, called a Mahayuga, with a total of 8.64 million years. One thousand complete Yugas cycles form one day in the lifespan of Brahma. The total human years are 8,640,000,000 or 8.64 billon years. The lifespan of a Brahma is 100 years. The formula completes with 8.64 billion years * 360 days per year * 100 = 311,040 trillion human years. Current measurement calculates the age of the Universe to be 115 billion human years. The Hindu formula is complex. There are many interpretations available. At the end of the 311 trillion years Hindu philosophy states the Universe will merge back into *Source* and sleep. Before explaining the

Yugas there is a need to explain divine and human years as used in Hindu philosophy. Divine years are human constructs and are describing time when considering *Source*. *Source* is a state of eternal timelessness. Considering the sheer scale of divine and human years we can easily argue all that what we experience in the Universe or Multiverse can be in the now. For example 360 human years equate to a single divine year. Hinduism suggests Brahma is the creator of the Universe.

The four descending Yugas are calculated in divine years and then translated into human years. A complete descending and ascending Yugas cycle is 8.64 million years. There are one thousand cycles in a single day of the life of Brahma calculated to 8.64 billion years.

The descending Satya Yuga is translated as 4,800 divine or 1,728 human years. The descending Treta Yuga is 3,600 divine or 1,296,000 human years. The descending Dvapara Yuga is 2,400 divine or 864,000 human years. The descending Kali Yuga is 1,200 divine or 432,000 human years. A total of 4.32 million years. The Ascending Yugas equal the same total divine or human years. A full cycle of 8 epochs would be 8.64 million years.

There are many dates for the start of the first descending Yuga. Sri Yukteswar Giri wrote *The Holy Science* and provided calculations for the four descending Yugas. An equinox occurs twice a year when the sun crosses the equator and enters a sign of the zodiac. Each year the equinox rises in a different zodiac. The movement is called a precession with a full cycle passing through each zodiac as a divine year. Sri Yukteswar Giri suggests a full cycle of equinoxes through each zodiac takes 24,000 divine years equal to the descending and ascending Satya, Treta, Dvapara and Kali Yugas.

The Surya Siddhanta is an Indian Sanskrit astronomical text which dates from the late 400 CE. The Surya Siddhanta states the Kali Yuga began on February 18, 3102 BC. Aryabhata was an Indian mathematician and astronomer and was born during the Kali Yuga in 476 AD. He wrote the Aryabhatiya at the age of twenty three. In the Aryabhatiya he calculated a Mahayuga to be 4.32 million years.

The first Yuga measurement is estimated to have started in 11500 BC. This by no means should be interpreted that life did not exist prior to this date. It must be remembered what exists as knowledge now is what has survived. Life has existed since the dawn of the Universe. It is cyclical. Life evolves and dissolves. The Yugas offers an interesting depiction of cycles and can be used to compare against past, present and potentially future human experience.

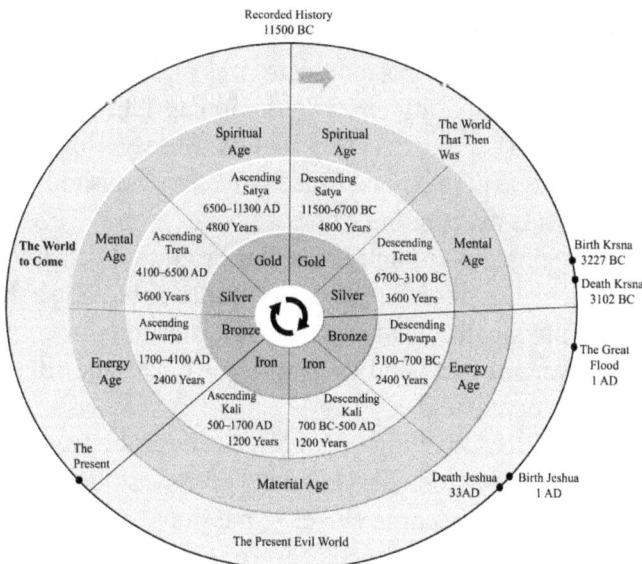

Figure 15: The Great Cycles and Ages

Humanity entered form into a state of love and balance. This was described as the Golden Age. The Satya Yuga was preceded by the Krita Yuga which means to create.

The Krita Yuga was described as an age of truth and perfection. A time where there was no religion and where all humanity was in balance with no need for religious ceremonies or rituals.

During the descending Satya Yuga the contentious and objectionable concept of the caste system emerged but was regarded as flexible. Humans were far taller and larger, powerful, sincere, honest and youthful. True sovereign free will existed.

The descending Treta Yuga although meaning third is the second of the Yugas. A time when frequency started to diminish. A time of emperors, dominance and the urge to conquer the world. Wars were a reality and weather patterns changed. Oceans and deserts are formed. Humanity started to develop impaired awareness and inner knowing diminished. Humanity embarked upon agriculture, labour intensive work and extracting metals. Average lifespan of humans was said to be one thousand to ten thousand years.

The third descending Dvapara Yuga is the age where humanity engaged in activities that promoted pessimism, ignorance, laziness, criminality and doubt. Humanity became physically weaker. Diseases, discontentment and further warring between each other. An average lifespan was a few centuries.

The fourth descending Kali Yuga is described as an age of darkness and ignorance. Humanity became sinners, lacked sincerity, virtue, become slaves to passions and physically a pale reflection of what they were in the Krita and start of the Satya Yuga. Society fails with deceit and hypocrisy. Knowledge destroyed or lost and scriptures are hidden.

Humanity eats animal meat and engages in unrestrained sexual practices. The environment becomes polluted, water and food become scarce. Wealth is heavily diminished. Families become non-existent. Average lifespan of people is barely 100 years. The descriptions also state by the end of the Yuga some lifespans will be as low as 20 years.

The four descending Yugas have ascending opposites where the ascending Yuga epochs offer vibrational shifts to support the re-emergence back to *Source*. Some Hindu measurement states humanity has been traversing the Kali Yuga since 700 BC.

The Yugas are interesting descriptions of ages, epochs or cycles and the loss and reawakening of spiritual content. Sri Yuktesar Giri suggest we are exiting the ascending Kali Yuga and entering the Dvapara Yuga. The frequency of the ascending Dvapara Yuga is greater. It is interesting when comparing the description of the Kali Yuga to our current human experience. There are no coincidences only synchronicities. These cycles offer concepts for reflection. It is interesting symbolism a two meter tall statue of Kali is located outside CERN, the European Center for Research in Particle Physics in Geneva. The statue may symbolise the CERN desire to recreate the GOD particle through the acceleration, annihilation transformation of subatomic particles in the Large Hadron Collider (LHC).

The Yugas start by stating a great culture proceeded Humanity. One such date offered by theologians is 3,894,000 years ago where a civilisation of humans were happier, taller, and lived longer. By contrast, modern scientists currently date Genus Homo to 2.5 million years, Homo sapiens 300,000 years. Hindu cosmology abstracts time in cycles called Kalpas (cosmic rounds), Mahayugas (great ages) and Yugas (ages). Each great age is divided into the four descending and ascending Yugas.

Are cycles implicit and impact everything universally? The answer is subjective. We move between Yugas not physically but energetically through our developing frequency or state. As we expand we move through energetic states which expand our inner knowing, self, perceptions and awareness of *All That Is*. Our spiritual development is not limited nor confined to the states defined in the Yugas. We can be of an expanded infinite state of higher vibration akin to Krita or Satya Yuga yet experience physical life that may be universally traversing the denser Kali Yuga.

For example if we operate in a low vibrational energetic state of fear, hate, separation, anger and violence the frequency will be that of the Kali Yugas, regardless of where the cycle states humanity is passing in current time. Adversely if physical life is calculated to be traversing the Kali Yuga our personal expanded frequency may overwhelmingly be of infinite love, unity, joy, bliss, power of self and *Source* consciousness and be emitting the state of Satya Yuga. We can move through these depicted states of being through the journey to self and unlocking *The Book* of knowing, connectedness with all that exists at any time, during any concept of cycles or epochs through free will.

Can we become impure in that Satya Yuga?

From a place of complete connection, balance and awareness humanity always has free will choice. Humanity also possesses ego. Some will lead, others observe and the rest will follow. It is an individual free will choice which state or frequency they emit. The Yugas are descriptions of repeating energetic frequency cycles. It is all wavelength frequency manifestations of energy. If we accept the concept of ages, epochs or cycles we assume they are implicit to life on Earth no matter the level of personal expansion. Yugas or energy cycles occur as constant perpetual motion of imposition should we allow their frequency to govern our own state. Cycles are not implicit and will impact those in alignment with their frequency.

For example a person can be in living during the Kali Yuga yet within emanate the Satya frequency. From expansion comes connection to higher frequencies and then on. Hinduism or any philosophy should not be taken prescriptively. Age of scripture is not necessarily evidence of validity. Consume knowledge from other perspectives, religious, esoteric, spiritual and metaphysical. They all should be investigated and have validity when approached without dogma.

Yugas as with all conceptual cycles are human creations and reflect energetic shifts in the Universe and consciousness of humanity. It is our free will and strength of belief in defined structures that create the prison of human consciousness and energetic expression into these cycles. Cycles are repetitive in the universal theatrical construct and may simply be an exceptional measurement of human evolution in consciousness and cyclical behaviour. It is useful to remind ourselves there have been many cycles of life on Earth before modern humanity. To assume humanity as we currently understand it was the only intelligent life on Earth is a nonsense. Expansion is dependent on what was described in the main body of this book. We determine our frequency individually regardless of the Yuga or cycle the Universe is said to be traversing.

The objective of the whole or in this case our human experience is to move individual frequency and vibration through the journey into self toward a re-emerged infinite state. As greater numbers of humanity expand the more powerful the frequency will impact upon the overall state of the collective experience.

What is a psychic and mediumship reading?

An answer is best offered by those who provide psychic and mediumship services to others.

> "Mediumship is an energy driven exercise. The frequency of my energy raises to a higher point than in a psychic reading. My job, as a conduit, is to focus on fleeting disruptions in the energy around me. All my senses are used during a session as energy patterns may come through in various different ways. There is a language that is expressly mine that involves imagery and symbols that I interpret. The info contained within can be figurative or literal. It is used to guide me and not necessarily impart important information. With mediumship I have experienced hearing spirit; seeing spirit (sometimes in 3D), sensing or feeling spirit; tasting whatever they are trying to get me to taste and smell whatever they are wanting me to smell so as to guide me to a specific topic. The 'how' this all works is actually none of my business. I have never understood it. Since I was born with this ability it has always been a normal part of my life. I

cannot explain what I have never had to
learn. It is as natural as breathing."

Tracy Baker

"First and foremost I must be as clear a
conduit as I can possibly be. This means I
must deal with whatever is in my own energy
(frustrations, worry etc.) so that I may lift
my frequency to experience others' energy
patterns from a higher vantage point. This
higher vantage point allows me to see how
they are using their focus (read: power); to
offer guidance on how to move themselves
from where they are to where they want to
be, and to assist them by offering the tools
to begin living the life they came here to
live. Other aspects of psychic readings
may include any and all life topics. I am
not a deliberate prognosticator as I know
that events can be included or excluded
by a simple choice either conscious or
unconscious. However, there have been
times where prognostication comes through
but again the results of those predictions
are predicated on the choices the receiver
makes up to the point of possible fruition. As
everything is energy it stands to reason that
sessions are energy driven. To me it is akin
to picking up puzzle pieces of someone's
energy and helping to construct the most
preferred picture."

Ara Parisien

What is happiness?

The Dalai Lama is often referred to as his holiness similar to the pope and other professed persons of divinity. The term holiness should be avoided as it purports false divinity and a state of worship to another. They are humans just like you. They have chosen to commit their lives to the journey of self-discovery. A journey open to everyone if we wish to embark upon it. Spiritual practitioners are here to nurture stages of our personal journey but are not there for worship or to place on a pedestal for perceived unattainable heights of enlightenment. Through constant meditation, prayer, inner reflection and balancing ego is self-awareness and spiritual expansion achieved.

> "...happiness is determined more by one's
> state of mind than by external events...
> If you want others to be happy, practice
> compassion. If you want to be happy,
> practice compassion.... Compassion can
> be roughly defined in terms of a state of
> mind that is nonviolent, non-harming, and
> non-aggressive. It is a mental attitude based
> on the wish for others to be free of their
> suffering and is associated with a sense of
> commitment, responsibility, and respect
> towards others."
>
> The Dalai Lama

To develop happiness there will be an inevitable a recognition of a *Source* of *All That Is*. This realisation is unavoidable. Meditation, prayer, inner reflection and the balancing of ego develop three important states. These states are Inner

Peace, Forgiveness and Gratitude. Without these three internal states the external pursuit for happiness may be an aloof feeling no matter how much we change the mind or compassion we seek to externally exhibit.

For peace to be attained the inner journey will force the confronting of our ego and self-importance. Peace is a state of inner grace. To be within your core and emit outwardly this state. It does not mean we becomes saintly or holier than thou. We rediscover humility, create an ability to laugh at ourselves in a non-deprecating way and develop the personality. The objective is to develop internally the frequency of grace rather than ego and self-absorption. To overcome the external conscious barriers and shift intent to the higher self and knowing. The frequency is not holy, divine nor exceptional but a higher state of being and regaining sovereignty of our own power. It is an awakening and more importantly understanding and accepting the 'I' is not of this physical realm. The process is constant with perfection not a goal nor achievable. Expansion is the objective.

Contentment is an outcome of inner peace. Contentment is knowing you are where you need to be, at the right time and with all that is needed. Be content internally and to dispel the hungry ghost. The material will align and come into perspective delivering contentment. A lack of contentment is the pursuit over all else the material desires. Discontent is the sense of lack, dissatisfaction with every new gain or accumulation, feeling inadequate or inferior and fed by further immersing into the mind. The inner journey removes the sense of discontent by shifting the external consciousness and mind to a life guided by inner peace, knowing and presence. The seeking and chasing of the material over all else will no longer be the driving factor in life. Goals and life objectives and desires are pursued with balance and peace knowing they will come to pass. Peace and contentment is a state of being, stillness of inner gentleness and grace. It is to be content.

Forgiveness, is critical and a practice we find most difficult. Forgiveness is not forgetting nor is it asking for the embrace of someone who has committed heinous crimes. There are those who are able to achieve this state within the heart and it is to be admired. We need to simply accept and understand every spirit has its own journey. If we hold anger and resentment as energetic load impacting expansion and the inner journey. We often hold onto energy from hurt and negative actions of family, friends and colleagues. The journey to self must incorporate forgiveness within the self and others daily. If we are honest a list could be drawn up of many we hold inner resentment for a past actions or words. Life is expected to offer these experiences as we share the space with billons of spirits moving along their journey of actions, words, thoughts, intents and perceptions manifest through free will. A prayer of forgiveness is recommended daily to increase inner frequency and remove energy created by long held resentment of those present or past.

> If someone of something has hurt me in the past, consciously or unconsciously, I forgive them and free them.
>
> If I have hurt someone or something in the past, consciously or unconsciously, forgive me and free me.
>
> If I have hurt myself in the past, consciously or unconsciously, I forgive myself, I free

myself, I forgive myself , I free myself, I
forgive myself, I free myself, for my benefit
and the benefit of all my relationships.

And so will it be.

Gratitude is the thankfulness to the self and spirit for every
sign, synchronicity, number, symbol, event, people and place
we are guided to. A state of inner reconnection brings peace
and a natural urge to be grateful for every moment of our
experience. We are eternally guided once spirit is requested
to walk with us in life. Life will start to become one of
peace and a gentler flowing when gratitude is expressed.
We experience the physical and all it offers which will push
the frequency in and out of balance. This is natural and part
of expansion. The pursuit of perfection is for those who are
living under a false sense of personal ego.

Giving gratitude daily for the experience, guidance, love
and protection to the infiniteness of possibility is offered
for consideration. Recognise what is in front of you and not
what is perceived as lacking. Focus on lack will only deliver
more of the same. Focus on constant accumulation will never
offer happiness and contentment. Gratitude of what is, has
been and will be. The majority may never give gratitude
on a daily, weekly or monthly basis and reserve them to
thanksgiving, Christmas or other annual celebrations.
Happiness is not a hope, a desire for something better or
compassion as these are external actions. The foundation
of true happiness is a derivative of peace, contentment,
forgiveness and gratitude. Change the personal Universe
and not be distracted by the assessment of another.

Can someone or something be holy?

Humanity has a tendency to bestow the state of holiness, deity or divinity on others or objects for reverence and worship. This is a major challenge for humanity. We look externally when the answers are internal and released if the mind and heart are ready to receive. Study the philosophies of others offering guidance, knowledge and practices to start the personal journey. The objective is not give your power away through a lifetime of unconditional or unquestioning devotion to another. We have nurtured an environment where we look to political, religious or spiritual leaders for guidance and have become sheep. Traditional doctrines and new age practices suffer the same challenge.

There is no human among us who can claim to be holy or possess divinity or is a messenger of whatever god they deem to be in communication. Some of those who enter the theatre have open connections and vibrate higher frequencies and are here to assist our inner growth. This can be attributed to only a few. We all originate from the same *Source* and expanse of energy.

An object or deity through the power focused upon it can manifest from the great un-manifest or astral plane. They hold the sum of all the energy given to them often from the heart of the devotee. This does not mean these objects, person or places are divine. We should respect the energy given to each of them as we would anything a person may cherish or value if life. The energy is of devotional love. The objective is not to see any object, place or person as a source of divine energy and become a devotee.

We should be cognisant of anyone who assigns themselves or accepts the label of holiness or divinity. Behind their public face they likely do not behave as the flock perceive them to be. The rule applies to every position from president, prime minister and politician and into every section of society. Roles in society are not an indication of superiority but pedestals we bestow upon them through awe and a lesser than perception. We should cease looking to and creating religious and spiritual leaders and become sovereign in our true nature. Institutions, positions and rules are for control and removing personal power and awareness. There are no rules, controls or masters of our infinite spiritual destiny. There is no purpose in creating the prison of perception. We all return to the same state when the experience ends.

What is an Astral Plane and Astral Travel?

There are numerous descriptions of dimensions and planes of the physical and ethereal body ranging from the Hindu Lokas to the Seven Cosmic Planes. The cosmic planes are not physical planes but energetic or vibrational frequency. The esoteric realm promote numerous definitions of planes including the astral. One such example is the seven cosmic planes. Planes are energetic planes of manifestation. They are vibrational frequencies or manifest matter and un-manifest all possibility. From the great un-manifest or dark matter we can create any form we desire through the persistent focusing of energy and thought. These forms are often said to exist in the ethereal or astral plane.

The Seven Cosmic Worlds or Planes are similar to the Qabalah Tree of Life. A plane or world refers to states or frequencies of matter represented as planes. The planes shift upward through meditation and inner advancement from the Physical toward Logoic or Kether. The lower planes are those of dense matter of the physical and into more subtle less matter consciousness states as faster and higher frequency energy.

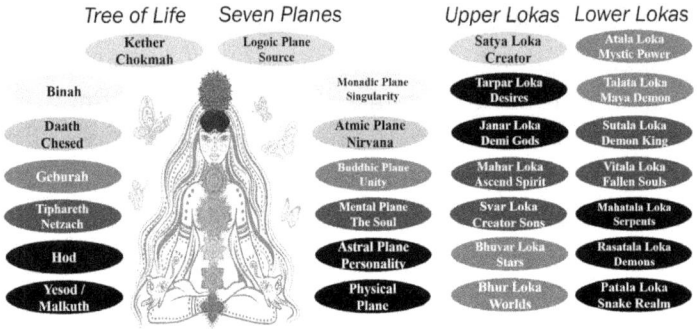

Figure 16: The Planes of Experience

The first plane is the physical plane of the material and the body. This deals with the identification with the body. The second is the Astral Plane corresponding to the emotional and personality. From this plane progression advances to the Mental Plane of the Soul. The Mental Plane is twinned with Tiphareth or formless spirit consciousness. The fourth Buddhic Plane represents consciousness Unity with the Soul and mapped with Geburah. The fifth Atmic Plane is achieving nirvana or spiritual plane. The sixth Monadic Plane is Singularity of Binah of full understanding. The final seventh state of Logoic Plane is Kether which is *Source* consciousness.

Hindu Lokas are another approach that describes fourteen worlds. Lokas in Sanskrit means World. The Lokas expand the notion of realms. The Lokas in alignment with the Qabalah Tree of Life and Seven Planes progresses toward the Creator. The Lokas differ in that they present realms of lower tendency such as the practices described in

Malkuth, Yesod and Hod. These lower realms of the Lokas move to occult practices where manifestation of Astral beings from the un-manifest and nurtured through feeding the forms thought and energy from sacrifice. If our personal energy is at the same frequency of the lower realms they can manifest and be traversed. It is important to note these are not *Source* realms or states. The lower Lokas are formed by those who operate in the Theatre and the worlds remain within it. These vibrational energetic states are accessed when we open our perception and awareness to the wider spectrum of what we describe as the 'unseen'.

Planes and realms of energetic vibrational frequencies exists within the theatre but not in the realm of *Source* consciousness. The cosmic planes, Lokas and abodes are observed when a person astral travels. We are able to see subtle forms, realms, past, present and future possibility beyond our spectrum when our inner state has been elevated. Satanic and demonic planes or serpents are human creations through persistent and focused manifestation of energy. Belief sustains these frequencies or wavelengths of form. The astral is the subtle body which through meditation and concentration we can, whilst remaining grounded, free the consciousness to travel within these energetic frequencies. These are not in the spirit realm of *Source* as that is a realm of love, not mind, logic nor demonic. Astral travel allows the observing of fantastic realms of possibility and what has been manifest by every lifeform in the Universe through positive or negative intent. The concept of 'as above so below' states we are a microcosm of the macrocosm. What exist around or above us exists within us. We are everything and everything is us. We can create from the great un-manifest and traverse planes of energetic existence. There is no separation. It is all one and felt. These levels exist in the theatre where belief create planes and lower frequencies.

"Each experience is according to an individual's belief structure to a) show them where they are in the grander scheme of things or b) to allow them time in the playground to play out their fears in a safe manner. I say fears because much has been labelled about astral travel, as in where all the disembodied evil spirits eternally reside. Some of the places are quite fearful and can be experienced by anyone aligned with those fears/beliefs. Astral travel is when an aspect of soul traverses outside the physical vehicle to learn, grow and expand. Typically, when we sleep is when this occurs. I must preface my remarks by saying there are infinite possibilities and explanations as to who, what, why, when, where and how this happens. Many spend much time on deliberately making it happen. To me, this is ego consciousness driven where proof, tangible proof is required. Astral travel occurs virtually all the time and to me it is the soul knowing exactly where it needs to be, doing exactly what it needs to do, for perfect reasons that may not be required to rest in my awareness. I simply trust it. There have been many nights I have been aware of astral traveling where I delivered sessions (all night long in dream state) or where I went to classrooms to learn from the divine team. I am sure there are infinitely more

times that I am unaware of and that is fine by
me. I am hard pressed to tamper with or force
the perfection of that which already exists for
my benefit."

Ara Parisien

What is the Soul?

Esoteric thinkers and spiritual philosophers state the human
body can be separated into many energetic layers from the
spirit, soul, etheric and astral body. We create abstractions
for the mind to understand the indescribable and unknowable
infiniteness of the inner spirit. From an academic sense
they are useful but when connected these are irrelevant as
we feel the spirit as one and not through mental layers. In
his book *The Nature of Man* Rudolf Steiner describes the
mind as the processor of thought, the body consisting of a
life force and a sensory body or ether-body. He states the
ether-body gives life to and preserves the physical body
during the lifetime and is also associated with the life-body.
He goes on to write the sentient-soul is what receives soul
sensations and is dependent on the ether-body. He further
notes a presence of the soul-body or sentient-body.

A finer element of the ether-body supporting unity
with the sentient soul. We come to the evolved higher
member of the soul, intellectual-soul or the mind-soul.
The intellectual-soul integrates with the sentient-soul. The
compartmentalisation continues to the consciousness-soul
which is the imperishable element or what is referred to
as the infinite spirit. This infinite spirit element holds the
self-existent nature of the spirit, rising above the sentient
soul. Rudolf Steiner also refers to this as the spiritual-soul.

Figure 17: The Theosophical Soul

"Thus three members have to be distinguished in the soul as in the body: sentient soul, intellectual soul, and consciousness-soul. And just as the body works from below upwards with a limiting effect on the soul, so the spiritual works from above downwards into it, expanding it. For the more the soul fills itself with the true and the good, the wider and the more comprehensive becomes the eternal in it. To him who is able to "see" the soul, the radiance which proceeds from a human being because his eternal element is expanding, is just as much a reality as the light which streams out from a flame is real to the physical eye. For the "seer" the corporeal man counts as only part of the whole man. The physical body, as the coarsest structure, lies within others, which mutually interpenetrate both it and each other. The ether-body fills the physical body as a lifeform; extending beyond this on all sides is to be perceived the soul-body (astral form). And beyond this, again, extends the sentient soul, then the intellectual soul which grows the larger the more it receives into itself of the true and the good. For this true and good cause the expansion of the intellectual soul. A man living only and entirely according to his inclinations, his likes and dislikes, would have an intellectual soul whose limits coincide with those of his sentient soul. These formations, in the midst of which the physical body appears as if in a cloud, may be called the human aura. The aura is that in regard to which the "being

of man" becomes enriched, when it is seen as
this book endeavours to present it."

Rudolf Steiner

Osho an Indian spiritual speaker who was also known as
Acharya Rajneesh, Bhagwan Shree Rajneesh, and now
as Osho offers a description of the seven bodies as the
Physical body, the Etheric body, which is energetic and
not solid as the physical body. The Astral body as vapour
and transparent.

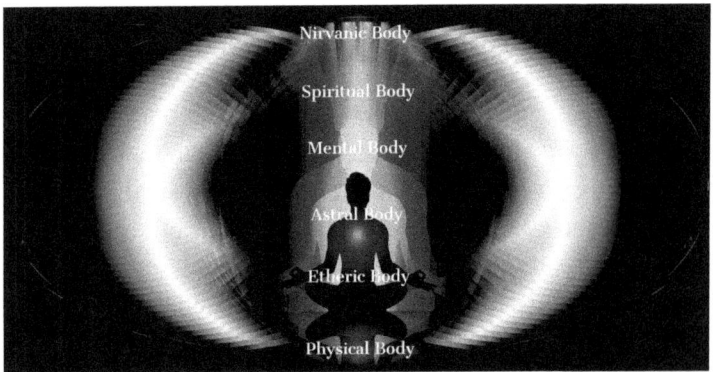

Figure 18: The Osho Bodies

The Mental body is described as the last of the lower plane
bodies and one that looks downward. Yoga is a practice that
moves the self into the fifth Spiritual body which drives
focus upward. Fire is a symbol of the spiritual body as it
flows upward whereas the other four including mind are
water which flows downward. The sixth is the Cosmic
body the removal of ego and into Brahma the expanse of
the Multiverse. The seventh is the Nirvanic body which
represents a state of non-being and integration into *All
That Is*.

Yogic philosophy offers the Pancha Koshas which means five sheaths or abstracted human body. The following Koshas exist within the body. The physical body is represented Annamaya Kosha and is the visible outer self. We identify with the Annamaya Kosha. It is the external body of the senses and as a result we feel joy and pain through it.

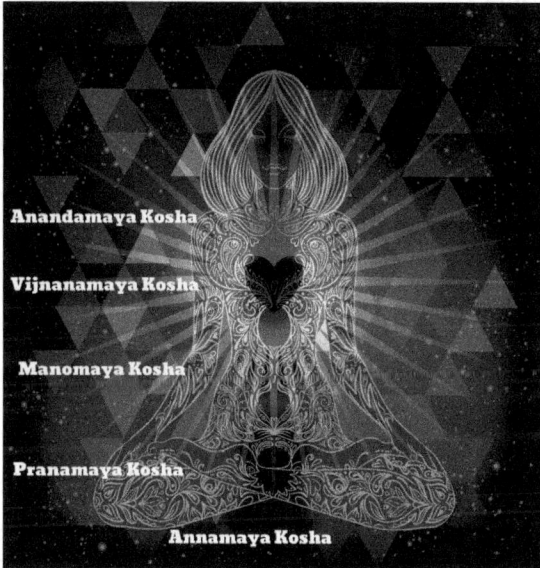

Figure 19: The Koshas

The Pranamaya Kosha is life force or Prana of the body. It comprises the internal systems and circulation. We control the state of the Pranamaya Kosha through breathing or Pranayama. The aura emits from the Pranamaya Kosha. Some among us can seeing auras with their open perceptions. The Pranamaya Kosha is said to survive death for a short time and is temporary. The Manomaya Kosha is the inner perception and intuition. The mind causes detachment from the Manomaya Kosha. It is the subliminal subconscious. Yogic philosophy suggest to energise the Manomaya Kosha the Pranamaya Kosha and Annamaya Kosha must be quietened through deep relaxation. Persistent practice allows the intuitive and subconscious self to rise.

The Vijnanamaya Kosha resides deeper with the conscious body and governs inner growth, ethical and moral behaviour. The Vijnanamaya Kosha is the presence that seeks to shift awareness into the esoteric from the physical observed world. This Kosha is the action of emerging spirit pressing upon the surface self. The Anandamaya Kosha is the core and is the animator of the body or the infinite spirit itself. All the previous Koshas are expressions of the one. The Anandamaya Kosha is a state of bliss and joy. It is the he true spirit in unity with *All That Is*.

Persistent meditation allows all the sheaths, bodies and abstractions of the soul to unify as that is the reality. There many philosophers from Swami Vivekanands, Gautama Buddha, Osho, Sri Aurobindo, Ramana Maharashi, Ramakrishna, Rudolf Steiner, Carl Jung, Alan Watts and the more controversial Helena Blavatsky. The ultimate reality is there is little significance other than academic curiosity of the various bodies as we are infinite spirit, a fractal of *Source* and *All That Is*. Upon meditating we do not feel our separate layers or abstractions. We feel the wholeness of unity of the spirit. We enter the fantastic realms of possibility as one spirit. We are not cognisant of the many depicted sheaths but traverse all abstractions seamlessly and without sense of their existence. It is true the body has an energetic aura which exudes from the energy or ether-body. The vessel is all energy. Everything is energy. Our aura changes constantly. We do have an internal foundational frequency mirroring our inner state and reflected as an aura.

The foundational aura can change in an instance when we have moments, period or outbursts of emotion and reverts back when we are in harmony. For example we may have a golden aura reflecting an inner graceful state then experience a period or moment of anger, worry, stress or unhappiness which may change the aura colour to grey or black.

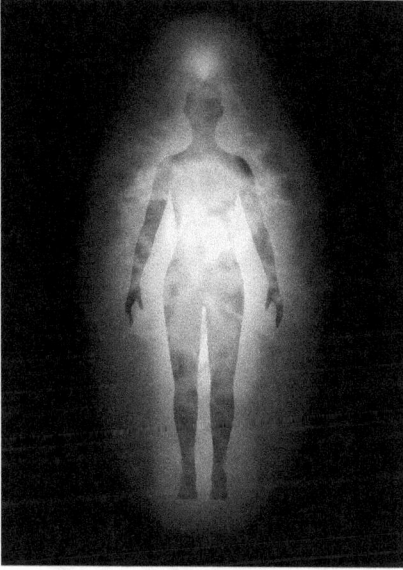

Figure 20: The Aura

The interactions of the soul-body, sentient-body and others are academic and interesting topics for discussion and observation. Rudolf Steiner also offers many layers of the soul. The soul is the spirit. The body is energy. The Universe is energy. Our spirit is energy. *Source* is energy. Energy vibrates at wavelength frequencies creating form and dimensions. The concept of the many layered souls is academic and purely subjective. Rudolf Steiner also describes the 'I' as being in the soul and belongs to the consciousness-soul. The 'I' is the infinite spirit and every abstraction of the soul.

"The "I" of a man, which comes to life in the soul, draws into itself messages from above, from the spirit world, through intuitions, just as through sensations it draws in messages from the physical world. And in so doing it fashions the spirit world into the individualised life of its own soul, even as it does the physical world by means of the senses. The soul, or rather the "I" lighting up in it, opens its portals on two sides; towards the corporeal and towards the spiritual."

Rudolf Steiner

The physical body is the vessel in which the fractal infinite spirit experiences being human. Energy is the body and is presented as physical by our perceptions. Science has accepted the truth the body is energy and objects emit fields. The field is the aura as a projection of the etheric body and is connected with all that exists including other beings. The soul or astral is stated by esoteric philosophy to be that which absorbs all experiences an extension of the infinite spirit. Others state the existence of the mental body which is an abstraction of the mind surface consciousness. It is not important the definitions used as ultimately there is only one point of energy and awareness. The aspects discussed are in complete unity and there is no separation. The infinite spirit within is the higher self and the transcending and eternal aspect. The physical a temporary vehicle. Understanding and expansion is devoid of complexity and is simple. Humanity wishes to make it complex and becomes drowned by detail.

How much is predestined?

Life has an element of what is called fate or predetermined nature of events, occurrences, challenge or major crossroads. These cannot be defined as a fixed percentage as life is predominantly free will including the choice to discover and fulfil the life intent or purpose. A spirit can enter a life with many predesigned challenges for quantum leaps in expansion whilst others may have a few. Predetermination in reality describes transcendental intent for the lifetime or purpose and is not to be confused by fate or destiny which are illusions. Upon birth into a human body or any vessel the Intent is unclear due to rapidly imposed degrees of forgetting. The discovery of purpose so many seek is presented through the only transcending journey of inner reconnection. Through stillness and reflection the purpose or intent will emerge. Free will is critical as it determines choice. The choices we take determine if the life is immersed in ego, mind and material existence or is directed toward the higher self. Choice determines if during life there is a loss of self or a reconnection. Free will is ownership and responsibility of actions, words, thoughts and intent. Predetermination and destiny is created through every free will action.

Many seek purpose. This is due to loss of inner connection. Reconnection offers a window to what drives the soul and our reason for being. The objective is to direct the nature of life whilst experiencing it through the true self. A method is to reconnect with the heart and allow it to work in synergy with mind and listen. There are other complimentary approaches. It takes time, patience, learning and guidance. The rest is free will. Free will is sovereign when formed from a position of true and open expanded awareness not influenced by external programs and systems of control, dogma, doctrine or human created beliefs. We cannot escape the physical in life but the beauty is to experience the challenges from a state of knowing and expansion. The greater the inner sovereignty the truer free will determines the experience.

In short finding the purpose or life intent does not mean we will fulfil it. That is a journey we drive from within. The spiritual rebirth of humanity and all life in the Universe is initiated through self. Unhappiness comes from imbalance, blind immersing into physicality, domination of mind and body from the heart creating a misalignment from self. Life is not predetermined and is created by the self. The only truth is following the inner nature of the self to create balance. The purpose is to be of service to others, to love, non-judgement, peace and to support each other in manifesting beautiful experiences and a world worth a revisit. The inner spirit and heart is the source. What is left behind will be experienced again. Delusion is to think upon the end of a life we will not return for another sojourn to experience. The likelihood is our spirt may choose to do just that. Create now within self and externally. Create what we seek to experience as we may return for another adventure.

What is good and evil?

The definition of good and evil is subjective and dependent on indoctrination. One culture may see another practice as evil whilst others may not. The judgement is subjective and based upon a personal view and perspective. The question should concentrate on how actions manifest and are deemed evil or good. Actions are free will. Actions are a choice of the individual borne from positive or negative intent.

Simple definitions of good can be an action, word or thought to evolve oneself, serve the greater good with sincerity and integrity. Bad can be categorised as selfish, agenda driven, controlling, insincere, separating and manipulative. The definitions of good and evil are perceptions with origins based on our state of expansion or dimensional consciousness. Free will becomes sovereign as conscious expands to higher states of perception and awareness.

An expanded states of consciousness detaches us from physical ego constructs, influences and programs. Free will from an expanded state can only reflect true vibration which is implicitly sincere and of love. When immersed in the physical or third dimension state of awareness the ego material, political, cultural, societal, dogma, doctrines and agendas offer fruit for their power. The foundation of free will determines the state or intent of action be that from ignorance or not. Those in low vibrational states are not always bad by intention. Their perceptions and expansion is stunted and are led by others directing practices that will further limit awareness and sovereignty of spirit. Good and bad are dualities manifest within *All That Is*. The objective is to change our personal Universe, remove energy that attaches duality reducing its imposition on the greater whole. Raise the inner vibration and frequency to lessen the influence of duality. Duality has no place in true home and is an involution of the theatre. The power duality has over humanity is a direct result of the energy given to it in this paradigm.

If intuition and heart are ignored the surface conscious acts through desire, ego and the material causing actions of negative outcome yet not intended explicitly to be bad. Mental, desire, ego and material hold influence as inner consciousness remains stagnant or dimmed. Mental intelligence is not a precursor to greater expansion but is the processor and curious to question the external reality and reflect upon it. The paradox is excessive mental ego intellectualism creates greater blocks to expansion than one with a lesser intellect. Intellect can breed ego and blindness though the notion of cleverness and better than perception. Ethics are relative to cultures, where ethical societies exhibiting greater violence and aggression than one with traditional but non-violent tendencies. Harmony, peace, grace, good will, kindness, giving and sovereignty of self is true existence.

What is self-realisation and what follows?

Self-realisation is not fully possible in form. The journey to self presents continuing states of awareness or realisation. A journey of eternal expansion. There is no limit to realisation as the infinite has no end. The journey will naturally, if allowed, flow into connectedness and intuition of spirit. A state of becoming and energetically shifting awareness. Developing a detachment from the material and becoming an observer of the Universe and engaging with it from a different space. We expand onward from this space from what is commonly called an enlightened state. A subjective change and an inner feeling that arrives at any moment in the journey. It is dependent upon the inner awareness and intellectual ego how fast we allow enlightenment to emerge. The objective is not to try but allow. To allow the emergence of the higher self, removal of ego, surface consciousness and identification with the physical. Patience, practice, persistence and allowing are needed to engage in the journey. The journey is not a race. Allow resources to be presented for knowledge, perspectives, study and reflection to support inner feelings and developing sovereignty. Follow no person, doctrine, belief or personality as this practice serves restriction. Grow and expand, catch every lapse, accept and continue to a place of inner peace, harmony, contentment, perception and love.

Does change prevent self-realisation?

Human and any form is an experience. We enter an appropriate vessel to interact and engage with the physical world in which it inhabits. This vessel or human body is not the real self. Identifying with the physical as *All That We Are* will prevent self-realisation. Removing this attachment and identification to it is a difficulty because of the mind. The idea we are not the body sees many respond with disbelief and see it as fantastic. The irony is those who dismiss the idea willingly consider we may be living in an illusion or generated Universe because it was proposed by a physicists. We change physically, emotionally, psychologically and mentally through external influences and study. Once we detach from being only the body and our internal belief systems the restriction to expansion is removed.

What is self-realisation and self-liberation?

Self-realisation is the inner journey from attachment and worship of the physical material expression to reconnection with the higher self, cosmic reality and *Source* consciousness. Self-liberation is an outcome where sovereignty of spirit is practiced, physical matrix and distractions have limited imposition on free will actions, words, thoughts and intent. It is a continual journey we cannot perfect or complete. We reach a point self-realisation with an awakened awareness and unlocking inner truth. Liberation of spirit develops, continues and progresses in life and phases between.

Does time exist and why is our time limited?

Time is a construct in the universal theatre. It exists for life to measure its place, state and progression of existence. Humanity within daily life assumes time as a linear sequence of events or occurrences, ageing with time and what is observed happens at that moment. Time is an illusion quoting Einstein "the dividing line between past, present, and future is an illusion". The preface of the book is to present an expanded view of *All That Is* and nature of the 'I'. The 'I' is infinite. It is not of time nor created from it. The 'I' experiences form in the theatre of the Universe. Time is a construct in which interaction is measured and observed through the physical. The Universe offers all possible experiences as timelines. They all exist and real. The timelines or possibilities we can experience and those in the now are created through free will. Our infinite spirit has no past, present or future. It is only now. The Universe is all possibility and presents us with timelines and potentials. Past, present and future possibility and timelines are created by forward projected cause and effect energy. They are all manifest in the now. The Universe is an eternal record of all possibility.

Alternate universes may experience different timelines of events and occurrence through other choices made in that reality. These all exist in the now of the whole, the *All That Is*.

Akin to a ball of elastic bands wrapping a winding web, a complex interlacing cluster of possibility beyond miniscule human perception. Remote viewing and Quantum physics as discussed in the main chapter of 'Time' are proving this reality and will continue along the path of discovery.

Time is not limited as the 'I' is infinite. All life is limited as the spirit determines when the purpose or the experience no longer serves and leaves the body. Life is not perpetual as this is a sojourn and a temporary adventure for a fractal for our infinite core. All life in the Universe is subject to the same principle. The theatre is an immeasurable stage of experiences. It is not home.

Everything has purpose. Once purpose is fulfilled or no longer serviceable the spirit will exit and return home. We agree the intent and duration of life. The inner spirit is never disconnected from home and will if it feels more can be achieved through a longer life create that reality. The opposite is also true. If the life can no longer serve a purpose the spirit may agree to exit.

When the purpose of life or energy for it diminishes the fractal of core spirit self knows it is time to leave and does so. Life can be diminished in any manner of ways. We can bring upon early demise through recklessness, suicide or be subject to the whim of another's free will choice to do harm. These are realities of the human third dimensional experience. Not all is fated and planned. Free will determines if we realise a greater state of consciousness and control over our life experience or we can be swept by external influences and whims of others to determine the longevity of life. The infinite spirit never dies and there is no limitation. We have many incarnations our true self chooses through need or to guide. Limitation is in the mind and a derivative of a need for expansion.

How important is positivity and optimism?

If we accept *All That Is* as energy and through the power of thought manifests form. Form is further abstracted as actions, words, thoughts, intent, events, cause and effect and experiences formed from matter. Positivity, negativity and optimism are expressions possessing energetic vibration or frequency. The energetic vibration and frequency of sufficient power of thought to support it manifests as outward or external experience. An overwhelming state of positivity, optimism and higher vibrational intent for life, actions and words will produce pleasant experiences. Concentration on negativity, fear, hate, separation, selfishness and insincere intent will manifest similar outcomes.

There are countless self-help books providing explanations and the need for maintaining a positive outlook for the sole objective of realising material desires and objects. A very limited view of energy focused on eternal gratification and the notion life will forever be blissful. These books ignore the reality that life will through cause and effect and design deliver challenges. If life was a constant state of happiness the spirit would not experience growth.

Duality is used for this purpose. Paradoxically duality exists in the Universe as a result of disconnection and power of ego actions and thus used to refocus humanity to regain reconnection to self. It is a self-supporting loop or a snake eating its own tail.

If the power of bad did not exist all that emanates from *Source* consciousness will have become fully aware and living with love intent vibration. This was the original state. This state is no longer present. From the moment ego and mind played their part the result formed duality.

An optimistic state will deliver through cause and effect a projected vibrational energy and experiences where it serves your greatest good. The infinite spirit is a fractal of our core *Source* consciousness. Positivity ceases to be solely focused on the material and moves to the spiritual.

Energy is universal and infinite with the simple rule. If we desire to project forward positive intent the present condition must be of that expression. There will be life challenges so we should not look at them as negatively but learn from them. Everything has cause or purpose. Nothing that exists is random, pointless or chance. All exists because of cause and effect. All that is unseen and seen is connected. All is one.

How do we raise consciousness?

The answer is whatever feels and resonates. There is no single prescriptive way or path on the spiritual journey. The journey is purely individual and must resonate with the seeker. Some may look for immediate guidance from a Guru, spiritual circle, group study, private meditation, prayer or from travel to the mystical places of the world. Embarking on the journey involves faith in what cannot be observed nor explained by the mental overlay. The process is gradual and challenging in that it will force us to confront the ego and external persona.

The persistence of meditation, tempering the mind, opening the heart, study, prayer, gratitude, forgiveness, asking the unseen to assist and guide to people, places, books and truth. We will be familiar with all these concept but uncomfortable conversing with unseen energies the mind has not yet accepted as existing. This requires trust and faith. We do not need to believe but simply trust. We should be willing and have the courage to confront ego, truth and should not feel this a simple task. It is in fact the hardest. We should start with what resonates as gently flowing water and introduce other practices as expansion continues.

If embarked upon with persistence and commitment to self the emerging feeling of contentment, harmony, awareness, healing, bliss and infinite connectedness will be experienced. Awareness and perception will change indescribably and not from an external book, holy or priestly person, doctrine or dogma but the higher self.

Connect with home from the physical experience. From this expanded perception observe the ease of which life can unfold and manifest. The purpose we all seek silently emerges naturally and the theatrical experiment becomes as clear as night and day. The hidden is presented, truth becomes clear and the infinite family assists in every moment.

Are spirit guides real and their purpose?

A fantastic notion indeed to accept unseen spirit energies of *Source* consciousness exist and are present in every incarnation. It is logical to assume when we chose to embark upon an incarnation as an infinite spirit we may have guides who assist energetically in the life. We can dismiss the existence of any form beyond the physical through egoistic blindness. The existence of the infinite, spirit realm and guides is not a debate in this book. Spirit guides work with the higher self to assist in realising the real intent for the lifetime and support balance with material ambitions we may have. Guides change but will always be present with our spirit and through stages of expansion. If we never expand from the initial state of ignorance the guide may remain unchanged.

As we expand guides will change depending on the state of awareness achieved to assist in the next stage of the journey. We may have a permanent guide with others entering to assist as awareness grows. There can be one or many at the same time. There is no end to possibility as everything is from the infinite. Spirit guides are an energetic interface of feelings, words, images, thoughts and always love.

The saying if you do not ask you do not get, is relevant. If we live immersed in the physical and mind the inner spirit struggles to emerge blocking assistance of guides. Spirit guides will as a result have a diminished impact and may simply observe. Once reconnection to self is established the awareness of spirit guides is a natural outcome and recognition not fantastic.

The inner journey, *Source* and guides ignite a life transformation of true free will and manifestation of events. All that originates from *Source* or home supports what is for the highest and greatest good of self and all those concerned. The presence of spiritual assistance and guidance will not assist to attain wealth or material successes. Yet if you ask enough and project sufficient energy the Universe itself may manifest what is persistently desired. Be careful what you wish for. Guides exist to assist in expansion to self and fulfilment of the life intent should we open up to them. Through the thinning veil and reconnection to the higher dimensional states home becomes apparent. Watch for synchronicities, people, places, events and symbols as these are methods by which guidance is presented.

It is not possible to articulate infinite possibility of which spirit guides are an expression. Human mind cannot explain with words or manner that which is ineffable and infinite. Awareness and understanding comes from feeling. Study, meditate, ask for guidance and allow inner knowledge to steer toward truth and remove illusions. We are never alone. Loneliness is a physical manifestation of separation from self and through that detachment to others. Loneliness is illusion as every second, minute hour of every day *Source* consciousness and guides are present. They patiently wait for us to call upon them for guidance, support and assistance. Love is ever present.

Do affirmations work?

Affirmations are positive statements used for self-improvement, to attract changes, desires and goal fulfilment. Affirmations use the underlying principle *You Are What You Think*. An example of an affirmation is 'today, I am brimming with energy and overflowing with joy' or 'my thoughts are filled with positivity and my life is plentiful with prosperity' or 'I am surrounded by wealth'. All intent, actions, words and thoughts are energy, vibration and frequency. We will attract no more than the frequency or vibration mentally, emotionally, physically and spiritually within. Affirmations align to universal law. Affirmations work when we are in alignment to the vibration of that which is sought. We cannot mislead the inner vibration. By repeating an affirmation and not truly being in the frequency and vibration of it will not make them become real.

Being in vibration is knowing implicitly within that it will come to pass. The frequency is of letting go and feeling inwardly, unreservedly and unwaveringly it will be. Affirmations should be built to match the frequency held within and switched to more expansive intents as we expand. The objective is to assert an intent in resonance to the feeling and one that is in misalignment. As we increase frequency we can introduce more expansive affirmations. Build upon them as energetic state increases. Selecting elaborate and attractive affirmations hoping they will change inner vibration is counter to universal Law. Counter to the infinite law is no action. Manifestation cannot work alone without a degree of action. Action creates powerful energy of intent to support the affirmation and its realisation.

The reality is an affirmation is a request to the infinite to bring into reality an experience, material or otherwise. Align the affirmation to the feeling in the present. As vibration and frequency expands replace with new affirmations. Continue in this manner toward a state where feeling it will just be is implicit. Inwardly manifest through true vibrational frequency and action and not a hope or self-delusion. For example if seeking better wellbeing an affirmation can be 'I am fit, I am strong, I am healthy' or 'Step by step and rep by rep, I am creating my ideal body'. Naturally action is required. Merely repeating an affirmation will not bring it into being. Energetic vibrational alignment will open opportunity, present synchronicity into the experience but action when these signs appear make them real. Affirmations are effective when practiced with the understanding energetic vibration must align with the statement and not the inverse.

And So The Story Goes...

There are many purveyors of spiritual, esoteric and metaphysical philosophy. They offer paths and concepts toward spiritual development. We can take the numerous philosophies on face value and assume the author practices what they preach. We are having a human experience. The external experience affects us in innumerable ways. We all experience periods of stress, anxiety and fear as well as the joys. Our intent is not to promote oneself as perfection as this is delusional. The objective is to be what you truly are, within to without, as far as is possible. The key is not to exhibit hypocrisy. We should recognise and accept these moments and expand to limit their imposition. We strive to live in harmony, contentment and peace within our inner being. Be that which you seek.

It should be said spirituality has become an industry. We all like the badge of being spiritual. We attend yoga classes, practice being present and meditation. A few attend Tarot card courses and immediately claim to be an intuitive on online and televised psychic channels. What does being spiritual mean? For me to be vibrating in spirit is to make it so critical to life it is as important as taking a breath. Without it life loses it meaning and purpose. To be spiritual is to maintain the constant conversation with the higher self, spirit and *Source*. It is the origin of strength and absolute trust. It is the recognition of the guidance that is given through our inner intuition. It is to understand there is no separation from the physical and the unseen. The belief what we do in glass towers has no relevance and is delusion.

The personal story that follows hopefully provides insight into the principles and perspectives offered in this book are not hypocritical musings. They are all implicit in my life. The story is offered in faith with the hope its message is received with love.

In early 2019 I started feeling a stinging burning in my chest. It appeared during cardio exercise. I would train through it and when I finished it would disappear. Over the course of a few months the burning sensation would persist and travel up into my throat. I consulted a doctor who initially diagnosed acid reflux. The doctor was also concerned it may be cardiac related due my family history. The Dr suggested I visit the local hospital emergency department. The hospital would perform blood tests to confirm if there was evidence of his prognosis.

The hospital emergency ward confirmed there was evidence of cardiac strain. After a few experiences over seven hours I left the hospital. There were many reasons for leaving which I will not share in this story. My intuition was telling me to leave. My heart was telling me that if this was going to go further it would be around my family. I never ignore what my infinite spirit through intuition gives as guidance. The inner voice will only guide decisions toward your highest and greatest good. It was the right decision for me.

In perfect synchronicity I was travelling to the UK the next day to attend a close family funeral. Upon arrival I went to the emergency ward at a specialist cardiac hospital. I informed them of the previous blood work and the stinging burning in my chest. I asked they check it again. I was admitted for further checks to discount a cardiac problem. This led to a series of unexpected events. I underwent multiple blood work, ECGs, ultrasound scans and x-rays to my stomach, kidneys and heart. The cardiac consultant suggested I undergo an invasive angiogram. This procedure would provide a comprehensive view of my heart and arterial health. During the procedure the surgeon informed me they had found a blockage in one of my arteries that needed attention. Stents were used to open the blockage.

The six days were traumatic and a shock. There were a number of blessings and guidance from spirit over the period. My family were present throughout. I was reminded how much love there was present. I was in constant conversation with the unseen grace of spirit and meditation. I was intuitively aware that if I went into the procedure I was walking out with a stent. I did not want to be right.

There were many moments of anxiety and sadness. This was not in the plan I would say internally to the unseen divine grace. As I lay in the operating theatre I was in meditation and conversation with the unseen. My third eye and crown Chakras were pulsing. I knew what was occurring was being guided although my surface consciousness did not want to accept it. From having acid reflux a series of events led to the discovery of a hidden manifesting problem. It was a blessing and an intended series of events the external human part of us does not see.

I was in the perfect place, at the right time, surrounded by love, passing through divinely intended events. I traversed the timeline with an implicit knowing that the grace of spirit was present as it is always. My conversation with the unseen was unceasing. Meditation was the source of calm. I stepped aside and allowed it to be. I had unquestioning trust in Source and those around me. It just was. It just is.

I underwent the procedure in a health care system that is available to everyone. It was not rationed depending on ability to pay, social or economic status. It supported the divine human right to be cared for when ill. It is what we are to evolve to understand.

These experiences changed a few aspects of my life. I was a different me. It inspired the completion of this book. It inspired the ending and starting of other aspects in my life. I am aware of what I am yet to experience. There is a journey in front of all of us. The principles and perspectives in this book are not the musings of an aspiring philosopher or guru. They are a part of me. Without *Source*, the spirit and transcendence there is no purpose. At least for me.

Bibliography

Sri Aurobindo, The Life Divine: Sri Aurobindo Ashram Trust, 2006.

Eben Alexander M.D, Proof of Heaven: Simon & Schuster, 2012.

Juan Mascaro, The Bhagavad Gita: Penguin, 1962.

Robert Schwartz, Your Soul's Plan, Frog Books, 2009.

Alfred Lambremont Webre, The Omniverse: Bear & Company, 2015.

A.C. Bhaktivedanta Swami Prabhupada, Bhagavad Gita As It Is: The Bhaktivendata Book Trust, 1983.

Dion Fortune, The Mystical Qabalah: Weiser Books, 2000.

Karen Armstrong, Islam: Modern Library, 2000.

Ara Parisien. Everyday Wisdom. Columbia: Ara Parisien, 2018.

Courtney Brown. Remote Viewing. USA: Farsight Press, 2006.

Sri Swami Sivananda. What Becomes of the Soul After Death? The Divine Society. 2015.

Anton Styger, Soul Liberation Experiences With Other Dimensions: StygerVerlag, 2016.

Dr N.C. Panda, Manusmrti Vol I & II: Bharatiya kala Prakshan, 2014.

Phulgenda Sinha, The Gita As It Was: Open Court, 1986.

Rudolf Steiner, The Essential Rudolf Steiner: Wilder Publications, 2008.

Todd Tremlin, Minds and Gods: Oxford University Press, 2006.

Karen Armstrong, A History of God: Gramercy Books, 1993.

Yukteswar Giri, The Holy Science: Martino Publishing Mansfield, 2013.

Caroline Myss, Sacred Contracts: Harmony, 2001.

Lydia Ross M.D, The Doctrine of Cycles: Theosophical University Press, 1949.

Alan Ross, Spirituality and Beyond: Ross Publications, 2004.

Walter Russell, The universal One: University of Science and Philosophy, 2013.

Lee Nichol. Essential David Bohm. 2002.

Rudolf Steiner. Rudolf Steiner Press. The Nature of Man. 2013

References

American Psychological Association. Divisions. Retrieved from http://www.apa.org/about/division/

Lord Krishna lived to 125 years old. Retrieved from https://timesofindia.indiatimes.com/india/LordKrishnalivedfor125years/articleshow/844211.cms

Did Jesus visit the Himalayas? Retrieved from https://www.neverthirsty.org/bibleqa/qaarchives/question/didjesusvisitthehimalayas

Why is Krishna Blue? Retrieved from https://isha.sadhguru.org/us/en/wisdom/article/whyiskrishnablue

Jesus Predicted in the Vedic Literature? Retrieved from https://www.stephenknapp.com/jesus_predicted_in_the_vedic_literature.htm

Einstein's Theory of General Relativity. 7 November 2017. Retrieved from https://www.space.com/17661theorygeneralrelativity.html

Dark Energy, Dark Matter. Retrieved from https://science.nasa.gov/astrophysics/focusareas/whatisdarkenergy

What is the electromagnetic spectrum? Retrieved from http://Earthsky.org/space/whatistheelectromagneticspectrum

Visible Light Spectrum—Overview and Chart. Retrieved from https://www.thoughtco.com/thevisiblelightspectrum2699036

The Dimensions of Consciousness. Retrieved from http://www.peaceinpractice.iinet.net.au/dimensionsofconsciousness.htm

How quantum trickery can scramble cause and

effect. Retrieved from https://www.nature.com/news/
howquantumtrickerycanscramblecauseandeffect1.22208

A New Scientific Experiment Involving Prediction and Multiple Universes. The Hypothesis. Retrieved from http://farsight.org/demo/
Multiple_Universes/Multiple_Universes_Experiment.html

The Farsight Institute. Los Angeles Airport Remote Viewing. Retrieved from https://www.youtube.com/watch?v=YMoyu3K0wtY

Why is Time Relative. Retrieved from https://www.sciencealert.
com/watchthefamoustwinparadoxofspecialrelativityexplained

Vyasa. Retrieved from http://www.newworldencyclopedia.org/entry/
Vyasa

AM vs. FM. Retrieved from https://www.diffen.com/difference/
AM_vs_FM

What Is Clairvoyance, Clairaudience,
Claircognizance And Clairsentience? Retrieved
from https://www.amandalinettemeder.com/blog/
whatisclairvoyanceclairaudienceclaircognizanceandclairsentience

Parallel Universes: Theories & Evidence. Retrieved from https://
www.space.com/32728paralleluniverses.html

What are the 11 dimensions in string theory? Retrieved from https://
www.quora.com/Whatarethe11dimensionsinstringtheory

Edgar Cayce. The Book of Life. Retrieved from https://www.
edgarcayce.org/the-readings/akashic-records/

New Scientist. Have we found evidence that we live in a
holographic Universe? Retrieved from https://www.newscientist.
com/article/2120209-have-we-found-evidence-that-we-live-in-a-
holographic-universe/

Robert L. Shacklett. Physics and the Law of Karma. Foundation
for MindBeing Research Editorial. Retrieved from https://fmbr.org/
editorials/

Morihei Ueshiba. The Art of Peace. Retrieved from http://www.
elise.com/q/quotes/ueshibaq.htm

Srimad Bhagavatam. The Life of Lord Kishna. Retrieved from http://www.bhagavatam-katha.com/

Dr. Courtney Brown, PHD. A New Scientific Experiment Involving Prediction and Multiple Universes. The Hypothesis. Retrieved from http://farsight.org/demo/Multiple_Universes/Multiple_Universes_Experiment.html

Alan Watts. Quotes. Retrieved from https://www.goodreads.com/quotes/59838-to-the-philosophers-of-india-however-relativity-is-no-new

Swami Vivekananda. Practical Vedanta and other lectures . Retrieved from http://www.ramakrishnavivekananda.info/vivekananda/volume_2/practical_vedanta_and_other_lectures/practical_vedanta_and_other_lectures_contents.htm

Nola Taylor Redd. Einstein's Theory of General Relativity. Retrieved from https://www.space.com/17661-theory-general-relativity.html

Einstein said that time is an illusion, and everything is actually happening simultaneously. What does that mean? Retrieved from https://www.quora.com/Einstein-said-that-time-is-an-illusion-and-everything-is-actually-happening-simultaneously-What-does-that-mean

NASA. Dark Energy, Dark Matter. Retrieved from https://science.nasa.gov/astrophysics/focus-areas/what-is-dark-energy

CERN. Dark Matter. Retrieved from https://home.cern/science/physics/dark-matter

Christopher Crockett. What is the electromagnetic spectrum? . Retrieved from https://earthsky.org/space/what-is-the-electromagnetic-spectrum

Jones, Andrew Zimmerman. Visible Light Spectrum Overview and Chart. Retrieved from https://www.thoughtco.com/the-visible-light-spectrum-2699036

Stephen Knapp. Jesus Predicted in the Vedic Literature? Retrieved from https://www.stephen-knapp.com/jesus_predicted_in_the_vedic_literature.htm

Shrimad Bhagavatam 1:4:1720. Retrieved from https://prabhupadabooks.com/sb/1/4/17-18

A.C Bhaktivedanta Swami Prabhupada. Speaks Hawaii on 20 January, 1974. Retrieved from http://btg.krishna.com/es/term/srila-prabhupada-speaks-out

Philip Ball. 'How quantum trickery can scramble cause and effect'. Retrieved from https://www.nature.com/polopoly_fs/1.22208!/menu/main/topColumns/topLeftColumn/pdf/546590a.pdf?origin=ppub

Andrew Cockburn. Long before drones, the US tried to automate warfare during the Vietnam War. Retrieved from https://www.businessinsider.com/long-before-drones-the-us-tried-to-automize-warfare-during-the-vietnam-war-2015-3

Ramakrishna Paramahamsa Ramkṛiṣṇo Pôromôhongśoe. Quotes. Retrieved from https://www.thoughtco.com/quotes-about-god-from-sri-ramakrishna-1770318

Billie Lue Fung, Divine Mind Intelligence. Retrieved from http://divinemindintelligence.com/

Jerry Humphries. Sense of Knowing. Retrieved from http://www.senseofknowing.co.uk/

Tracy Baker. Retrieved from http://www.psychictracy.co.uk/

SeeKen. The Art of Happiness: A Handbook for Living Summary by Dalai Lama. Retrieved from https://www.seeken.org/the-art-of-happiness-a-handbook-for-living-summary-by-dalai-lama/

Ara Parisien. Retrieved from https://araparisien.com

Visual Material

Anita Ponne, Yogi Meditating with Backdrop of the Cosmos, p147, JPEG, Royalty-Free Stock ID: 311364254, 15/03/2019, https://www.shutterstock.com/image-illustration/yogi-meditating-backdrop-cosmos-311364254?src=library

Irina Simkina, Hindu God Brahma Isolated on White Background, p134, JPEG, Royalty-Free Stock ID: 1055589062, 12/02/2019, https://www.shutterstock.com/image-vector/illustration-hindu-god-brahma-isolated-on-1055589062?src=library

Yulianas, Hindu Lord Vishnu Sitting on Lotus and Blessing. Supreme Being in its Vaishnavism Tradition is the Preserver in the Hindu Trinity -Trimurti That Includes Brahma and Shiva, p134, JPEG, Royalty-Free Stock ID: 1165254172, 12/02/2019, https://www.shutterstock.com/image-vector/hindu-lord-vishnu-sitting-on-lotus-1165254172?src=library

Yulianas, Lord Shiva in the Lotus Position. Maha Shivaratri, p134, JPEG, Royalty-Free Stock ID: 383985493, 12/02/2019, https://www.shutterstock.com/image-vector/lord-shiva-lotus-position-maha-shivaratri-383985493?src=library

Majcot, Angel Futuristic Background Wing, JPEG, Royalty-Free Stock ID: 94544146, 29/11/2018, https://www.shutterstock.com/image-illustration/angel-futuristic-background-wing-illustration-94544146?src=library

Sergey Nivens, Magic Book on a Blue Background with the Lines and Lights, p231, JPEG, Royalty-Free Stock ID: 63816586, 02/11/2018, https://www.shutterstock.com/image-illustration/magic-book-on-blue-background-lines-63816586?src=library

Zffoto, Dripping Heart Over The Water, p121, JPEG, Royalty-Free Stock ID: 111744533, Licensed 02/11/2018, https://www.shutterstock.com/image-illustration/dripping-heart-over-water-111744533?src=library

M-SUR, Reincarnation or Liberation - Traffic Sign with Two Options - Buddhist / Hindu Concept of Afterlife and Spiritual Cycles of Soul - Rebirth into Different Body vs Be Free and Liberated, p62, JPEG, Royalty-Free Stock ID: 507264289, Licensed 02/11/2018, https://www.shutterstock.com/image-photo/reincarnation-liberation-traffic-sign-two-options-507264289?src=library

Marcos Silva, Parallel Universe 3D, p84, JPEG, Royalty-Free Stock ID: 1052167430, Licensed 02/11/2018, https://www.shutterstock.com/pic-1052167430.html?src=library

Photos by D, Double-Slit Experiment Quantum Mechanical Phenomena, p85, JPEG, Royalty-Free Stock ID: 767262898, Licensed 02/11/2018, https://www.shutterstock.com/pic-767262898.html?src=library

Peratek, Allegory of Life and Death. Beautiful Mysterious Lady, p32, JPEG, Royalty-Free Stock ID: 1148461061, Licensed 02/11/2018, https://www.shutterstock.com/pic-1148461061.html?src=library

Xanya69, Yin-Yang Symbol, Ice and Fire, p177, JPEG, Royalty-Free Stock ID: 146573666, Licensed 01/11/2018, https://www.shutterstock.com/pic-146573666.html?src=library

Creative Icon Styles, Hand Icon, Prayer symbol, Stained Glass Icon on White Background. Colourful Polygons. P151, JPEG, Royalty-Free Stock ID: 1112344454, Licensed 01/11/2018, https://www.shutterstock.com/pic-1112344454.html?src=library

GiroScience, Matter and Dark Matter – Abstract, p110, JPEG, Royalty-Free Stock ID: 589120787, Licensed 01/11/2018, https://www.shutterstock.com/pic-589120787.html?src=library

Fouad A. Saad, Electromagnetic Spectrum - Visible Light, p118, JPEG, Royalty-Free Stock Photo ID: 560035945, Licensed 01/11/2018, https://www.shutterstock.com/image-vector/electromagnetic-spectrum-visible-light-560035945?src=library

Azur13, Red tulip resurrection in black white for peace love hope. The flower is a symbol for the power of life and soul and the strength beyond grief and sorrows. It also symbolises healing, Back Cover, JPEG, Royalty-Free Stock Photo ID: 474921658, Licensed 30/10/2018, https://www.shutterstock.com/image-photo/red-tulip-resurrection-black-white-peace-474921658?src=library

Novelo, Black Big Data Cube, Royalty-Free Stock Photo ID: 151300544, Licensed 27/10/2018, https://www.shutterstock.com/pic-151300544.html?src=library

VS148, Abstract Artificial Intelligence. Technology Web Background. Virtual Concept, p218, JPEG, Royalty-Free Stock Photo ID: 728178127, Licensed 27/10/2018, https://www.shutterstock.com/pic-728178127.html?src=library

Kindersps, Futuristic Digital Landscape with Particles Dots and Stars on Horizon, Computer Geometric Digital Connection Structure, Futuristic Blue Abstract Grid. Intelligence Artificial, JPEG, Royalty-Free Stock Photo ID: 684149035, Licensed 27/10/2018, https://www.shutterstock.com/pic-684149035.html?src=library

Yulia Glam, Abstract Shiny Background, JPEG, Royalty-Free Stock Photo ID: 114842389, Licensed 27/10/2018, https://www.shutterstock.com/pic-114842389.html?src=library

Gorbash Varvara, Meditation concept. Woman Ornate Silhouette Sitting in Lotus Pose Over Night Sky Background, New Age, Inner Light, Sacred Geometry, Kundalini, Chakra, Natural Healing, p272, JPEG, Royalty-Free Stock Photo ID: 424393570, Licensed 27/10/2018, https://www.shutterstock.com/pic-424393570.html?src=library

Titima Ongkantong, Man Meditate Dark Abstract Circle Background, Yoga. Beam. Ray, p271, JPEG, Royalty-Free Stock Photo ID: 402695833, Licensed 27/10/2018, https://www.shutterstock.com/pic-402695833.html?src=library

Olga Borysenko, Lotus Flower Icon, p269, JPEG, Royalty-Free Stock Photo ID: 169947248, Licensed 27/10/2018, https://www.shutterstock.com/pic-169947248.html?src=library

Yulia Ogneva, Isolated Hand Drawn Arrows Set, JPEG, Royalty-Free Stock Photo ID: 692835079, Licensed 23/10/2018, https://www.shutterstock.com/pic-692835079.html?src=library

Transia Design, Girl with 7 Chakras, p265, JPEG, Royalty-Free Stock Photo ID: 180707540, Licensed 23/10/2018, https://www.shutterstock.com/pic-180707540.html?src=library

Gorbash Varvara, Woman Ornate Silhouette Sitting in Lotus Pose. Meditation, Aura and Chakras, p224, JPEG, Royalty-Free Stock Photo ID: 280877510, Licensed 23/10/2018, https://www.shutterstock.com/pic-280877510.html?src=library

Apatpoh, Arrows Vector Collection with Elegant Style and Black Colour, JPEG, Royalty-Free Stock Photo ID: 503152339, Licensed 23/10/2018, https://www.shutterstock.com/pic-503152339.html?src=library

DeoSum, Human Energy Body, Aura, Chakra, Energy, p274, JPEG, Royalty-Free Stock Photo ID: 64018174, Licensed 22/10/2018, https://www.shutterstock.com/pic-64018174.html?src=library

Zanna Art, Heart Chakra Activation Concept. Man with Shining Aura. P51, JPEG, Royalty-Free Stock Photo ID: 733686082, Licensed 22/10/2018, https://www.shutterstock.com/pic-733686082.html?src=library

Gorbash Varvara, Woman Ornate Silhouette Sitting in Lotus Pose, Meditation Concept, Over Colourful Watercolour, p147, JPEG, Royalty-Free Stock Photo ID: 303136676, Licensed 22/10/2018, https://www.shutterstock.com/pic-303136676.html?src=library

Zanna Art, Chakras set, JPEG, Royalty-Free Stock Photo ID: 420127420, Licensed 22/10/2018, https://www.shutterstock.com/pic-420127420.html?src=library

By liseykina, Infinity Clock with a Heart Shape, p101, JPEG, Royalty-Free Stock Photo ID: 91303181, Licensed 22/10/2018, https://www.shutterstock.com/pic-91303181.html?src=library

NASA images, Colourful Deep Space. Universe Concept Background, p70, JPEG, Royalty-Free Stock Photo ID: 781457584, Licensed 22/10/2018, https://www.shutterstock.com/pic-781457584.html?src=library

By Duda Vasilii, Raster Version. Human and Alien Hands Silhouette, p94, JPEG, Royalty-Free Stock Photo ID: 83691517, Licensed 22/10/2018, https://www.shutterstock.com/pic-83691517.html?src=library

Zanna Art, Human Aura with Seven Sparkling Chakras, p79, JPEG, Royalty-Free Stock Photo ID: 417002542, Licensed 22/10/2018, https://www.shutterstock.com/pic-417002542.html?src=library

Cherezoff, Wall Inside Torus, JPEG, Royalty-Free Stock Photo ID: 267690263, Licensed 07/10/2018, https://www.shutterstock.com/pic-267690263.html?src=library

Muamu, Tree Like Heart / Realistic Sketch, p42, JPEG, Royalty-Free Stock Photo ID: 70348678, Licensed 07/10/2018, https://www.shutterstock.com/pic-70348678.html?src=library

Artdock, Vector Ornament, Decorative Celtic Tree of Life, p17, JPEG, Royalty-Free Stock Photo ID: 345099080, Licensed 07/10/2018, https://www.shutterstock.com/pic-345099080.html?src=library

Krissikunterbunt, Hand Drawing Person in Meditation Pose on White Background, p222, JPEG, Royalty-Free Stock Photo ID: 1174095358, Licensed 05/10/2018, https://www.shutterstock.com/pic-1174095358.html?src=library

By Lars Poyansky, Detailed Sephirot Tree of Life, Kabbalah Scheme Isolated on White, p141, JPEG, Royalty-Free Stock Photo ID: 437276272, Licensed 5/10/2018, https://www.shutterstock.com/pic-437276272.html?src=library

Inspiration

Tracy Baker

Tracy truly believes in providing a pathway to the light for those searching in their lives and through guidance is able to provide a natural opportunity for reflection, whilst exploring matters of career, love, home, family, work, relationships, spiritual healing and development.

tracyatpsychictracy@hotmail.com
www.psychichtracy.co.uk

Ara Parisien

Ara Parisien is a Medium and Spiritual Teacher whose mandate is self-empowerment. She assists individuals to step into the life they came here to live. For over 30 years she has delivered seminars, workshops and conducted individual and group readings for people all over the world. Through her powerful messaging she provides the tools to live a fuller, more meaningful life.

araparisien@gmail.com
www.araparisien.com

Jerry Humphreys

Jerry is the *psychics' psychic*. Jerry is an international psychic medium, animal communicator, counsellor, hypnotherapist and Reiki master of over 25 years. He has appeared on TV and radio, runs teaching and development workshops, paranormal, mind, body and spirit events and clearances. He is the CEO for an online publication. Jerry works with his psychic ability to offer guidance, compassion, healing, openness and truth.

psychic@senseofknowing.co.uk
www.senseofknowing.co.uk

Rosa Oh

Rosa is an energy healer and Reiki master. She has provided energy treatment internationally. She engages with pure spirit energy to heal imbalances and create a positive universal flow of light throughout the body. Through her compassion, love, grace and empathy she provides holistic health and wellness to our global family.

rosaoh214@yahoo.com

Carol Clarke

Carol has seen auras since early childhood and was able see things which were invisible to others. She began to be able to hear people's thoughts and to see angels and guides around them. At the age of sixteen that she decided to do readings for friends. At the age of twenty Carol started doing readings remotely and has global client portfolio. Carol performs soul energy and past life readings and helps people to find their purpose as well as giving guidance to life problems.

welshseer15@aol.co.uk
welshseer@hotmail.co.uk

All That We Are

www.ingramcontent.com/pod-product-compliance
Lightning Source LLC
LaVergne TN
LVHW051622080426
835511LV00016B/2119